BULLSH*T COMPARISONS

BULLSH*T COMPARISONS

A Field Guide to Thinking Critically in a World of Difference

ANDREW BROOKS

FOOTNOTE

First published in 2024 by
Footnote Press

www.footnotepress.com

Footnote Press Limited
4th Floor, Victoria House, Bloomsbury Square, London WC1B 4DA

Distributed by Bonnier Books UK, a division of Bonnier Books
Sveavägen 56, Stockholm, Sweden

First printing
1 3 5 7 9 10 8 6 4 2

A CIP catalogue record for this book is available from the British Library.

ISBN (hardback): 978 1 804 44083 4
ISBN (ebook): 978 1 804 44084 1

Printed and bound in Great Britain
by Clays Ltd, Elcograf S.p.A.

MIX
Paper | Supporting
responsible forestry
FSC® C018072

To Barra, Sol and Göta who are sweet darlings beyond compare.

Contents

What Makes a Bullshit Comparison?

What is Bullshit?

Bullshit survives in the nearshore between truth and lie, something that is slippery and dishonest, yet not as salty as a baseless fiction. An eighteen-year-old who had dropped out my high school once bragged he had a brand-new BMW X5. He then turned up outside our local nightclub in a brash, gleaming silver SUV with the music pumping. This guy was a bullshitter. As my impressed friends piled into the warm, white leather interior for lifts home, it all seemed true. Maybe he had got rich after flunking out of school? In the cold light of day, I found out he only had it for that one night. It was his boss's car. A boss he had been chauffeuring round. So, what he'd said was a nearly-truth. Not a full-blown lie, but a twisted misrepresentation of reality with the aim of amplifying his own social standing. He was a young man conflating looking after his employer's flash BMW with having his own car. It was youthful, silly and arrogant, and a sort of lie that couldn't be sustained. It was bullshit.

The origins of the term bullshit are uncertain,[1] but we know for sure that there is a lot of it floating about. Some is

---

[1] The *Oxford English Dictionary* attributes it to a 1916 T. S. Eliot poem 'The Triumph of Bullshit'.

easy to spot. Other instances require more insight and critical thinking. A bullshit comparison is a particularly misleading type of mistruth, because comparing two different objects can tie fact and fiction together. This book will help you spot these misleading comparisons concealed in plain sight, and unpick arguments that at first glance appear to use robust data or compelling metaphors, but actually present a distorted not-really-true version of reality. Before unpacking what makes for a bullshit comparison, it will help to expand the definition of bullshit in general terms. We encounter all manner of sort-of-lies through our daily lives and tend to forgive or forget them: ignoring the ludicrous tabloid headline based on a grain of truth, dismissing the overly enthusiastic sales patter of an estate agent, or refusing to give credence to the greenwashing claims of an oil company. That is not to say we tolerate the abundant could-be-truths. They can have real consequences and forever tarnish reputations. Two modern American presidents are infamous for their bullshit.

During his administration, the US enjoyed more peace and economic well-being than at any time in its history and he worked harder than any president to build peace in the Middle East,[1] yet the first bullshitter-in-chief is more notorious for what he said he *didn't* do in the White House than his political accomplishments. Bill Clinton is best remembered for his personal relations with Monica Lewinsky rather than his policies. He was tried in the Senate and found not guilty of the charges brought against him. Clinton sidestepped the issue in his Grand Jury testimony using carefully worded explanations, such as 'it depends on what the meaning of the word "is" is.' He later apologised to the nation for his actions, claiming to have answered questions truthfully and legally accurately, but admitting to not volunteering information and having had a relationship with the young female intern that was 'not appropriate'. There is now no doubt about his sexual indiscretions in the Oval Office, but in the late 1990s he skilfully rode a wave of bullshit and continued to have unprecedented popular approval ratings.

If Clinton is notorious for one defining moment, the 45th president is known for permanently inhabiting the intertidal zone between fact and fiction. Donald Trump is, by his own admission, a 'I say what's on my mind' kind of guy concerned with constructing a could-be-true narrative that reinforces his worldview. The examples are myriad: misrepresenting his conduct towards women, the unbuilt border wall, casting doubt over Barack Obama's citizenship, distorting the scale of his inauguration crowd, and disputing the lost election. He elevates bullshit to an art form. His medium is the media and like a potter moulding clay, he readily manipulates the press: 'If you do things a little differently, if you say outrageous things and fight back, they love you.'[2] Provoking controversy results in free publicity and is catalysed by exaggeration. A Trumpian claim might start with a kernel of truth but grows into a forest of lies.

When Trump complained at the start of his presidency that Obama ordered his phones to be wiretapped, he was not really trying to persuade people that this was true. He was a bluffer doubling down in his acrimonious dispute with Obama. There was no evidence this had happened, yet it was almost conceivable given the tension between the president and his predecessor. Also, Obama was faced with the impossible task of proving a negative claim, because you can't evidence that you didn't do something. Trump's bet paid off. He was further testing his accolades in the media and the Republican Party to see if they would debase themselves and blindly repeat his claim. They did and this untruth consolidated his power base.

Clinton and Trump's brands of bullshit were very different. The adulterous Bill always kept his foot planted in the literal truth while misleading his electorate with, for example, the carefully constructed sentence 'I did not have sexual relations with that woman, Miss Lewinsky,' as what transpired did not meet the dictionary definition of sexual relations. Trump is brazen and weaponises bullshit as a powerful political tool. This continues to be his modus operandi. He uses it to draw a line between 'us' and 'them' in society: those who believe him or accept his twisted reality and those that reject the discourse.

Bullshit takes many forms. It can be seemingly credible and robust, or just shallow and brittle. The Clinton example could not be more different in its execution to the 'BMW outside the nightclub' ploy, which had hardly been thought through at all: as soon as the car went back to the boss, the bullshit was exposed. Clinton's words were finely crafted, disciplined and served him well. It is difficult to fathom how much of Trump's proclamations are pre-planned or off the cuff. Either by design or intuition he is the bullshit artist par excellence. What is common across all three examples is that what makes bullshit toxic isn't that it is slapdash, but that it is a misrepresentation: it is looking at reality through the distortion of a dirty window.

Metaphors, Models and Metrics

Bullshit is a problematic word. An offensive, visceral noun or verb that evokes disgust or a sneer. Invoking it in a book that promotes critical thinking is intended to be both powerful and playful. It draws attention and provokes a reaction, but is not used without restraint, rather it is used because it can help explain toxic miscommunication in the most important of contexts.

Politics is fertile ground for corrosive nearly-truths. While the presidential examples illuminate how it is used by the world's most powerful men to protect and bolster their status, more widely its proliferation across the political landscape is unsurprising. Politicians are expected to know something about everything from defence to culture, economics, healthcare and justice. It is understandable that they often get caught out on topics for which they are unprepared. They are faced by circumstances that demand they speak without knowing what they are talking about.[3] A good leader should be self-confident enough to say they don't know the answer, but that isn't something that plays well in 24-hour news cycles. When confronted with a hot microphone they must wing it with a half-truth, rather than risk losing face. In such circumstances a bullshit comparison can aid a politician.

While most folks may know what plain old bullshit is when they hear it, it can be harder to spot when cloaked by comparison. A comparative device gives authority to a mistruth. It destabilises our cognitive ability, by giving structure to the sort-of-lie. Donald

Trump uses comparison in this way to build more persuasive arguments. When he faced ninety-one criminal charges in 2023, Trump insisted he was not afraid of prison and likened himself to a famous inmate: 'I don't mind being Nelson Mandela, because I'm doing it for a reason.' The comparison with the dignified Nobel Peace Prize-winning South African was absurd: one was imprisoned for leading the fight against apartheid, the other faced criminal indictments and civil trials spanning allegations he inflated his wealth, misclassified hush money payments to women, tried to overturn the 2020 election loss, and hoarded classified documents.[4] The former was imprisoned for upholding his beliefs and leading a movement for justice, the latter was trying to save his reputation and avoid a custodial sentence. Yet by bringing his personal legal challenges and the anti-apartheid leader's struggle together, Trump used a comparison to structure his political statement and give it more strength than if he had merely said, 'I don't mind going to prison, because I'm doing it for a reason.' By drawing a moral equivalence and placing himself alongside Mandela he disorientates the audience, who may wonder if Trump has a point about the wider political context of the charges being brought against him.

Trump was using Mandela's imprisonment as a *Model* for his own political struggles. This is one of three forms of comparison discussed through this book, and the others are *Metaphors* and *Metrics*. Think of them as the three Ms Now, imagine we are comparing a great pizza. We could use a metaphor and say: 'This pizza is a slice of heaven!' or compare it to the model of an outstanding pizza: 'This pizza is almost as good as that at Sorbillo in Naples,' or use a metric to evaluate its flavour: 'This pizza is in the top five I've ever tasted.' Each comparison conveys that the pizza is delicious and are all reasonable, non-bullshitty ways to make a comparison.

With this scheme in mind, the next three real-world examples from British politics illustrate how the three Ms are used to make bullshit comparisons by voices from across the ideological spectrum. All are common in political communication and can be used spontaneously or be part of a pre-planned strategy to take the upper hand in public discourse through powerful sound bites. For instance, in 2022 the British Home Secretary, Suella Braverman, used the following invidious metaphor when talking about the government's response to undocumented arrivals in the UK: 'The British people deserve to know which party is serious about stopping the invasion on our southern coast.' Comparing an increase in migrants or refugees to an invasion, or as others have suggested, a 'plague' or a 'swarm', is both a toxic use of language and deeply inaccurate. The arrival of immigrants seeking to improve their livelihoods or displaced people looking for asylum is in no way akin to the arrival of an enemy army, the spread of disease, or an influx of flying insects.

Metaphors are deeply embedded in our patterns of speech. Their careful employment can give texture and added meaning to the written or spoken word,[5] but also may be crude comparative devices that are used to misdirect attention. Politicians, journalists, academics and authors are professionals that work carefully and deliberately with language to convey particular meanings, report facts or articulate new messages, and thus have a responsibility to deploy metaphorical comparisons sensitively. Metaphors can help professional writers and public figures communicate to a wider audience, but are also a blunt tool that can be put to work to hammer home a misleading comparison. Politicians that are guilty of calling migrants invaders, or marauders, or depicting them arriving in floods or streams, are trying to whip up nationalistic fervour.[6] Most of them cannot literally think that poor and vulnerable foreign people will bring death and disease upon the constituencies they represent. Such damaging metaphors and other anecdotal parallels are the everyday untruths that proliferate as bullshit comparisons in public discourse. It may be understandable that in colloquial and everyday language, metaphors pepper language to articulate meaning, and add flair and spice to arguments, but when they are used in formal contexts we should expect them to be deployed with foresight and bring clarity to communication.

Second is the category that spans between Metaphors and Metrics: Models. These are the comparisons where one object is seen as a standard to which others are compared. For instance, was the war in Afghanistan like the one in Vietnam? Is Tom Brady a better quarterback than Joe Montana? Could Britain follow the Singaporean model of development and growth? Some of these comparisons make sense, others are bullshit. The last arose during the Brexit debates, as proponents of economic liberalism argued that when Britain left the European Union it could become Singapore-on-Thames. The basic geographies of the tiny Southeast Asian city-state of 5.4 million, which is marginally smaller in size than New York, and the northern European nation that is 338 times larger with a population more than ten times its size, were so fundamentally different that this comparison made no sense. The conditions of a low tax base, high foreign investment, diplomatic neutrality, and a strong legal framework that enabled Singapore's economic growth miracle over the last half-century, are not a formula that could be replicated in the mature and diverse British economy. Nor was there a thought-out strategy for UK growth that compared to Singapore's disciplined urban-centric economic master plans. Since leaving the EU, Britain's economy has stagnated rather than boomed.

Remainers as well as Brexiteers have peddled misleading comparative models. *The Economist* compared Britain and Italy and satirised the arch-Brexiteer Prime Minister Liz Truss as the leader of a tumultuous 'Britaly', which like its Mediterranean counterpart had become 'a country of political instability, low growth and subordination to the bond markets'.[7] Truss was pictured as the lady Britannia with a pasta fork in place of her trident and a pizza for a shield on the front cover of the magazine. Inigo Lambertini, the Italian Ambassador to the UK, riled at the misrepresentation of his nation and responded with an open letter that criticised the comparison for recycling 'the oldest of stereotypes' and failing to appreciate the successes of the Italian economic model.[8]

Third are Metrics, the codified comparisons that take the form of league tables and rankings that dominate policymaking. Politicians are ever eager to hold their departments of state to account against new performance indices. Many comparative metrics start off well intentioned. Like other forms of bullshit, their origin can be located in the truth, yet there is always the temptation to manipulate the comparator to meet political priorities. League tables for schools, universities and hospitals became popular in Britain under the premiership of the centre-left government of Tony Blair. They began with good intentions, to raise standards in healthcare and education, but as soon as new measures of good and bad performance were established, managers began to shift their resources to a narrow focus on these indicators rather than taking a holistic view to improve conditions in the hospital wards and classrooms. This is a phenomenon known as Goodhart's Law. An adage attributed to the British economist Charles Goodhart, which can be expressed simply as: 'When a measure becomes a target, it ceases to be a good measure.'[9] Blairite league tables provoked anxiety and concern across the government, and changed behaviours, sometimes for the worst. Health service providers adjusted their case mix – the conditions they treated – to boost performance, rather than concentrating on local needs.[10] Despite these long-observed concerns, politicians continue to champion comparative metrics and shift targets, or cherry-pick indicators to advance their political agendas.

This political use of metrics can be absurd. In 2012, Michael Gove, then Education Secretary in the centre-right Conservative-Liberal Democrat coalition government, argued every school should be rated above average, yet it is impossible for everything in a population to be above the average. When grilled on this absurdity by the Education Select Committee, the following farcical exchange took place:[11]

Chair: . . . if 'good' requires pupil performance to exceed the national average, and if all schools must be good, how is this mathematically possible?

Gove: By getting better all the time.

Chair: So it is possible, is it?

Gove: It is possible to get better all the time.

Chair: Were you better at literacy than numeracy, Secretary of State?

Gove: I cannot remember.

More recently, in 2023, the former chief inspector of schools, Sir Michael Wilshaw, poured scorn on the Ofsted rating system used to judge schools which rated almost nine out of ten state schools in England 'good'. Wilshaw was deeply critical of the way in which the school comparisons are made:

> Ofsted says that nearly 90% of schools are good. That's nonsense. That's complete nonsense. Having seen some of the schools judged good over the last few years, I would not say [they] were good. When I've been into some of these schools and then I've seen the [Ofsted] report, I've felt like going to Specsavers and getting another pair of glasses because they were not good and it's giving false comfort to parents.[12]

His comments matter, because he is arguing that the comparative system is distorting the quality of the education provided. It is promoting mistruth and concealing from parents the real conditions of the schools their children attend. The ways in which comparative metrics can distort educational outcomes are explored in depth in Chapter 5.

Bullshit comparisons are far from confined to politics and government; they can be found everywhere from families to the workplace, across history and geography. It is best to think of comparisons as a continuum rather than the three Ms as distinct categories. Metaphors blend into models, and some metrics are orientated towards measuring performance against a pre-conceived 'best' model. Comparisons really are all around us and many of them are deeply unhelpful. Even the most pressing topics like climate change are obfuscated by comparisons. The metaphorical term 'greenhouse effect' is a misnomer. A real greenhouse is designed to preserve heat and have a positive effect on the life developing within. Emissions of carbon dioxide and other 'greenhouse gases' are trapping heat leading to dangerous warming, but not only warming. Some regions are impacted by localised cooling, drought and flooding – heating isn't the only impact of climate change. Secondly a greenhouse can be quickly cooled, by removing panes of glass. There is no such quick fix to remove carbon from the atmosphere; it is a thickening layer that will continue to grow for thirty years after emissions are cut to zero.[13] The simple metaphor elides the wicked problem of global climate change.

At a more personal scale, parents compare their younger and older children even when they know it lowers their self-esteem. Maybe one is the model child for others to follow, or perhaps they compare their individual performance against a standardised metric. Online click-bait celebrity rankings litter the internet, presenting cruel and divisive opinions as agreed facts in new metrics of star power, harming the mental health of media personalities, and leading to abuse, bullying and harassment within communities of fans.[14] Comparisons abound. And yet despite their prevalence, comparisons are all too often shorn of context and present anecdotal points of view and dubious data as objective evidence. They simplify differences and provide leverage for ideology. Divisive comparison drives irresponsible competition, damages well-being, and blunts responses to pressing social and environmental issues. We need to stop and think critically about comparison.

A Field Guide to Comparison

This book is a guide to understanding the ways that comparisons misdirect attention. Across three sections – *People*, *Place* and *History* – *Bullshit Comparisons* advances a critical understanding of comparisons. *People* starts with the personal and explores comparison within the family home, then progresses to the ways in which famous individuals are compared and venerated across sport and politics, all too often without thinking about the wider social relations that makes them great. Lastly, it considers what comparisons between dogs and their owners can tell us about attitudes towards race and class. On an individual register we unfairly compare ourselves to other people without thinking about the broader context of our circumstances. Maybe someone else is richer and healthier, because of the advantages they enjoyed growing up: financial support, better schooling and diet, opportunities for exercise and travel or perhaps just the uncontrollable contingencies of genetics and events have moulded their lives. Social positioning leads to success and failure rather than triumphs being defined by individuals that can be atomised and compared. This section explores these dynamics and is a sociology of bullshit comparisons.

If a subject is concerned with change through society, it is sociological. Whereas as change across space and between places is geographical and change through time historical. The second section on *Place* is home ground for me. By discipline I am an academic geographer. Studying geography at degree level is not rote learning flags or a city's major industry or river, but being immersed in a subject alive in complexity that seeks to untangle connections between environment and society. In an age of climate change and globalisation we need people who have the critical ability to range across topics spanning from modelling atmospheric processes, and understanding natural hazards, risk and resilience, to contesting social inequality and mapping urban development and cultural change.

My teaching leads me to ask my students to compare places, and to think about the real engines of change that drive uneven development. Here I challenge them to undertake *relational* comparisons. For instance, if comparing the development of Britain and Kenya, their respective affluence and impoverishment is not simply due to their natural environment or the characteristics internal to those two societies, but rather their wealth depends on their different relations to the world at large. In this example, the international relations include a history of British colonial exploitation of Kenya, as raw materials were extracted from Africa to boost Europe, but extend further to the present-day subordinate political situation of Nairobi within the global economy. Today, Kenya principally provides cheap agricultural goods, natural resources and a safari destination for the world market. This is primarily because decades of underdevelopment during British colonialism stymied education, orientated the economy towards supplying cheap goods like tea to global markets, blocked the emergence of local industry, and established a tradition of big-game hunting and Western tourists driving round in Land Rovers spotting elephants and giraffes.[15] We can't sensibly compare aspects of life within these countries without foregrounding this wider relational context. The *Place* section of this book provides a geographical illustration of the ways in which popular comparison of places, ranging in scale from universities, to hospitals, to cities and countries, isolates them for analysis without adequately reflecting the wider web of relations that make that place a success or failure. These chapters further show how we can render this broader relational landscape of uneven development to explain the reasons for spatial differences.

As a geographer, fieldwork is at the heart of my professional practice, and this is a field guide to comparison developed out of two decades of real-world research. Going into 'the field' isn't just about slinging a backpack over your shoulder, flying somewhere exotic and setting out to interview people. I've done my fair share of international boots-on-the-ground research from street markets to rural communities and government offices. Throughout this book there are examples from my research in African societies including Mozambique, Sierra Leone, South Africa and Zambia[16] as well as Hong Kong, India, Portugal and at home in the UK. *The field* though extends beyond visiting places to do first-hand research and can stretch back into the past. Old media sources, historical documents, online catalogues, other archival sources and even statues also helped me understand the uses and abuses of comparison. These methods anchor the third section. *History* casts backwards to see the ways in which a selective reading of the past often uses comparison to promote certain politicalised worldviews.

Lessons from history are manipulated to change perceptions of the present. Historical comparisons pepper contemporary debate. Tensions between the American Right and Left are like the Civil War.[17] Russia has laid waste to Ukrainian cities as the Nazis did in the siege of Stalingrad.[18] Emmanuel Macron is following in the footsteps of Napoleon Bonaparte.[19] Some such analogies make sense; others are stretched beyond breaking point and lack credulity. An influential well-educated speaker can selectively pull down an example from their mental library to bolster an argument. Boris Johnson was a master of this. He would reach into the Classics when he wanted to add intellectual ballast to an argument. Two examples that bookend his premiership demonstrate his craft. Soon after taking office in 2019, during a speech at the United Nations General Assembly in New York, he compared Brexit to the eternal torture of the Greek hero Prometheus.[20] Three years later when he resigned as prime minister he likened himself to Cincinnatus, the Roman leader who 'returned to his plough' at the end of his tenure, only to later return to high office in Rome in the face of a later crisis[21] – a prophecy which in Johnson's case has yet to be realised. When speaking off the cuff his classical metaphors would wrong-foot an interviewer unfamiliar with ancient Greece or Rome and convince the public he was a deep thinker, or at least bamboozle them into assuming he knew more about a topic than he really did. Johnson is also keen on comparisons between himself and his great hero and role model, Winston Churchill, and this bullshit comparison is examined in depth in Chapter 3.

Unmasking Comparison

As the arguments build in complexity and consequence through the chapters, they tear away at the distorted mask of comparison to bring you face to face with bullshit. Coming away from this book will advance your approach to critical thinking, but will not just enable you to recognise invidious comparisons, it will instil the ability to think relationally and enable you to use comparisons effectively. The second point is important as this isn't a nihilistic argument against comparisons. They are part and parcel of our intellectual furniture but need to be carefully positioned and used honestly. At key moments in this guide, the effective uses of comparisons are highlighted to demonstrate how metaphors, models and metrics can be powerful tools for communicating challenging ideas or casting light on injustices. Relational comparison can bring order to a chaotic world. Without comparative data there would be no evidence to challenge gender pay gaps, plot patterns of disease infections, identify the worst polluters or highlight disparities in educational outcomes. Thoughtful lessons from history can help policymakers avoid the pitfalls of the past. Comparisons are necessary and can trigger discussion over new ways to address global challenges ranging from climate change to public health and social inequalities. So, while primarily highlighting the bullshit comparisons that confuse, this book also intends to cast new light on comparisons that kindle understanding.

This book is framed by the notion of bullshit and as such is also a contribution to an emerging school of work whose foundation was Harry G. Frankfurt's essay *On Bullshit*.[22] This philosophy of bullshit preceded David Graeber's *Bullshit Jobs*, a work of economic anthropology that exposed the proliferation of empty and pointless white-collar employment, and the data scientists Carl T. Bergstrom and Jevin D. West's *Calling Bullshit* that shed light on the manipulation of quantitative information to support doubtful claims. Critical work on bullshit has tackled serious topics with robust analysis, but also a shared characteristic has been to use humour and creative insight to debunk myths. This guide follows in that vein and contains dark examples of corruption, conflict and misogyny, but also lighter studies of sports, pets and tourism that showcase the full spectrum of bullshit comparisons.

This book straddles across sociology, geography and history to detail the proliferation of bullshit comparisons in public discourse drawing on diverse examples from around the world. Comparative bullshit uses mistruth to impose authority on statements and categorisations by focusing on difference. Comparison is the rhetorical hinge that connects fact and fiction, where one object is established as being a standard for others to be measured against. Thus, bullshit comparisons are often rooted in power dynamics dominated by affluent Western males. Dismantling such comparisons undermines capitalist, colonial and patriarchal power. The detrimental social dynamics of comparison can be experienced on everything from an interpersonal register to the world scale: an African migrant can suffer marginalisation on the basis of gender within her household, and within globalised society be prejudiced against as someone from the peripheral Global South. The personal and political are not wholly independent spaces. As the two presidential examples illustrated, there are connections between the intimate social lives of authority figures and their ability to shape history. Hence this book maps the nested connections between comparisons across progressively wider geographies and deeper histories. So let me guide you through the world of bullshit comparisons.

PART I

People

CHAPTER 1

Did His Brother Cry Like This?

Understanding social comparisons

Comparison Begins at Birth

Go-bags packed and lined up in the hall beside the front door. Waiting for days in anticipation. One holdall for the expectant mother with comfy clothes and all the personal effects needed to help smooth labour. Another for the soon-to-be newborn with fresh Babygros, squares of soft blanket, miniature hat and mittens. And this time around, a third small suitcase for the little toddler, about to become a big brother. His red plastic case is shaped like a fire truck and stuffed with changes of clothes, fluffy toys and favourite books ready for a day away with family. The anticipation builds as the due date arrives and passes. It was only ever a pencil cross on the calendar. Baby will come when he's ready. Each hour brings us closer. The imminent arrival of a second child is no less exciting than the first, though the unknowns are fewer, and the sense of anxiety is lower. What is certain is that a growing household will make comparisons inevitable.

He arrives into the world with a scream, pulling air into his lungs for the first time. Followed by cries, loud, sharp and rasping, filling the delivery room. Echoing off the tiled walls. The wails reverberate and are answered by wordless smiles and tears of purest joy and exhaustion from Mum and Dad. And then a question from the midwife: 'Did his brother cry like this?'

As the second follows in the footsteps of the first, how can you avoid measuring one child against the other? There will be constant reminders in reused high chairs, hand-me-down jumpers and much-loved old toys being newly discovered. At what age will the key milestones of walking and talking be reached? Earlier or later? As they develop from boys to young men, who will be taller, do better in sports, achieve more at school or have the most successful career? It is not just parents that grapple with comparisons. There could be family likenesses, common features and mannerisms that draw comment from loved ones. Acquaintances may confuse the two. Teachers' opinions can be framed by the experiences with older siblings. Younger children have to escape the long shadow of prejudgement.

From the outset, as a parent you draw on your experiences of the first to help with the care of the second. In the time-bending early weeks, where day and night blend together in a haze of endless nappy changes, late nights, early-morning milk and top-and-tail body washes, you remember which soothing skin creams worked, what position was best for feeding, and how to be as gentle as possible with fiddly clumps of cotton wool damp with warm water. The experience is a godsend. Some tasks are easier second time around, others harder. The younger one feeds much better and his little tummy and thighs plump up quicker with rolls of squidgy baby fat, but he needs more warm human contact – you can hardly put him down as he always wants to be held close. Since day one we try not to, but it is ever so hard not to slip into comparisons.

Sibling Rivalries

The Kardashians, Chris, Luke and Liam Hemsworth, Venus and Serena Williams, John F. Kennedy and his brothers Robert F. and Ted, Rudi and Adi Dassler (German founders of rival Puma and Adidas sportswear companies), Emily, Charlotte and

Anne Brontë, Romulus and Remus of Ancient Rome. History is full of famous siblings. Inevitably we are drawn to compare them. Who is the most liked social media icon? The better actor? The greater tennis player? The stronger politician? The wealthier businessman? The finer novelist? The more powerful leader? It is something of a guilty pleasure to compare rich and famous families and contrast their reputations. We are drawn to think about them as rivals rather than celebrating their collective achievements.

Closer to home, what is the problem with comparing siblings or cousins? With tiny babies and toddlers, it surely does no harm, and it is fun to think about how new little people fit into a broader, big family picture. This is true. There is such enjoyment to be had in exploring likenesses and shared traits, but problems start when children begin to feel constrained by these comparisons.

An easy way to think about how comparison can limit children is to take the fictional characters of Bart and Lisa Simpson. The older boy is rogue, charismatic, adventurous, mischievous: an extrovert. His sister is disciplined, shy, conservative, well behaved and an introvert. *The Simpsons* leads us to make comparisons between them and their oppositional personalities, intelligence and social skills. In the episode 'Bart vs. Lisa vs. the Third Grade', Bart neglects to study for a school test and scores so low that he is demoted to third grade. Lisa prepares so well that she is promoted to third grade. With the two in the same class, they become rivals and wind each other up, but the episode ends happily as they are forced to work together when lost on a school trip. While this is a comic exaggeration, we can think of real-life Barts and Lisas and, as we compare them, we begin to conceptualise them in relation to one another, and in turn polarise and exaggerate their differences and defining character traits. We often think of brothers and sisters in this way and rather than considering them as individuals, pigeonhole them as 'the smart one' and 'the dumb one', or the 'bookish' and 'sporty' child. Our judgements feed back to kids and can affect them and reinforce these differences. They think of themselves as less clever or less athletic, breeding self-doubt and narrowing their potential.

Not only can comparison cause self-doubt to take root, it may damage relationships between siblings as one becomes jealous of the other. Many parents endeavour not to take sides or play favourites, and to always love them equally, but this can be easier said than done. Children squabble. They fight over who sits where, who has a favourite teddy bear, whether to go to the park or play in the garden. For the kids tussling over toys or snacks, it's hard. For the parent trying to mediate, it's torture. It is all too easy to take sides and bend to the will of one rather than the other, to do the same again and again, and for a pattern to emerge. This can foster jealousy and further reinforce lopsided comparisons between well-behaved and naughty children. What is better is to consider how to equip youngsters with the attitudes and skills to form caring relationships. Not to compel them to always agree with one another, but also not be hung up on being right or wrong, or winning or losing, and to listen to each other, think about how they are different from the other person and resolve their disputes together. This advice is easier written down than deployed amid a full-scale multi-child meltdown.

Many grown-up siblings still have a hurt child inside them. Damaged by embarrassment, resentful of the attention their brother or sister received, or unable to live with their inferior record in some long irrelevant test or competition. Why even try if you can never measure up to the golden child? Childhood comparisons and relationships can impact well-being long into adult life. We are both the same and different to our siblings. These key notions are used from an early age by young people to describe and reflect upon their own sense of self. Our identity is closely tied to being part of a group, having a sense of belonging as a duo, trio or more. The intimate connections and at times unsettling separations of childhood help define who we become. We are both dependent and independent. The young model themselves on those that are a little older. Our associations with those of the same generation, and especially having brothers and sisters, is incredibly important in shaping our self-identification, our own sense of who we are in relation to others. In research, these comparisons usually take a back seat relative to the psychological and sociological studies that overwhelmingly focus on parent-child relationships.[23]

It is true that parents are the strongest force in shaping children through biology and socialisation. Fundamental characteristics pass downwards via nature and nurture. From the genes and hereditary factors that influence who we are, like the distinctive bumps, valleys and folds of an ear, or the pleasing curve of a smile; to the environmental variables that shape who we become: the home we grow up in, or the older generations' ideas of the ways to behave in different situations. Our self-identity is primarily formed in relation to Mum and Dad and then further moulded by broader relationships that span space and time. After parents, the rest of the household is incredibly powerful in shaping personality. If you have siblings by birth, marriage, adoption or co-habitation, your lives are interconnected. Past, present, real and imagined relatedness shapes personality. Sibling relationships are among our most enduring and give our identity light and shade throughout life, but in the early years they are powerfully formative. This includes both how we learn from and influence our brothers and sisters, and the ways in which our parents and other persuasive adult voices compare us and talk about us in relation to one another. Later, adult sisters and brothers retell stories of their childhood. Even if they grow apart, they still cast their minds back to how they were compared to one another, such that the significance of early comparisons can influence self-identity throughout life.

Comparison is a near inevitable outcome of siblings' common experiences. Whereas parents are of the previous generation, children are nearly always members of the same, be that today's Gen Z, or earlier Millennials, Generation X's, Baby Boomers or the stoically named 'Silent Generation' born from 1928 to 1945. Siblings are unique in that they normally get a near identical start in life, before going on to live different and separate lives. So, from starting off in the shared home, to attending the same schools, to living through parallel cultural moments and entering similar job markets, there are ready points of reference to calibrate how one child is turning out relative to another. It is taken for granted that the younger is compared to the older. Being compared to a brother or sister, who becomes the model child, is the most fundamental comparison in the human experience with tremendous influence on self-identity. *'Why can't you be more like your brother?'* might just be a few throwaway words, yet they may be among the most effective influence over young lives.

Even outside the family, comparison seems inescapable. Competitive parents measure their daughters' and sons' performance against their local peers, and they peg their achievements against metrics, rather than considering their success and achievements on their own merits. Comparisons extend across neighbourhoods, schools and on into adult life. It is the responsibility of parents, teachers and others who play key roles in child development to think carefully about how and when they compare young people. A lazy comparison might make it quick and easy for adults to discuss and categorise kids, but it can have hard hitting and enduring impacts.

Happiness should be the goal of raising young people. Children who are content in themselves and have the opportunity to live every day full of joy is what matters rather than their relative performance measured on any scale. Comparison can breed self-doubt, sow the seeds of jealousy, build negativity and damage parent-child and sibling relationships. One of the drivers of comparison is that mothers and fathers want to push their children to achieve as much as possible, and pitching one child against another can motivate them both to do more. This intention comes from a good place, but grown-ups can go too far down the competitive path, bringing comparative devices from adult life: market forces, rankings, league tables and, worst of all, the relentless individualism that seems to be a hallmark of contemporary society to bear on their kids. A competitive childhood may enable some to flourish, but can also lead children to become preoccupied with pleasing parents rather than themselves. Failing to meet expectation can stifle their confidence and autonomy. Now and then, some gentle competition can spark kids to do better, but the objective should be a rising tide that lifts all boats rather than a sink or swim approach to raising children.

Nurturing children together can be both the means and the goal of parenting, rather than reifying their relative performance measured by any standard.

Girls and Boys

The birth of a second child brought intragenerational relations into sharp focus and spurred me to look beyond geographical renderings of difference to the social roots of comparison. Being responsible for the care and development of two young lives and helping them on the same initial trajectories, while enabling both boys to follow their own distinct paths, means balancing the needs of each individual against the dynamics of family life. But that isn't the full picture. The subsequent arrival of a baby girl injected more joy and glorious chaos into our household and brought me face to face with history's greatest divide: the different ways in which women and men are treated, the opportunities, challenges and discrimination they encounter, and the ways in which they are compared.

Although we treat her just the same, beyond the home our daughter will face different pressures to her brothers, from what to wear, to how to navigate the transition into womanhood. With two male siblings she inherits many boyish Babygros printed with the dinosaurs and diggers that are coded from month zero as masculine. You try and look past the pattern, but some just don't seem to suit her as well. She is gifted onesies and dungarees with butterflies and elephants from doting aunts and grandparents and part of me thinks they fit a little better, although I know this is silly. I'm no ecologist, but I'm well aware there are just as many male butterflies and elephants in the world as female ones; moreover, I'm sure it was the same for the dinosaurs. As for diggers, the machines lack sex, but the association with physical power and construction being a male-dominated profession gives this simple motif significant loaded and gendered meaning.

What makes baby girls and boys different? After anatomy and birth weights, the developmental waypoints: gross motor skills, talking and other milestones are framed by gendered comparisons. Does 'baby boys are more adventurous' or 'girls walk earlier' have a foundation in fact? And if so, does it even matter? One of my nephews was a very late walker, much slower than his sisters, but now a teenager he competes in 100-metre sprints in national athletics competitions. Developmental differences between the two sexes are small, and we tend to exaggerate disparities between the female and male infants we are familiar with and then extrapolate from a handful of intimate encounters and impose that perception on the whole population. So the example of my slow-to-walk athlete nephew is not particularly helpful. A child's genetics and life experience primarily determine behaviour and development rather than sex.

Across the gross motor skills, from sitting up by themselves, to crawling, to cruising between pieces of furniture using a sofa or coffee table to navigate like an old mariner uncertain on their sea legs, and on to the big one of walking, some parents convince themselves there is a general pattern that boys are ahead of girls or vice versa. It has long been observed in the scientific literature that social influences are more important than sex differences in determining when girls and boys learn to walk, with both sexes generally starting around month fourteen.[24] Instead, there are lots of could-be-true gendered differences in performance that are culturally reproduced. For instance, there is a tendency for parents to overestimate their sons' development and underestimate their daughters' ability, and while this might be related to the marginally greater weight of baby boys, it could also mirror the wider social relations which cast female performance in an inferior light. This is an example of the gendering of female and male performance, showing the social construction of feminine activity as inferior to male, even when it has little or no difference. That these detrimental, bullshit comparisons start so early hints at the deep structural gender inequalities that mark society.

Thinking about young children as individuals rather than trying to fit them into a comparative frame based on their gender is a healthier way of viewing their progress. Some children will master their motor milestones early, others will be later, and some may miss out on developmental stages altogether. It is not uncommon for kids to never crawl and instead learn to bottom shuffle before walking. The rate at which a child develops mobility is affected by many factors such as their genetics or family history. If they come from a family of bottom shufflers, they are more likely to be late to walk, but their temperament may also be important, as can their experiences and opportunities. If a baby has not spent much time on the floor, maybe because they have had mobile young lives being carried around from place to place, travelled often in car seats and buggies, or lived in a tiny apartment with limited floor space and no garden, then they will not have had the same chances to learn experimentally. Also, it could be that parents give boy and girl babies different exposure to opportunities to explore independently, and these freedoms and constraints can shape their progress.[25]

Whereas girls are wrongly perceived as being later to walk, male children do tend to be later talkers.[26] Even at the tender age of eighteen months, girls have larger vocabularies than boys, although other sociocultural factors are more influential in shaping patterns of speech than any correlation with sex. A child's home environment and exposure to language at a young age has much more impact on the variety of words they use. In potty training, girls learn faster, acquiring the control two to three months before boys.[27] In other areas there can be sex differences in behaviour, but these are less significant than divergences in physical development. Males tend to weigh more at birth, but females catch up by the time they are toddlers. Then in relative terms they move ahead in toddlerhood.[28] Across the eighteen years of childhood, every kid's personal development is different, with each life story marked by chapters of growth spurts and pauses. Ultimately every child grows and develops at their own pace and nurturing parenting and a wider circle of care bring the best out of them.

Self-Image

Developmental milestones extend beyond early years and mark the rights of passage that announce the transition to adulthood.

One station on the journey to womanhood is a girl's first period. For Gen Zs and Millennials, Judy Blume's fiction has been a guide for many girls, and some boys, navigating complex subjects such as family conflict, bullying, body image and sexuality. In the film version of her classic coming-of-age novel *Are You There God? It's Me, Margaret,* the eleven-year-old Margaret (Abby Ryder Fortson) is desperate for her period. 'I'd die if I didn't get it before sixteen!' she wails to her mother (Rachel McAdams). 'Honey, you'll get it exactly when you're supposed to get it,' her mom sagely advises. And yet when every female classmate around Margaret is getting their period, it's hard to be patient and cool.

Margaret's frustrations stem from a desire to fit in, as well as a concern about her own development and a worry that she will be left behind as a child, while her peers move forward in their increasingly adult bodies. She prays 'just let me grow and get my period, just let me be regular and normal like everybody else, please, please, please'. A first period depends on the rhythms of a unique body clock, but young lives are calibrated by cultural comparison and the desire to be like the others in their school classes. Another first that makes young people incredibly self-conscious is the age at which they lose their virginity. Unlike the period, this is something within most, although tragically not every, individual's control and can be no less anxiety-inducing. Social comparison amplifies the pressure on young sex lives. Here, the casting of sex as a single specific heteronormative act of penetration is unhelpful.[29] Rather, thinking about sexual experience as a spectrum of moments, which women and men navigate incrementally, exploring forms of contact and emotional engagement progressively can enable people to build consensual, trusting and loving relationships rather than turning losing one's virginity into some sort of competition.

Beyond the bodily, there are a whole suite of life moments that signify progression and change. Learning to drive, leaving school, moving away from your parents, getting a job or going to university, getting married, buying a home, and having children. These life stages do not happen in a linear and planned fashion and different people transition back and forth. You skip getting your driving licence until your late twenties, or have to retake school exams, you boomerang back to your childhood bedroom after a failed move away, a gap year or two interrupts progression into employment or higher education, you do better without university, you find that different types of emotional relationship are more important than traditional marriage, a recession and being part of a generation that missed out on an asset boom has robbed you of the dream of home ownership, and the opportunity for parenthood never came your way or did not fit with who you are. All this great stew of opportunities and contingencies that are the ingredients of life nourish comparison.

In adulthood, it is easy to feel envious of the kid at school whom you always bettered in exams, who is now earning much more money, and maybe even getting that flash BMW for real. Parents in their sixties will for more grandchildren, probing their childless daughters to be more like their sisters that have already extended the family into the next generation. At work, I see first-hand colleagues that have come to academic life late after being in government or industry feeling anxious about their new early-career profile, and older students that have deferred study struggle to fit into class. These mature members of the university community should be self-confident in their status and life experience rather than comparing themselves to their new colleagues or classmates or downplaying their new professional or freshman status to their wider social circle.

For millennials, Facebook and Instagram became public journals that enabled more celebration and comparison of social achievements, while also being anxiety-inducing spaces where the digital version of a person is curated to present something half a step better than reality. The audience for this better self spans both close friends and family, but also distant acquaintances, like former classmates and ex-partners. Being addicted to these intimate forms of social media is like constantly living through a digital high school reunion. There is a lot of fun to be had, and it can be rich and insightful to share stories, yet this is always a vaguely off-centre social history. Social media accounts quite literally filter life, giving an opportunity to step off the solid ground of fact into the murky waters of bullshit. From the retouched photo to the carefully curated holiday snap, and the half-true announcement of a new professional achievement, a new lean, smiling, nearly-you is put out there for an audience to consume and compare.

Anyone on digital platforms can be stymied by virtual comparisons, and the wider social pressures of 'keeping up with the Joneses' are anxiety-inducing, but these pressures fall unevenly on women and men. From their mid-twenties onwards, there is tremendous expectation around marriage, motherhood and linked to this achieving a certain career stage before maternity leave, which constrains young women's lives in a way which men just don't experience after entering their third decade. Waves of feminism have forced us to think differently about the roles of women and men in society. From a first wave at the turn of the twentieth century that pushed women's suffrage, access to education and family planning. To the second-wave feminism of the 1960s that expanded the remit for equality to sexuality, family, work, reproductive rights and domestic abuse. Through to a third that since the 1990s furthered the female liberation movement and promoted feminism as an identity. And, although debated, a fourth wave began around 2012, with a focus on sexual harassment, body shaming and rape culture. A key component was the use of social media, not just as a space for competitive individualism and self-promotion, but as a place to highlight and address these concerns and take collective action. Despite the progress in women's rights, we need to do more to make the burdens they shoulder something that is equally borne by men. Reducing the pressure exerted through competitive comparisons is part of the solution.

Beyond Binary

Bullshit is *bull*shit. It isn't cowshit. It is no coincidence that it is gendered. Irresponsibility towards the truth is something of a male speciality.[30] Men can be happy talking bull, comparing things they don't know much about. They might not truly know whether Manchester United have a worse defence this season than last, or be unsure if Patrick Mahomes should make MVP ahead of any other football player, as they haven't been watching enough of the English Premier League or the NFL, but they want to be in on the conversation. They can safely give an opinion, and it can be a forceful one based on little evidence: a bullshit opinion, as the repercussions of this within their peer group are limited, unless they happen to be friends with the coaching staff of a rival football club or a member of the Associated Press. This cockiness with opinions is what Trump would dismiss as locker-room talk, the type of boastful, lurid, chauvinistic conversation prevalent in all-male spaces. In the UK it might be known as pub chat, talking bollocks, banter or *bants*.

This is not to suggest that either bullshit in general, all mindless banter, or bullshit comparisons specifically are a uniquely male foible. Rather that men are more confident in floating various thoughts and attitudes to hear themselves say things and see how their audience responds. What they say may not reveal what they really think, as they may take an experimental or adventurous approach to a topic. So, conversations are not always about concrete personal beliefs but about social positioning. To demonstrate this cognitive disconnect, let's go back to the migrant example in the introductory chapter. Alongside Suella Braverman, another prominent Conservative politician who took a hard line on migration was former Immigration Minister, Mark Harper. In 2013 he infamously sent trucks carrying mobile billboards into racially mixed neighbourhoods warning illegal immigrants to 'go home or face arrest'.[31] But this same minister was the next year forced to resign after it was found that he employed a cleaning lady who was an undocumented migrant. His hard man posturing about the evils of migration were a populist ploy, when at home he enjoyed the benefits of low-wage female migrant labour. It is difficult to take his hard-line rhetoric seriously when he himself doesn't check the credentials of his own foreign cleaner. Both Harper's and Braverman's tough language is assertively masculine and laced with bullshit.

A person can embody 'masculine' qualities and be a woman, and the same applies to a man taking on 'feminine' attitudes.

Gender identities, instead of being separate, are really two parts of a whole. Yet in the Western world, gender is seen as either man or woman; there is gender dualism even though there are many prominent small-c socially conservative figures that span this dualism in their public-facing roles. Bullshit comparisons can be used to reinforce gender roles in a way that reproduces a heteronormative worldview. People that don't fit neatly within male/female comparative categories, including those who are trans, non-binary and intersex, face stifling prejudices.

Lives that differ from the norm can be difficult for outsiders to understand. Heterosexuals tend to believe that within same-sex couples there is a more masculine and feminine member and that they perform the same stereotypical gender roles. They might think, 'Who's the man?' in a lesbian or gay partnership, as if a couple couldn't function in the twenty-first century without a male patriarch.[32] This comparison is unhelpful on two registers. Firstly, it reproduces a misogynistic notion that there is housework and defined roles that should be rigidly coded male and female, and secondly it reduces same-sex households to being an imperfect facsimile of a heterosexual model. Research suggests that same-sex couples have more equal relationships rather than falling into differentiated 'husband' and 'wife' roles,[33] but also that gender roles are fluid within gay or lesbian couples, as indeed they are within heterosexual relationships. As Judith Butler argued, 'Gay is to straight not as copy is to original, but, rather, as copy is to copy.' No matter who you are biologically or where you are on the sexuality spectrum, all gender is performance. There are, for example, butch/femme differences within some lesbian couples, but these need not correlate with the division in housework between masculine and feminine defined jobs. Reversing the comparison and learning from same-sex couples can unveil how heterosexual norms are constructed and destabilise the patriarchy.

This chapter has taken an initial, personal perspective on comparisons across the family, school and relationships. Much of the critique of comparison has centred on the ways in which they reproduce established social norms and values that embolden the first born or early developer, and cement a male-dominated and heteronormative worldview as a model to which everything else should be compared. These norms and values are not fixed laws but fluid, dynamic and prime for reinterpretation. Moving from these familial settings, the next chapter goes to the intense competitive arena of elite sports. Whereas this first chapter highlighted how intimate personal comparisons can shape and stifle individual development, in the next chapter our perspective expands to consider how young athletes are compared against other competitors, both past and present, who are usually unfamiliar to them. The individual performance of strangers is measured and metricised in a world in which behaviour is strictly regulated within the field of play. This should make for fruitful and meritocratic comparisons of sportspeople, but even in this more objective arena, comparison can be deeply problematic. Inappropriate and unfair comparisons can crush development as emerging talent is measured against established greats. Pressure is projected in high definition by exposure on a televised global stage. Individual success can overshadow the importance of teams in building the platform for achievement. Sport is an entertainment industry that celebrates charismatic stars and one that privileges the achievements of sportsmen above sportswomen, who are diminished by comparisons that reinforce patriarchal social relations.

CHAPTER 2

Is Messi Better Than Maradona?

Living in the shadow of comparison

The Greatest of All Time

Will there ever be another Michael Jordan? Bill Russell, Magic
Johnson, Kareem Abdul-Jabbar and LeBron James all feature
in the GOAT (greatest of all time) conversation, but it is always
Jordan who comes out on top as the undisputed standard-bearer
of the NBA.[34] A basketball talent so mercurial his name has
become a cipher for achievements that almost transcend the limits
of human capability and become a shorthand for expressing
excellence in other sports. He is both *the* model basketball player
and *the* model elite athlete. To take just one example, in the NFL,
Patrick Mahomes's outstanding early-career achievements are
compared to Jordan's despite their sports being so different.[35]
Jordan is the undisputed all-time American superstar and one of
a handful of global names whose reputation stretches beyond his
sport into a wider cultural context.

In Brazil, every talented teenage racing driver is the next
Ayrton Senna. Indian cricket dreams of another prodigious
sixteen-year-old Sachin Tendulkar striding gracefully down
the wicket. Any brilliant young Canadian hockey player

will be compared to Wayne Gretzky. An exciting new talent can ignite a whole sport. Stories spread like wildfire as an unknown is transformed through the heat of competition into a household name. Even before any records are broken for the first win, goal or championship, the sporting public tries to set the trajectories of rising starlets against the career arcs of accomplished megastars. Television pundits and pub bores alike love to compare across generations. It makes for great banter. Even when self-declared experts are drawing on hazy memories of yesterday's men to inform their opinions of today's newest talents. This all seems like good harmless fun, but there is a darker side to sporting comparisons. Being the heir to a champion's legend can be a burden too great for young shoulders to bear.

When a seventeen-year-old Lionel Messi burst on to the world stage in 2004, commentators and ex-professionals were aghast and quick to compare him to compatriot Diego Maradona who, alongside Pelé, consistently ranks as the greatest of all time. Messi himself has always played down the comparisons. Clearly, he does not welcome the parallels: 'Even if I played for a million years, I'd never come close to Maradona. Not that I'd want to anyway. He's the greatest there's ever been.'[36] When Messi eventually won the World Cup in Qatar in 2022, his hitherto disappointing international record finally matched the glories of Maradona, who carried an average Argentina side to victory in 1986. Despite his astounding record, the persistence of the comparison riles some who see the late Maradona as an untouchable all-time great, the ultimate model Argentine footballer. His former teammate, and later assistant coach of Argentina, Héctor Enrique, believes he is beyond compare: 'There will never be anyone like Maradona again, not even if Messi wins three World Cups in succession or scores a bicycle kick from midfield.' Messi will always be the one that follows *El Diego*. There is no counterfactual reality where we can see how Messi would have fared without the Maradona comparisons. Perhaps he has been spurred on to emulate him; maybe on the international scene he struggled to escape the expectations of a nation that for more than a decade fixated on

'Leo' leading them to a World Cup win like the original *'El Pibe de Oro'* (Golden Boy)?

Crushed by Comparison

In the autumn of his career, Messi joined Inter Miami. His transfer to the new David Beckham-owned Floridian franchise drew celebrity fans: Kim Kardashian, LeBron James and Serena Williams came for his debut, showcasing the rising popularity and glamour of soccer in the United States. Inter's heron pink number ten jersey quickly became one of the most in-demand items of sports apparel of all time.[37] Messi has long been the ultimate contemporary frame of reference. The model for the emerging talents of Argentina and Barcelona, and for small, quick dribbling, young forwards in other teams. Across his career, many good players and some not so good ones have stood comparison: Pietro Pellegri was dubbed the Italian Messi, Gai Assulin the Israeli Messi, Lee Seung-woo the South Korean Messi, Ryan Gauld the Scottish Messi, Giovani dos Santos the Mexican Messi, Ryo Miyaichi the Japanese Messi, and Erik Lamela the next Argentine Messi. Some of these men have gone on to have success or still have time to flourish, others would only be remembered by the most dedicated football fans. Perhaps the most infamous 'new Messi' soon followed him on to the field of play.

Just over two years after his own debut at the Camp Nou, the website Foot Mercato published an article titled 'Bojan Krki': le futur Messi?' Bojan, as another seventeen-year-old, broke Messi's record as the youngest ever Barcelona player. He had excelled at *La Masia*, the club's famous academy, bagged 900 goals for Barça's youth sides, and went on to appear 104 times for the first team and score thirty-six times. Like Messi, Bojan was an out-and-out attacker most at home in the same number ten role. Knitting together attacks and using his vision and passing range to deliver the ball to teammates. The two were close in stature as well as style of play, both being five foot seven inches tall. There was even a passing resemblance and genealogical research uncovered that they were fourth cousins. Playing alongside

Messi, he helped Barcelona claim honours including three La Liga titles and two Champions Leagues. Despite the obvious similarities, Bojan's career did not continue like a photocopy of Messi's CV.

By the age of twenty-one his best football and greatest achievements were behind him. Bojan was crippled by anxiety. He was unable to match the talents of Messi. In an interview at twenty-seven he reflected on his career: 'It all happened very quick,' Bojan says. 'In footballing terms it went well but not personally. I had to live with that and people say my career hasn't been as expected. When I came up, it was "new Messi". Well, yes, if you compare me with Messi . . . but what career did you expect?' Despite his own record being incredible in and of itself, he stalled under pressure: 'With me, it was a dizziness, feeling sick, constant, twenty-four hours a day. There was a pressure [in my head], powerful, never going away. I started to feel this powerful dizziness, overwhelmed, panicked.' Bojan suffered an anxiety attack on the eve of the 2008 European Championship, but this was covered up as gastroenteritis, because in football any form of mental ill health is perceived as a weakness. A move away from the intensity of Barcelona and the ever-present comparisons with Messi failed to revive his career. His first four years playing at Barcelona 'conditions everything'.[38] Bojan became a globetrotter, gradually progressing down from the zenith of world football, moving to Roma, AC Milan, Ajax, Stoke City, Montréal Impact and finally, after two years at Vissel Kobe in Japan, he retired at the relatively young age of thirty-two.

Bojan now works back at Barcelona nurturing the next generation, including Lamine Yamal, who at sixteen broke Bojan's record to become the club's youngest goalscorer, and seventeen-year-old Marc Guiu who has already been compared to their leading striker Robert Lewandowski.[39] Guiu scored thirty seconds into his debut, after which he 'went from 40,000 followers to a million overnight on Instagram', Bojan says. 'That's madness. "How nice, how incredible, a million followers!" But that's hard to manage, transformative.'[40] Their mentor will have to use all his experience to protect them from the pressures of the global fame that accompanies playing for the most famous club side in world football.

In sports writing, comparison is a shortcut to capture the readers' attention, but as Bojan's experiences illustrate, misjudged words can have long-term impacts on mental health. For a journalist under pressure to file a match report at the final whistle or to fill the column inches on a slow news day, pitching someone as the next big thing can give a humdrum story a sprinkling of stardust. But the young – sometimes child – players in the words of Bojan 'need a good shield'. In the media, pundits need to think carefully about how they build new reputations so that developing players can rise to their promise tomorrow rather than sink under the weight of expectation today. It was sad that the great Alfredo di Stefano missed the World Cup through physical injury in 1962, but what about the youngsters who never made it to the finals as they felt overwhelmed and mentally shattered? In the same way that nobody wants to see a player miss the game of their lives through a broken leg or a twisted ankle, neither should we accept that younger players be crushed by unrealistic expectations and their anxieties abetted through comparisons. Mental health needs much more attention in elite sport as one in three current and ex-footballers have suffered from depression or anxiety.[41]

Sadly in football, comparison has contributed to some deeply tragic moments. As a teenager, Martin Bengtsson seemed to have it all. He made his professional debut at seventeen for Swedish club Örebro SK and went on to captain the national under-17 side. The striker was expected to be the next Zlatan Ibrahimović, the famous Swede with an intimidating record as one of the most decorated forwards in football. There is a picture of the two of them together with Zlatan smiling, towering over a pale and sombre child Martin, arm wrapped around his shoulder. By nineteen he was at Italian side Inter Milan, a club Ibrahimović scored for fifty-seven times. Bengtsson had always dreamed of playing in Italy, but reality did not meet his expectations. He felt lost. His footballing performance was the only way in which he was valued at the club. Then his performances declined due to injury. The relentless routine was like a 'prison' from which he saw no escape: 'I needed someone to talk to, and not just to say, "Try harder" or "Think positive."' As he explains, the competitive pressures to get better results came at the expense of his wider social development. He became increasingly depressed and saw no way out:

'I was too proud, probably, to just say, "Hi, I am not made for this." I was too ashamed and this shame led to a suicide attempt . . . I prepared razors in the bathroom the night before, I think it was 21 September 2004. I went up in the morning and cut myself in the wrists and arms and I started to bleed. I got into my room somehow and I fell there.'[42]

The Inter youth academy was ill-equipped to deal with the drastic act. A therapist came to talk to him but offered only empty words: 'You are a football player at one of the biggest clubs in the world, earning a lot of money; you have a car.' And the last thing she said was: 'You can fuck any model you want.' Bengtsson retired from football soon after and became a musician. He now tours Sweden speaking to young footballers about the psychological challenges of elite sport.

The Ballon d'Or

Lionel Messi has had a remarkable career despite the comparison to Maradona that dominated his early years. As his performances developed and his achievements accumulated in his twenties, he was increasingly compared to Cristiano Ronaldo, another world-class talent who enjoyed parallel success. They share similar records, having played most of their careers in the Spanish La Liga and both are among the world's highest-earning sportsmen, with incomes from salaries and sponsorship in excess of $100 million a season. They have regularly broken the fifty goals a season barrier, won ten European Golden Shoe awards (six for Messi and four for Ronaldo) for leading scorer, and most incredibly have a combined seventy-eight major trophies (Ronaldo thirty-four, Messi forty-four). For more than a decade they dominated football, and any other great player was compared to these two rivals. As the World Cup winner and current French captain Kylian Mbappé explains:

You do always compare yourself with the best in your sport, just as the baker compares himself with the best bakers around him. Who makes the best croissant, the best pain au chocolat? I think Messi has done Ronaldo good, and Ronaldo has done Messi good. For me they are the two best players in history, but I think that one without the other might have not remained the best far ahead of the others for fifteen years. Maybe they would have let themselves go at some point.

In the 2018–19 season, Mbappé was competing with Messi to be the highest scorer in Europe, but noticed that no matter how well he did, Messi always appeared to get ahead of him:

I'd score two, he'd score three; I'd score three, he'd score four. It was so crazy that I talked to Ousmane [Dembélé, Mbappé's friend and Messi's teammate at Barcelona]: 'It's not possible! Is he doing it on purpose? Does he check how many goals I score?' Dembélé told him: 'Of course he's watching you!'[43]

That season, Messi won the European Golden Shoe for the third successive season after scoring three more goals than Mbappé.

Every year, Messi and Ronaldo are brought together on football's glitziest night out. So 12 January 2015 was a familiar occasion in the Kongresshaus, a nineteenth-century concert hall on the shore of Lake Zurich. That year was notable for a low point in male fashion. The two footballing greats were seated next to each other in the most outrageous suits, like a pair of flamboyant peacocks showing off their status. Messi's was a metallic burgundy three-piece with matching bow tie and black shirt, Cristiano Ronaldo's a gloss midnight blue round-lapelled tuxedo with low-coat waistcoat. Ronaldo ruled the roost that year. The pumped and preened, bronzed, six-foot-two

Portuguese winger triumphantly claimed the prize of the Ballon d'Or for World Player of the Year. Together, he and Messi have won thirteen Ballon d'Or trophies (eight for Messi and five for Ronaldo). Their duopoly is incredible as, in addition to winning, both featured in the top three nominations in all but four years between 2007 and 2023, phenomenal individual achievements in a team sport.

Their Ballon d'Or pre-eminence and the award itself have not been without controversy. Some consider the solo prize represents everything that is wrong with modern football: an exercise in vanity and individualism fuelled by commercial interests to build up the cult of celebrity. The award is voted for by national managers, captains and journalists. It favours certain types of players (attackers) and teams (famous ones). Politics between rival clubs and nations twists the credibility of the results, but the event attracts interest at an otherwise quiet point in the football calendar. The comparison of elite players feeds the social media machine and provides a topic for fevered debate among football fans. This and other MVP (Most Valuable Player) awards are subjective and as much a popularity contest as a meaningful metric of who has contributed the most to a team's success. Speaking in 2014, Thierry Henry questioned why the unrivalled Spanish national team's historic run of victories in the 2008 and 2012 European Championships and the 2010 World Cup were never recognised: 'I'd like to have an explanation of the fact that no Spaniard has won the Ballon d'Or over the last four years. The game is too focused on the individual. Stars are fine. But within the team, not without.'[44] A generous interpretation would be that the multiple Spanish stars – Andrés Iniesta, Sergio Ramos, Xavi and others – split the vote, but another would be that the behind-the-scenes FIFA politics promoted Messi and Ronaldo as they were established as the high-profile, commercially attractive sporting celebrities. Either explanation highlights the absurdity of the individual ranking.

The Ballon d'Or rewards vanity and promotes individual achievement over that of a team. As the ultimate means of comparison, it feeds aspects of modern football that many fans hate: the celebrity culture, the inflated egos, the commercialism; worst of all it may hamper good football. Players actively target the accolade. They are even incentivised by commercial sponsors. Brazilian star Neymar will reportedly receive a £750,000 bonus from Nike if he wins the coveted gong, although this is on top of the huge £36 million a year he already gets for promoting the brand.[45] You cannot get inside the mind of a footballer, but Ronaldo's comments leave you wondering if it influences how he plays. For instance, his choice to make a comfortable pass to a better-positioned teammate or take a long shot for the winning goal? Ronaldo has spoken about his obsession: 'That second Ballon d'Or was one of the most beautiful moments in my life,' he explained in the documentary film *Ronaldo*. 'But my ambition ends up always wanting more, always wanting more.'[46] When he won his third for the 2014 season, he unleashed a howling '*Siiii*' a huge 'Yes' of celebration. It is almost as if the Portuguese captain's lone moment on a winter's night in the Swiss Alps in his shiny blue suit was worth more to him than his triumph alongside ten other men in the brilliant white of Real Madrid, as they defeated city rivals Atlético Madrid 4-1 in the Champions League final in Lisbon the previous summer. Beyond all else, the award represents the triumph of an individual trying to escape the collective glories of a team. This is a fallacy. As Henry argued, success in modern football is built upon unified action and discipline, and players working selflessly for a shared victory, not seeking an opportunity to showboat for the highlights reel. Creativity is vital, but for players like Ronaldo and Messi to flourish, those around them must execute their own roles to perfection. The Ballon d'Or exemplifies how in a hyper-commercialised team sport, players are individualised, compared and incentivised to strive for their own glorification.

Sports Entertainment

Comparison with the past can be overbearing for fledgling sportsmen, and subjective rankings can inflate individuals' celebrity status above the reputations of great teams. Sport is an imperfect meritocracy, and although in fair competition the cream rises to the top, outside of sporting arenas names are made and destroyed by the surrounding media and culture: via advertising deals with clothing brands, through the words of journalists, in the comments of players and managers, and increasingly across social media. The role of an agent or an image consultant is as important in shaping careers as a coach with their training tips. The purity of sport is diluted through commercialisation, but many fans know this and are reconciled with the ways in which live events have become pay-per-view sports entertainment. Theatrical flourishes beyond the field of play: fireworks, half-time shows and performers in mascot suits are a crowd-pleasing circus. This razzmatazz frames professional sport as a pursuit only for a portion of society. Commercialisation has hyped up some elite sports and fuelled comparisons, crushing and elevating careers, but there has been a stark omission in my argument so far, that is so commonplace in sports writing, that it is all but taken for granted.

The comparisons have all been stories of sportsmen. The four waves of feminism have had little impact on the world's sports fields. Sadly, for emerging female athletes there are fewer forebears. Fewer greats of sport for comparison. Fewer icons to inspire young girls to achieve the unimaginable or to motivate women to try harder every day. There is also less media attention, less sponsorship and less of a theatrical carnival surrounding women's sport. This is not for an absence of female attainment at the elite level, but because the doors to the Parthenon of sporting immortality are marshalled by male gatekeepers. Across sports news desks, governing bodies and the advertising sector that does so much to boost the status of elite sport, the whole industry is a patriarchy. When female superstars do break out into popular consciousness, all too often they are compared to men rather than other great women.

At Pinehurst golf course in North Carolina, towering longleaf pines cascade over sand-based ridges separating to form glades in the valley; it is a beautiful place to host a competition. Here in 2000, Michelle Wie first made headlines at just ten years of age. She entered the USGA Women's Amateur Public Links Championship and became the youngest player to qualify for an amateur championship event. Four years later she was 'the most vaunted golfing prodigy since Tiger Woods'. The Korean American stepped on to the first tee of the 2004 Sony Open to become the youngest ever person to play in a Men's PGA Tour event. Former world number one, Ernie Els, who played against her that January week, said at the time: 'She's a true phenomenon. I was lucky enough to be around when Tiger Woods came out; I saw him when he was an amateur, and a lot of what I saw from Michelle reminds [me] of what Tiger used to do. I don't think I have ever seen a lady golfer who swings the club as well as she does.'[47] Playing in her native Honolulu, she missed the cut at her first attempt by just one stroke. From the outset, the excitement about Wie was not just that she was a prodigious child golfer, but that she was a female who could compete with males. The comparisons with Tiger Woods and other men grabbed global attention. Sony likely got more name-checking publicity from her 2004 appearance than they had since they launched the first Walkman.

Over the past two decades, Wie has won five women's LPGA titles, including the 2014 United States Open, and she made eight starts in men's PGA Tour events, but never made the cut. Though she has had a very good career in women's golf, she is not in the top fifty list of golfers with the most LPGA Tour wins or in the Hall of Fame. She does though remain one of the most famous female athletes. Since first stepping on the fairway in front of the world's cameras, she has been a commercial dream. In 2006 she was the sixth-highest earning golfer in the world with an income of $20.2 million, most of it earned off-course, and like Woods's endorsements, a lot of that cash came from Nike. Her other sponsors have included Kia and McDonald's as well as Sony.[48] Her entry in men's events garnered great publicity and as she grew up, she continually attracted attention for her looks. Wie feels she has been misunderstood and too much attention has been paid to her appearance on the course: 'If I wear a short skirt, it's not because I'm trying to be revealing. It's because I really don't like the feel of a skirt breaking on my mid-thigh.'[49]

Now in her mid-thirties, Wie no longer competes in male events. On the one hand, the comparisons with male golfers, especially

Woods, helped boost her image, land major sponsorship deals and ultimately raised the profile of women's golf. She has reaped the benefits and become an incredibly wealthy celebrity. On the other hand, her entry into men's competition overshadowed more successful female golfers and attracted controversy, including the use of sponsors' exemptions which allows the big-name brands that support golfing tournaments to invite players that might not otherwise be qualified. Wie has always been coy in discussing the invites and competition with male golfers. She has a degree in communications from Stanford University and makes regular TV appearances as a pundit, so is adept at managing her public image. It is difficult to know how the comparisons have affected her game, but back in 2008, speaking after her eighth attempt to make the PGA Tour cut, she said: 'Whether it's a women's or men's, shooting a good round, the feeling you get after shooting a low score, it's the same. I'm really excited to play some good golf.'[50] Suggesting that first and foremost she is a sportsperson that just wanted to achieve her best.

Objective and Subjective Comparison

As the pioneering female tennis player Billie Jean King said, 'Women get the attention when we get into the men's arena, and that's sad.' Michelle Wie's story is a prime example of this. She is better known for how she did in comparison to men than for her achievement in women's sport. To escape this prison of comparison, female sport needs to ascend to an even footing. One way in which to advance the profile has been to campaign for equal pay. The US women' soccer team has demanded the same remuneration as their male counterparts, who have only tended to make up the numbers in international tournaments, like the World Cup, a competition the US women have won a record four times, although they had a disappointing performance in 2023. The women's team are a great commercial success and generate double the men's revenues for US Soccer. Co-captain Megan Rapinoe spearheaded the fight for fair pay and argued that their campaign was about wider gender equality: 'It's actually about women everywhere being treated equally and respectfully in the workplace'[51]

In 2020, Rapinoe won the *Ballon d'Or Féminin*, also known as the Women's Ballon d'Or. Like the male prize, her achievement was a subjective popularity contest as well as a recognition of sporting prowess. It is difficult to argue with her award. Rapinoe seems to have it all: a World Cup-winning captain who has gained as much praise as an outspoken advocate for LGBTQ+ rights and gender equality. After turning down an invitation to the White House, she lambasted President Trump live on CNN: 'Your message is excluding people. You're excluding me, you're excluding people that look like me, you're excluding people of color, you're excluding Americans that maybe support you.'[52]

Rapinoe was only the second ever winner of the female version of football's top individual prize. The previous year, Ada Hegerberg, a Norwegian striker for Olympique Lyonnais, claimed the inaugural award. Sadly, the long overdue moment of equal recognition was overshadowed by controversy. After accepting she was asked by the host, French DJ Martin Solveig, if she 'twerked': the infamous sexualised dance fad. The question was horrendously ill-judged and bordered on harassment. You can never imagine a man like Messi or Ronaldo being so shamed in their moment of glory. The Norwegian star answered with a firm *no*. The audience was stunned, the camera panned to Mbappé who was there to collect the young player award and his appalled reaction said absolutely everything. A huge backlash against Solveig followed on social media. In later interviews, Hegerberg tried to turn the conversation away from the outrage and argued the importance of the award: 'Obviously, it's an individual trophy, but it's still a symbol because we're talking about women's football. That's basically the biggest sport in the world and it shows that we're going some right direction as well.' She further talked about how she wanted to be a role model for young girls, and how her older sister, who is also a professional footballer with Paris Saint-Germain, spurred her on to do well: 'We've been pushing each other, supporting each other, since we were little kids. She's one of the people who has meant maybe the most for me in my life and my career because she always was there to help me and we're still best buddies today and sisters, so we have a special bond.'[53] For the Hegerberg girls, some gentle competition, alongside working together, helped them rise to the top of the world. Those personal comparisons that began in childhood were foundational in shaping their lives for the better.

The greatness of Jordan, Messi, Wie or Hegerberg represents a form of meritocracy and their achievements and disappointments are linked to objective measurable performance within agreed and established rules. Yet their superstar status is by varying degrees also subjective. Primarily their status comes from athletic ability and winning championships, but their reputations are also the product of a sports entertainment industry that does not consistently make fair comparisons between sportswomen and men and instead is led by subjective valuing of appearance and charisma. A miasma of objectivity shrouds subjective reality. As one of my geography colleagues, Kevin Lougheed, illustrates when he teaches an introductory course on scientific research methods. His class includes a lecture slide from a Scooby-Doo cartoon. Infamously, every episode of Scooby-Doo has a penultimate scene in which the four teenage members of Mystery Inc. – Fred, Shaggy, Daphne and Velma – unmask the seemingly supernatural antagonist to reveal a real person in a costume, a suspicious character introduced at the beginning of the show. Kevin's unmasking slide is captioned 'Oh objectivity, let's see who you really . . . Oh! It was subjectivity all along!' The same goes for comparing sporting greats. We can list all Maradona's and Messi's footballing achievements to try in vain to produce an objective, metricised comparison, but ultimately it comes down to a subjective assessment. Who comes out as the all-time greatest player was the footballer we liked most all along.

If sporting comparisons are wreathed by objective measure of performance, greatness in other walks of life are nakedly subjective. In the next chapter we move to the fields of government and cultural, where the achievements of great people are fraught and contested. Here comparisons of greatness extend beyond the contributions of key individuals – artists, celebrities, politicians and scientists – and reflect unequal power relations within society and their continual, selective veneration of certain male leaders.

CHAPTER 3

Who is the Greatest Ever Briton?

What comparing great people reveals about society

100 Great Britons

Crossing Westminster Bridge, the temperature drops as cool air is funnelled along the River Thames. The breeze is welcome in the summer, offering relief from the heat trap of tight city streets. In winter, the damp chill bites at exposed skin, coats are pulled in tighter and footsteps quicken. Heading to the North Bank, the Palace of Westminster stands smaller than you imagine, and yet remains a powerful emblem of the British political establishment. Beside the House of Commons, there are twelve statues around the green of Parliament Square. One woman and eleven men. They are not arranged regularly like hour marks on a clock face but form a boomerang-shaped curve bordering the gardens. At the south-west corner is Nelson Mandela. Moving clockwise, Robert Peel is next, the first of five nineteenth-century prime ministers, then Abraham Lincoln, Mahatma Gandhi and Benjamin Disraeli. A recent 2018 addition is the lone female, Millicent Fawcett, leader of the suffragettes. Then another six politicians. The last

49

of these is the most venerated figure: Winston Churchill occupies the corner opposite Big Ben in a buttoned great coat, collar raised against the wind, face set against the world.

Churchill was crowned the 'Greatest Briton in History' in a 2002 BBC poll that garnered over a million votes. The greatness of Britain's wartime hero was reaffirmed. As a spokeswoman said, 'Everyone's delighted with it.' The public had chosen from a list of one hundred figures. Churchill's celebration was widely anticipated, but rather than delighting *everyone*, the contest led to discontent about how greatness is compared. *100 Greatest Britons* was flawed in method and design. Isambard Kingdom Brunel came second, ahead of historical luminaries including Charles Darwin and William Shakespeare. Brunel was a great railway engineer of the Industrial Revolution. A worthy inclusion in the top one hundred, but a surprise runner-up, his elevation boosted by a campaign led by Brunel University students and some 'sophisticated' voting tactics to get their man to the top spot. If they had been successful, as they very nearly were, this would have been rather awkward for the BBC. The unintended elevation of Brunel illustrates how comparisons can be rigged. Picking the greatest Briton was a glorified parlour game, but the legacy is not so trivial. For the casual historian looking back at the widely reproduced BBC metric, Brunel's podium finish will not be remembered as a voting anomaly.

Much more concerning than the polling methodology was the reaction to the long list of one hundred, which had been drawn up following a survey of 30,000 people. Of the hundred chosen, only thirteen were women. There were no Black Britons. Freddie Mercury, who was often assumed to be white, was the only non-European. These omissions garnered no comment on the BBC story announcing the list, which fails to mention the gross gender imbalance or lack of representation of non-white people.[54] Today it would be unimaginable to list a hundred significant individuals so lacking in diversity. There was no place for Shirley Bassey, Agatha Christie, Millicent Fawcett, Rosalind Franklin, Elizabeth Fry, Stuart Hall, Audrey Hepburn, Noor Inayat Khan, Ben Kingsley, Salman Rushdie, Mary Seacole, Wilfred Wood or

Virginia Woolf. Some of these names might be unfamiliar; and that is the point. Lists like the BBC's draw attention to under-appreciated figures as well as comparing established greats such as Darwin and Shakespeare. Furthermore, the list included the objectionable historic figures of Enoch Powell, who espoused fascist and racist views, and Robert Baden-Powell, who as well as founding the scouting movement has been accused of executing an African chief who had surrendered as a prisoner of war and been promised safe treatment.[55] The inclusion of Enoch Powell was noted for personifying 'the British bulldog spirit for some right-wingers' according to Helen Haste, an expert on cultural icons at Bath University quoted by the BBC in 2002.[56] An ill-judged remark that seems absurd today. Public lists like this matter, as rather than just measuring greatness they spark debate, draw attention and fossilise reputations. Who is in the conversation is as important as the identity of the winner.

Churchill and Johnson

Two decades on from *100 Greatest Britons*, Winston Churchill continues to gather adoration. In 2014, Boris Johnson wrote a celebratory biography *The Churchill Factor*. Not only was this book gushing in praise, it was relentless in building a favourable comparison between the then Mayor of London and Britain's wartime leader. As Will Lloyd of the *New Statesman* writes:

> This was the point of *The Churchill Factor*. To kick enough biographical sand in people's eyes until, when they looked up, they could no longer see where Churchill started and Johnson ended. Churchill's detractors are 'snobbish' and a 'teensy bit jealous' – like Johnson's. Churchill's writing was a way of 'dramatising and publicising himself' – like Johnson's. Churchill's disloyalty to party colleagues was 'magnificent' – like Johnson's. It becomes absurd. 'In habits', Churchill – and I can't find another biographer who has made this claim – 'superficially resembled a Bertie Wooster figure'. Just . . . Like . . . Johnson.

He is absorbed by blurring the lines between his subject and himself. Amplifying Churchill's qualities as a leader, journalist and national hero has a halo effect for Johnson, the writer-politician, as he is associated in some voters' imaginations with this model icon.

Despite mainstream veneration, Churchill remains a divisive figure. When, in 2020, the Black Lives Matter movement shook the United States and reverberated around the world from Minneapolis to Melbourne, and Philadelphia to Paris, effigies of historical racists were attacked by protesters seeking social justice. Churchill's statue facing Big Ben became one of the key sites of British protest. After a weekend of being plastered with slogans: 'All lives can't matter until Black Lives Matter', 'Churchill was racist'. Johnson, now prime minister, rallied to protect his hero. In a high-profile *Telegraph* column, he passionately declared he would defend the statue 'with every breath in my body', though it was under no serious threat of falling. The polemic defence of Churchill's statue made the protection of colonial-era monuments a law-and-order issue and further fanned the flames of an ongoing culture war that threatens to polarise British society. Similar cleavages already divide America where civil war symbols bisect communities. Throughout the world, the legacies of other disputed icons – King Leopold II in Belgium, Francisco Franco in Spain, Queens Victoria and Elizabeth II in Canada, Cecil Rhodes in South Africa and James Cook in Australia – are fiercely contested as they pose difficult questions about identity. Churchill attracts love and anger. By offering undying support, Johnson courted popularism through the refracted comparison with a divisive relic of an imperial past.

Churchill's status as a resilient and determined leader also resonated across the Atlantic. At the same time, as cities around the United States erupted in protest, Donald Trump visited a Washington church, posed with a Bible, and called for an end to the disturbance. The president's photo opportunity had required the dispersal of Black Lives Matter campaigners by police armed with tear gas. A White House spokesperson made a ridiculous and ill-judged comparison as he argued that this choreographed media stunt was an important symbol of strength for Americans akin to Churchill's visits to bomb-damaged London.[57] Churchill's heroic wartime reputation and unwavering 'never surrender' stance against Adolf Hitler is familiar to every Briton along with many in America. What is less well known in London and Washington is how Churchill was equally forthright in his defence of the British Empire and flippant in his disregard for foreign lives.

Like Baden-Powell, Churchill was at the forefront of aggressive imperialism. As a young man he bragged of shooting three 'savages' in the Sudan. He defended British atrocities including the first concentration camps that led to the deaths of 28,000 white Afrikaners and 14,000 black South Africans during the Boer War. Once a Member of Parliament, he demanded the expansion of empire championing the belief that 'the Aryan stock is bound to triumph'. He was a social Darwinist who believed in racial hierarchies and eugenics, with the British pitched as winners in this global contest.[58] When Secretary of State for the Colonies, he unleashed the notorious Black and Tan paramilitary forces that savaged the Catholic population of Ireland in the 1920s. Later, when Kurds rebelled against British rule, he said: 'I am strongly in favour of using poisoned gas against uncivilised tribes . . . [It] would spread a lively terror.' In 1931 when out of government, he was campaigning against Indian self-rule and bluntly argued that the vast majority of Indians 'are primitive people'.

It was the Indian subcontinent that bore the very worst of Churchill's leadership. He vehemently opposed home rule for India and said the following in a Cabinet meeting about Mahatma Gandhi's advocation for self-determination: 'Gandhi should not be released on the account of a mere threat of fasting. We should be rid of a bad man and an enemy of the Empire if he died.' His horrific disregard for Indian life was later realised on a much greater scale. In 1943, a famine broke out in Bengal killing up to three million people. An unimaginable number, but to help render the scale of this disaster, throughout the Second World War, approximately 450,000 British civilians and military personnel died. The Nobel Prize-winning economist Amartya Sen demonstrated the Bengali deaths were a result of imperial policies. As colonial subjects starved, British officials begged the prime minister to redirect food supplies. Churchill refused and raged that it was their own fault for 'breeding like rabbits'.[59] These twentieth-century global atrocities might be unfamiliar to many Britons, but one man who will be well aware of the details is Winston Churchill's biographer: Boris Johnson.

Faced by the Black Lives Matter protesters in 2020, who called for a reappraisal of Churchill's legacy as part of a wider campaign for racial equality, the then prime minister ignored their voices and redoubled his support. Having harnessed his reputation to Churchill's, Johnson leveraged the wartime leader's legacy as part of a wider polarising popularist identity. Brand Boris encapsulates a nostalgia for British greatness on the global stage. This was an imperial greatness. Britain's comparative wealth, power and status was derived from colonial trade and the exploitation of Africans, Indians, Irish and others around the world. His vision of Britain continually casts back to the Second World War and pitches Britain's leading role in the global conflict as the defining moment in national history. This celebration of Britain's wartime endeavours and 'blitz spirit' is a very popular trope, and the ways in which countless contemporary cultural and political moments are compared against the events of 1939–45 are explored in Chapter 12.

Johnson's Churchill-inflected nationalism won him a general election and is associated with a particular individualistic patriarchy. The pairing of a Nation and a so-called Great Man is a long-standing association that feeds the myth that major change can be willed by the strength of one heroic figure alone. Donald Trump wanted to follow in the footsteps of the founding fathers and single-handedly 'Make America Great Again', Gaullism has become its own grand political identity in France, between a metaphor and a model, to which other aspirational leaders compare themselves.

Through the Brexit referendum triumph and his electoral victories, his selective British nationalism and a sense of his own manifest destiny have been key ingredients in Johnson's pitch to the electorate. At the end of 2020 when Britain exited the European

Union, one of his Conservative MPs spoke triumphantly in the House of Commons and favourably compared Johnson to Winston Churchill and even Alexander the Great![60] Remarks that look ludicrous given his ignominious exit from the Palace of Westminster less than two years later. While the Churchillian self-confidence and masculinity have had a strong resonance with a big proportion of British society, today's voters are not the flag-waving masses of the 1950s that re-elected Churchill. An increasingly multicultural society populated by many decedents of colonialism and shaped by cultural globalisation means black, white, Asian, British or European citizens increasingly want to rethink the nation's relationship with heritage and challenge symbols of empire like the statues of Parliament Square. Ultimately it was Johnson's own party that ousted him from power, in a portentous moment that demonstrated individuals that aspire to greatness are dependent upon wider scaffolds of support.

Great Men around the World

What does it mean to be a great? The British television programme and mass public vote were just the first in a whole raft of national *100 Greatest* . . . contests. Across the last two decades there have been thirty-nine around the world, from the BBC's original in 2002 to the most recent one in Slovakia in 2018. Each reflected the character of the cultural and political history of a different nation, but there are also important commonalities that tell us more about what is most valued in these high-profile interpersonal comparisons.

Some of the national winners have been international household names and among the most famous people in world history such as Charles de Gaulle in France, Nelson Mandela for South Africa, and Leonardo da Vinci from Italy. Others were more obscure. The greatest Indian was B. R. Ambedkar, an important politician and reformer, who was chosen after the much more recognisable Mahatma Gandhi was excluded. Gandhi would have overwhelmed the competition and detracted from the surprise, or at least the competitive element of the show's format.

Elizabeth II and other living royals were similarly excluded from the British show. Brazil's contest followed a football-like knockout structure where competitors were compared against one another, and the surprising victor was Chico Xavier, a spiritist medium. On the Discovery Channel's *The Greatest American*, the winner was not, as might be expected, President Lincoln, Washington, Franklin or even Martin Luther King Jr., but someone more at home on the small screen, former TV actor turned politician Ronald Reagan.

The US show aired in 2005 shortly after President Reagan's death, which led to an emotional surge in voting support. His son, Ron, told Discovery that his recent passing may have been a factor in his father's success and observed that, 'I'm sure he would be very honoured to be in the company of these great gentlemen.' In retrospect, the elevation of Reagan does look like an anomaly and an unreasonable comparison, but his accomplishment has subsequently been used by conservative commentators, such as biographer Paul Kengor, to embellish his reputation. Like the British original, the US version has met sustained criticism for the way in which it compiled the long list of historical figures and for a heavy weighting towards contemporary celebrities: Ellen DeGeneres, Mel Gibson, Rush Limbaugh, Michael Moore, Martha Stewart or Dr Phil are unlikely to feature in a long list of 100 greatest Americans published today. Some of these figures have waned from the forefront of public consciousness, others have had their reputations tarnished.

Despite the US contest being nearly two decades old, its legacy continues. The Israeli-born artist Jac Lahav used the Discovery production as a jumping-off point to develop his own high-profile series of more than thirty portraits of famous figures in a celebration of American life as being layered in history, lore and imagery that has toured galleries from the Richmond Art Museum in 2010 to The Slater Art Museum in 2023. This is an evolving canon that explores how such competitions are a contested cultural legacy. Lahav's thoughtful intervention is not intended to be an objective attempt to find a singular great American and the portraits are a critical reflection that such a notion of a unified great is unobtainable. As Lahav says, these comparisons reflect 'the push and pull between who are the people that we see as being great Americans and who actually achieved greatness.' Mirroring this ambiguity his collection includes new names such as Ruth Bader Ginsburg, Afong Moy (the first Chinese woman in America), Charging Bear (aka first nation leader Little Big Man) as well as a tongue-in-cheek portrait of his own dog, the Instagram star pug: Momo.[61]

Moving the camera lens further back to span across all thirty-nine national televised competitions, there is one trend that is more striking above all others, and this is becoming a defining theme across the people comparisons in the three initial chapters, and that is a total absence of female winners in any national competition. Not only have there never been any female outright winners, but women consistently make up a tiny proportion of the long lists of a hundred candidates for every nation that has ever run the comparative contest. Even if the British competition were to be relaunched today with the inclusion of the late Elizabeth II, her certain victory would be an empty one for feminists. It is only her unearned hereditary advantages of birth and privilege that transcend any gendered disadvantage.

Who is included for discussion in these comparisons sets the limit for debate and can reflect unacknowledged biases that evolve within society. *100 Greatest Britons* under-represented women and excluded ethnic minorities, thus reproducing British national identity as primarily male and exclusively white. Outrage from the black community led to the publication of an alternative list of the hundred greatest Black Britons in 2004, topped by the pioneering nurse Mary Seacole. After Black Lives Matter surged into global consciousness in 2020, a new list of '100 Great Black Britons' was published, but this time around the book that emerged from that project was a collective celebration that includes new role models and previously little-known historical figures, rather than a glorified popularity contest with a single winner like the BBC's poll. The urgency of this type of project is underlined by a recent survey that found most UK adults could not name a single historical Black British figure.[62]

If there were further doubt as to the necessity for more of a national conversation over who is publicly celebrated, we can circle back to Parliament Square. The statue of Fawcett was only erected after a long feminist campaign to improve the representation of great British women in public life. The other eight British statues continue to calcify national identity as white and male. Alongside them, three of the four great foreign leaders – Gandhi, Mandela and Lincoln – may represent ethnic diversity and voices for democracy, equality and liberty, but the effect is diminished as they share Parliament Square with the South African prime minister Jan Smuts, a staunch advocate of racial segregation.

Rethinking Greatness

The point of the discussion of the comparison between Churchill and Johnson has not been primarily to determine if the characters of the two political leaders were indeed similar or different. Modern British historians have argued that Boris just does not match up to Winston. Dominic Sandbrook and Tom Holland make the point that Churchill's caddish father, Lord Randolph Churchill, a Tory popularist who cultivated mass appeal, was much more like Johnson than his son. Randolph was great at whipping up crowds with talk of the Queen and empire and called his opponents 'prigs' and 'misery guts', just the sort of thing Johnson barked at the opposition benches in the House of Commons. He was also a complete opportunist and a 'terrible man' that tried to blackmail the Prince of Wales, one of many unedifying scrapes this 'talented but utterly untrustworthy and unreliable man' found himself in. As Sandbrook argues, 'Boris Johnson models himself on Winston Churchill, but Lord Randolph would be a better comparison.'[63] He shares the human flaws of the father rather than the single-minded political vision of the son. Johnson's attempts to contort himself into a Churchillian mould to replicate a pattern of power were ultimately doomed to fail.

There is a could-be-true, but isn't really, likeness between the two journalists-turned-prime ministers, so then yes, when taken at face value, Winston Churchill and Boris Johnson is a bullshit comparison. However, the principal argument is deeper, and that is that Johnson's naked desire to be a new British national icon and reproduce the respect and power for which Churchill is famous is a deeply flawed and egotistical aspiration that replicates an outdated set of colonial, patriarchal and oppressive attitudes. The stoic Second World War leader was a diehard advocate for the British Empire, who espoused racist views, had a callous disregard for foreign life and was responsible for millions of deaths. Churchill's bullshit worldviews are no model for a leader in the twenty-first century.

From a starting point of asking 'Who is the greatest Briton?' this chapter exposed Churchill's role in imperial conflicts, atrocities and famines that were some of the worst moments in British history. Beyond Great Britain, in Ireland, Africa and India, he was a villain of his age, not a hero. Perhaps we can fix that toxic comparison and find another individual worthy of national adoration? Maybe a famous scientist or a writer or a different type of political figure? Ultimately it does not matter if, say, Darwin, Shakespeare or Elizabeth II were instead crowned the greatest Briton; all had human flaws, but rightly deserve to be celebrated alongside a wider, diverse and evolving body of outstanding individuals. Their greatness stems not only from their originality, but the circumstances of their birth, their connections to other scholars, artists and political leaders, and their lasting roles within wider global society. Individual comparisons spark animated, diverting debate, but a broader relational perspective on key women and men within history tells us not just about certain great people, but what is needed for a great society. As the example of Lahav's Great Americans and '100 Great Black Britons' illustrates, comparison can be an effective tool for drawing attention to those we don't always think of and may begin to help redress the social injustices of history.

More broadly, the worldwide '100 Greatest' comparisons of the last two decades were bullshit because although De Gaulle or Reagan could be truly the greatest Frenchman or American, the whole premise of this made-for-TV format was flawed.

The competitions for greatness reflected social attitudes when the contests were held rather than being objective and timeless litmus tests of achievement. Such exercises in comparisons serve as discursive tools that reflect a moment in time, and privilege certain people who are overwhelmingly male, charismatic, nationalistic and ruthlessly ambitious. They prioritise the individual over the collective, and as such were a harbinger of a wider social trend towards individualism. We are all daily pitched against one another in an increasingly comparative world. From the competitive way in which social media posts are liked and shared, via online reviews for everything from academics who get compared on RateMyProfessors.com to zoos on TripAdvisor, through to the ranking of achievements in education and work; performance-based measures direct us to compare. It is intuitive to understand society comparatively, but is it always helpful? Comparisons are all too often bad, lazy and dangerous, yet exert a powerful influence over everyday life. Contests and rankings influence our decisions, skew what we remember, and shape how we interact with people.

The previous chapter illustrated the ways in which female attainment can be overshadowed by male accomplishments and this pattern carries forward from the family home and local school to sporting arenas and the world's most established parliamentary democracies. The perception of greatness in sports in the second chapter reflected patriarchal relationships, the power of commerce through sponsorship, and the rise of sport-entertainment in promoting male achievement, as well as the triumph of individual reputations above team accolades. Greatness in wider society is also inherently individualistic. This is apparent in the electoral successes of the democratic leaders that make up a quarter of the '100 Greatest' national competition winners. Despite their individual popular mandates, their achievements are never just down to their unique qualities and charisma, but the strength of the party and broader movement behind them.

Finally, there is one last comparison associated with Winston Churchill to consider as it serves as a cameo of the next chapter. As well as being the 'Greatest Briton' and a foil for Johnson's self-aggrandising comparisons, Churchill is also renowned for being compared to a particular type of dog. In 1940 as Britain faced its darkest hour, a cartoonist for the *Daily Express,* Sidney Strube, drew a bulldog astride a map of the British Isles with a number ten tag on his collar, a steel helmet, and Churchill's head grafted on to the body with the caption 'Go to it'.[64] This was a perfect fit. Even his squat, stout physique, bald head and loose-jowled face gives him something of a bulldoggish appearance and it became the ultimate motif for his doggedness. This association was picked up by artists throughout the Second World War. It travelled across the Atlantic where a prominent poster featured another cartoon of a Churchill-faced bulldog astride a Union flag with the caption 'Holding the line' representing British resistance to the spread of Nazi Germany. While the image had been dreamed up by illustrators, Churchill's first pet had been a bulldog named 'Dodo' which he sold his bicycle to buy when a pupil at Harrow School.[65] With such a synergy between the image of a public figure and his pup, this raises the question, is it fair to compare people and their pets? Do dogs look like their owners?

CHAPTER 4

Do Dogs Look Like Their Owners?

How non-human comparisons conceal class and racial prejudice

Show Dogs

A pristine baize green carpet of AstroTurf awaits the contestants. Bright advertising hoardings surround the stadia. The booming echo of the tannoy fires up an excited crowd. Competitors from Belgium, Portugal, Russia, Thailand and the UK make their way to the centre, gracefully looping past the silver trophy. Anticipation builds. A nervous calm descends as the judge makes his way along the line for the first time, keenly looking each of them up and down: head, torso, leg. Seeking flaws in perfect bodies. The hushed tones of the TV commentators introduce the finalists one by one: a Samoyed, a Papillon, a Basset Griffon Vendeen, a Shih Tzu, a Boxer, an Irish Water Spaniel and a Scottish Terrier. The climax of Crufts Dog Show has all the theatre of a sporting final and the choreography of a beauty pageant.

The quest for an ever more perfect dog draws in competitors from around the world. Tens of thousands of dogs from more than 200 breeds compete at Crufts annually. Pedigree dog shows are not without controversy. Developing a pedigree is an attempt to retain and promote favoured genetic features. Concerns have been raised by animal welfare charities including the RSPCA and Dogs Trust which stopped attending Crufts in 2009.[66] Strict breed standards can promote dogs that have the right look, but the desired physical features may have ugly side effects or lead to genetic complications. Dangerously flat faces and excessive skin folds can lead to a low quality of life. Breeders trying to meet a certain model standard only mate sires and dams from the same breed and these parents may be closely related. Disease-causing genes can become prevalent as repeat inter-breeding rapidly narrows the gene pool and raises the risk of hereditary disease including hip dysplasia (a ball and socket that do not fit together), cancer and heart problems. Spaniels are liable to a chronic kidney disease, which is progressive, fatal and generally develops before five years of age. Dogs die on average 226 days after diagnosis.[67] Carriers do not express features of the disease, but if both parents have the mutated recessive gene, each pup has a 25 per cent chance of inheriting the life-ending disorder.

Dogs express genetic variability beyond the control of any pedigree breeder. Breeding problems are common in show dogs where owners are trying to achieve the perfect embodiment of a breed: the ultimate dog for comparison. Some highly acclaimed breeds expand from a small number of founder dogs, and if one or more carries diseased genes, particularly a champion male that sires multiple pups, it can spread across the population. Pairing strategies can help reduce disease frequency, but eliminating certain dogs from breeding further narrows the gene pool and leads to genetic bottlenecks. Correcting one genetic problem can create a new one. Even DNA tests are not a panacea. Tests are usually patented and often expensive and based on assumed relationships of disease susceptibility.[68]

Comparing dogs both in terms of selecting the best specimen within a breed, or finding the ultimate top dog is a big business. Dog shows feed into fashions in ownership, creating a buzz around certain breeds driving up demand and prices. Pedigrees such as pugs and French bulldogs have become highly prized. Some dogs, like Jac Lahav's Momo, are even icons of Instagram and TikTok with legions of followers. Unscrupulous breeders can cash in on short-term fads with irresponsible breeding strategies creating long-running genetic problems. Mixed breeds such as Cavapoos (a Cavalier King Charles Spaniel cross-bed with a poodle) that only emerged in the 1990s have become popular with suburban households as they are laid-back, loyal and sociable and have a cute teddy-bear-like appearance, perfect for family photos. Being a mixed breed reduces the likelihood of developing genetic conditions like chronic kidney disease, though the pups' characteristics are less predictable than the offspring of pedigree pairings. Cavapoos are much in demand and not cheap. Puppies cost £1,800 to £3,000, far more than less photogenic breeds.

Crufts itself is not a product of the social media age. The show has been running since 1891 and is as popular as ever. The event in Britain's National Exhibition Centre regularly attracts over 160,000 visitors and is televised across many countries. The 'best in show' competition is in effect the ultimate dog beauty contest; an attempt to compare all different shapes, sizes and characters and hold them to some subjectively defined notion of what is most desirable in a canine. There is a strange circularity to this. As with human beauty, past winners inform the judging criteria, then what is highly prized today sets the standard against which subsequent contestants are measured. Certain genetic characteristics become fixed as the most prized, either in that breed of dog or that category of person. The flip side of this is that those with different or opposing aesthetic qualities are lowly ranked.

In 2019, 'best in show' went to a Belgian Papillon named Dylan. Judge Dan Ericsson said he had been 'spoiled for choice', was drawn to a 'beautiful dog', who had 'everything you could look for in the breed', plus personality.[69] Accompanying a replica of the solid silver Keddell Memorial Trophy was a miserly cash prize of £100. There was also a bag of dry dog food thrown in from a sponsor. Owner Kathleen Roosens was delighted with Dylan's victory and had something more appetising planned as a special treat: 'You do know the saying: winner winner chicken dinner!'[70]

Kathleen and Dylan made a happy pair. Her neatly cut straight, fair, almost white, blonde hair and black-and-white two-piece skirt and top were coordinated with the papillon's award-winning, flowing white-and-black coat. There was something metaphorical in the tele-connected appearance. Around Crufts there are many human–dog doppelgängers. Angular-faced Afghan hounds with poker-straight locks and their saloon-fresh blonde keepers. Bichon Frises, like fluffy white clouds, and their snow-haired elderly owners. The towering Irish Wolfhound with a six-foot-six, lean and taut grey-haired handler. The wobbly, shaggy Old English Sheepdog with drooping whiskers around his snout held close by a stout man with a magnificent full moustache. Is it a truism that dogs look like their owners or rather that owners look like their dogs? Do beautiful people have beautiful dogs? What makes for an ugly dog and who owns them? Or is it unhelpful to read too much into human–dog likenesses?

Class

It is fun to make human–dog comparisons, but surface similarities are only the most visible aspect of complex relationships. It is doubtful that resemblances between potential pets and owners are the starting points for many decisions as to which breed of dog to take home, more likely when they align it is a happy coincidence. When someone chooses to share their life with a medium-sized mammal and realises that they are a dog person rather than a cat person, online tools such as the 'dog breed selector' by pet food supplier IAMS can help them decide. The IAMS app guides potential owners through questions on housing, outdoor space, children, experience, other pets, personality, barking, exercise, independence, obedience, size, grooming, shedding and qualities. Online comparisons provide only a snapshot and can never encapsulate the variance in individual dogs' traits, but they offer a baseline to work from. The output is a metric, a percentage match that recommends the most suitable breed, as well as some alternatives. For instance, if the preferences are towards the large, powerful dogs, the guide suggests Great Danes, Mastiffs or Rottweilers. Key physical and behavioural characteristics of these big dogs can then all be readily compared.

Dog comparison sites offer a relatively objective result, but miss the many unspoken influences that shape ownership decisions. Different breeds mark out social boundaries. Dogs can be tools of class distinction as well as objects of love. The aristocracy has long been associated with high-breed hounds. In 1892 the Duchess of Newcastle paid £200 at Crufts, equivalent to £20,000 in today's money, for a Borzoi named Oudar. The Borzois are a large, graceful hunting dog with wavy hair. Oudar was one of sixteen Borzois sent to Crufts that year by Nicholas II of Russia and was just the first of the duchess's thirteen Borzois.[71] The narrow-headed hounds became a symbol of affluence and taste. Czars would gift Borzois to European royalty at the turn of the twentieth century, however the breed came close to extinction in 1918 when many were slaughtered alongside their aristocratic owners during the Russian Revolution.

Back in Britain, along with a wax jacket, wellington boots and a Land Rover, the venerable Labrador is the hallmark of good country living. As at home out on the great estates as sleeping besides the kitchen Agas of the upper middle classes, the Labrador is a marker of reliability and status. In contrast, other dogs signal quite different qualities. The assertive, squat and powerful Staffordshire Bull Terrier, or Staffies, are commonly associated with white working-class youths, but this is not a positive relationship, as Ed West writing in the *Telegraph* puts it: 'Why is it that every time one sees a Staffordshire Bull Terrier walking down the street, the chances are the man at the other end of the lead has an IQ at sub-moronic level and a swagger that suggests an undeserved level of personal confidence? I've nothing against the dogs, but many of their owners are a waste of oxygen.'[72] The subtitle of this piece was 'why the underclass is bad for the environment' and West's barely contained rage clearly signals that some dogs are seen as emblematic of low-class status and he further discusses how Bull Terriers are associated with violence. Staffies have made headlines for aggressive acts, but the breed responsible for the highest number of personal injury claims and a third of all postal worker attacks is the well-heeled Labrador, a popular dog among stereotypical *Telegraph* readers.[73]

In town, landlords are known to add surcharges to rental deposits for those owning 'dangerous' breeds, including Staffies and larger dogs like German Shepherds associated with working-class identity. Labradors do not tend to feature in these constraints. In the US, poodles, terrier mixes, chihuahuas and Yorkies have been noted as gentrified breeds, like certain clothes, eating habits and decorating styles. Certain pedigree-breed pets are incorporated into patterns of consumption to display urbane good taste. In cosmopolitan cities, dog ownership is frequently associated with the growth in urban childless households – especially LGBTQ+ ones – and pampered pet dogs may be perceived, rightly or wrongly, as child substitutes.[74] The most bijou pets benefit from hotels, yoga classes, beauticians and even dog-food trucks. Williamsburg and Prospect Park, Brooklyn, have long been replete with Pamper Your Pet stores and dog parks, while dog-food trucks like Milo's Kitchen and Frosty Pooch move between hipster havens and pet-friendly parks.[75]

Housing can even be pitched towards certain dogs and their owners. At the Landsby Building in Wembley Park, London, 295 rental flats are available to human and animal tenants. But there is a catch. Pets have to undergo a selection 'interview'. One of the panel is Frankie the Cavapoo, who helps check if prospective dog tenants are sufficiently well behaved. On acceptance they are treated to a special collar, a goody bag and access to dedicated dog runs and dog agility classes. One-bedroom apartments start at £1,800 a month, with an additional £50 charge per month for (well-behaved) dogs. There is no knowing for sure what type of dog gets Frankie's tail wagging, but I would guess it is more likely to be those associated with middle-class identity. He is sure to be welcoming to a fellow Cavapoo with a genteel, well-turned-out, cosmopolitan keeper.

Reproducing Dogs

One of the tendencies in dog ownership is to raise generations of the same breed. Like the Duchess of Newcastle with her Borzois or Queen Elizabeth II with her famous Corgis, dog keepers often try to find a successor that closely compares to an original. Yet what happens if the flighty new puppy does not quite match up to the recently deceased loyal old dog? Now there is an alternative option. ViaGen Pets claims to be 'the worldwide leader in cloning the animals we love'. For any dog lover who cannot imagine another animal comparing to their departed companion, they offer to produce a genetic twin. The cost of this process is $50,000.[76] Initially customers purchase the option to clone their pets for $1,600 by having a vet collect a small tissue sample for genetic preservation. ViaGen then cultures new cells with the identical genetic make-up and freezes them until the client is ready to clone their dog. Once the new dog is produced by a surrogate, what happens next is an open question. How will genetically identical dogs with the same 'natural' ingredients develop as new companions when their nurturing will inevitably be different? Cloned dogs will be exposed to different behaviours, diets, stimuli and encounter new pathogens. How will their characteristics diverge from the original model? Will owners desperate to rekindle a lost companionship be disappointed with a new version that never quite compares?

The industry is still in its infancy so there are few experiences to discuss. ViaGen's site is full of testimonials where owners have purchased genetic preservations but are not yet in a position to clone their dog. Either the original is alive, or they are still mourning their passing, or they are saving for the procedure. One of the very first to take up this remarkable service was Roberto Novo, a celebrity hairdresser with clients including Britney Spears and Calvin Klein. To ease his pangs of loneliness he took delivery of a clone of his beloved French Bulldog Machito, and the genetic duplicate was subtly named Machi*two*. During the Covid pandemic they were pictured taking their daily exercise in New York with matching masks.[77]

Novo's attachment to Machito, and the lengths he has gone to to recreate him, demonstrates the intensity of human–dog relationships. Such intimate bonds make it intuitive that we infer that there are certain similarities among people who keep the same breed of dog. While owners might choose to compare their dogs using seemingly objective physical attributes – like those promoted at Crufts, or featured on comparison sites – ultimately the subjective values associated with dog breeds – what they say about the owner's identities, how they are a metaphor for their character – are more powerful in determining which puppies find a home in what community. The issue with dog comparisons is that when someone says they don't like a breed, often what they mean is they don't like the people associated with that dog breed. As Ed West openly stated. Comparing so-called better and worse dogs may become a proxy for expressing deep-rooted and discriminatory views. When this extends to unsavoury practices such as denying someone a home, not because they have a dog, but because they have a certain type of dog and thus must be a certain type of person, is when it becomes toxic. In the UK, 'high' and 'low' breeds of dog are part of the social fabric of class identity. There is a stench of eugenics that surrounds the comparison of humans and their dogs; horrid associations between breeding, superiority and status. Dog breeds standing in for class is bad, but what is worse is dogs representing race.

Racial Divisions

Back in 2009, I moved to southern Africa for a year's research. For the first few weeks I stayed with some white South Africans on the outskirts of Maputo, the capital of Mozambique. A few years earlier, they had come over the border from Durban and expanded their business in construction, capitalising on the investment boom in one of the world's poorest countries. They lived in a wire-fenced compound with parking for SUVs, piles of building supplies and several park homes; what would be called static caravans in the UK or trailers in the US. Being a South African enclave there was also an area to *braai* or barbecue; outdoor cooking is the national pastime. Alongside their 4x4s, their bricks and mortar, and their cabins and grills, they had brought with them their dogs. I had grown up around dogs. As a child we had a Golden Retriever who loved to bark, and though a soft soul, would sometimes scare strangers. Nothing I had ever seen in Britain prepared me for their South African mega-dogs, more like another species than a different breed. When I first saw them, I was stopped dead in my tracks. Sitting facing me, brooding, slobbering and imposing, were three huge brown Boerboels. A mastiff type of breed with short nut-brown hair. The dark bulks of their heads were massive hard spheres like motorbike helmets. Their haunches of taut muscle and sculptured legs looked more like the anatomy of racehorses than guard dogs. By day they rested in a shaded corner of the compound that I never dared approach. By night I was always sure to be dropped off right outside my park home door lest I encounter them. Their effect was terrifying.

Across southern Africa, the dog is a racially charged symbol.[78] The region has a troubled recent past and the legacies of apartheid, white-minority regimes and colonialism continue to mark society. Human–dog relations are entwined with identity as some pedigree breeds signal racial authenticity. One such breed is the Rhodesian Ridgeback, long associated with the big-game hunting that was the preserve of white colonialists. The Ridgeback has a raised spine and is a large, powerful, athletic dog known as the lion hunter. The nickname, which leads many to think that they actually killed big cats, is something of a misnomer. Ridgebacks tracked, teased and disorientated lions during the hunt, using their agility to dart away from slashing paws, and never directly confronted the quarry. Due to their further use in the colonial security services, Rhodesian Ridgebacks alongside other dogs such as purebred German Shepherds and Boerboels are seen as 'white dogs'. They embodied the cultural pursuits and violence of the coercive white supremacist regimes including those of Southern Rhodesia (Zimbabwe before 1980) and South Africa pre-1994.[79]

Into the twenty-first century, across postcolonial southern African cities, these 'white breeds' have replaced the colonial police as the first line of defence for wealthy private homes. Whereas once white cops in squad cars would roam privileged neighbourhoods, guard dogs now tirelessly patrol the limits of private property. They offer companionship to their predominantly white keepers and send a warning sign to the primarily black population beyond the walls. The aggression of white-owned dogs towards black bodies even extends to bloodhounds being trained on the scents associated with African men.[80]

Cape Town is the wealthiest part of South Africa. It has a Mediterranean climate, great food, acclaimed wine and endless ocean views. In the last quarter-century, the city has had a huge increase in wealthy residents and with them has come a growing population of guard dogs, alongside armies of private security guards, CCTV cameras and spiked walls. These dogs harass black domestic workers, cyclists and even schoolchildren. In the gentrifying Capri Village of the Cape Peninsula, black kids identify dog owners' homes as danger areas to be avoided at all costs.[81]

South African cities are divided spaces. There is extreme wealth and abject poverty. As well as the millionaires' rows of coastal Cape Town there are urban townships that are nearly exclusively black and have among the lowest life expectancy of anywhere in the world. The dog of the black city is the third of southern Africa's indigenous breeds. Alongside the pedigree Boerboel and Ridgeback, the Africanis is uniquely African. When the wealthy breeze past squalid townships in their sleek SUVs, they glance at these medium-sized, lightly built dogs, with slender muzzles, in mixed colours of black, fawn and beige. Africanis roam the fringes of poor settlements. Some are half-wild or ownerless like the pye-dogs of South Asia. J. M. Coetzee's 1999 Booker Prize-winning post-apartheid novel *Disgrace* explored the life of the men and women who live alongside these 'kaffir dogs', an epithet that combines an adjective so offensive as to be utterly intolerable.[82] Africanis are typically the offspring of less controlled breeding. They are a more 'mongrel' animal lacking in perceived refinement. In the eyes of grotesque racists their attributes compare to the human populations with which they live. The most bullshit of comparisons.

Evolving Human–Dog Relationships

Since the collapse of colonialism and the fall of apartheid, the racial divisions in dog ownership – though still present – have begun to break down across southern Africa. In Harare, the capital of Zimbabwe, since the 1990s the new black middle classes have protected their smart homes with the same vicious guard dogs favoured by the old white colonialist and post 'beware of the dog' signs on their imposing high gates. Protecting their property increases the insecurity of their neighbourhoods as children are exposed to the risk of dog bites and many worried parents opt for painful rabies vaccinations.[83] Jacob Zuma is unhappy with new attitudes towards dogs. In 2012, the then South African president argued that those who love their pets more than people suffered 'a lack of humanity'. He equated dog care with white culture and chided blacks that spent lavishly on their dogs, walked them or took them to the vet as rejecting African traditions.

Regimes of dog ownership have changed among black urban elites. The Zimbabwean author Shimmer Chinodya, in his short story 'Strays', traces the distinction between dog owners:

> A dog is a dog. The average African dog is a little less than that. The average African dog is a creature to be kicked, scolded and have missiles thrown at it . . . [whereas] . . . a European dog is more than a dog . . . It is a member of the family, with a personality, name, a kennel, a veterinary aid card and, of course, a budget . . . A suburban African dog in an aspiring middle-class household is something between the two. While it probably benefits from the example of its white neighbours, it remains a household appendage.[84]

In South Africa, some dogs have become fully fledged members of black families as Tinyiko Maluleke writes of his deceased companion:

> Bruno was tall, brown and handsome. Without fail, whenever I returned home Bruno would run to the

gate to welcome me – for 10 glorious years. On the last Thursday of February 2015, Bruno died. And I did something that is very unAfrican: I cried for my dog Bruno. What deed can be more unAfrican than an adult black male crying over a dead dog? If I could I would have avoided it, I swear. I would have postponed it until I had left the *dierekliniek* (vet).[85]

As Maluleke's intimate story illuminates, by sharing their new homes with dogs, loving them, caring and mourning their passing, a new generation of affluent black South Africans are challenging conceptions of identity.

It is not just the people in the human–dog relationship that are undergoing a transformation. The Africanis dog or 'Township special' has itself begun to have a change in status and is beginning to find a home in the white suburbs. The South African Breeders Association has sought to rehabilitate the Africanis as 'the real African dog', but this is solely a project of white South Africans that through the dog aligns whiteness with indigeneity and establishes the claim that whites are the rightful inhabitants of South Africa.[86]

Ex-president Zuma's critique of dog care by emerging black middle classes and white efforts to claim the Africanis bear witness to the enormous malleable power of the dog. No dog is intrinsically 'black' or 'white', it is a made-up distinction that serves political, security and cultural agendas. Dog choices are tied up with post-apartheid identity and not just their comparative physical attributes and behavioural characteristics. When breeds are uncritically compared as black or white, they are being used as a cipher for social and racial hierarchies. Across southern Africa, attitudes towards dogs articulate innermost anxieties and prejudices.

Dogs are the physical and ideological outriders of their owners. By selecting a dog, whether the owner likes it or not, they are choosing a new part of their identity. Whatever the intricacies of their human–dog relationship, other people will judge them on what that dog looks like, how they behave and how they compare to other breeds, even if this is a ludicrous comparison to make. Dogs are one of the most public aspects of identity. When out walking, a dog literally leads the way and makes a persuasive first impression. They help articulate high – and low – class status. Social status depends on many more factors, including identity, employment and education.

Choices of dogs are also as much about finding a breed that fits within established community values and class rituals as they are about making an objective comparison and finding the best type of dog. Across Britain in particular the national obsession with class and high and low status means that we are quick to view others' pets as powerful markers of their identity. We persistently make bullshit assumptions that could be true, but probably are not, about the content of people's character based on the animal on the end of their lead. Or maybe that statement is too human-centric and should be reversed: we make ill-informed judgements about the characters of dogs based on the physical appearance of their owners; either way you say it, the comparison sounds unfair on one species or the other.

PART 2
Place

CHAPTER 5

Why Are Some Universities Failing?

The tyranny of metrics

Start of Term

I was not very good at English at school, but I was very fond of my English teacher, Mr Roberts. He was tall with a craggy yet friendly face, and a brown-grey 'door knocker' beard and moustache that lent him a passing resemblance to Charles Dickens. Roberts would often say that the first week of September was his favourite time of the year. The 'Dog-end of Summer' as he put it. When every warm sunny day felt like it could be the last of the year. Those bright moments of borrowed extra summertime were to be cherished. He further professed that he eagerly awaited the return of his pupils to the classroom. At the time I had my doubts, given my class's limited appetite for Austen and Shakespeare. It was certainly a challenging comprehensive school for a good English teacher. A quarter of a century later, and after more than a decade at the chalk face, I must admit the start of a new academic year *is* perennially exciting. It feels especially so on warm and bright September days.

When the sun is shining, the beginning of the teaching year at King's College London feels like a festival. There are red flags and purple banners on the Strand for freshers' fair. New students queue outside with the warm sunlight on their skin. Inside reception there is an eager crush at the doors. Eighteen and nineteen-year-olds flood the corridors. Many fresh to London, all naïve to the chaos and opportunities of the first days of undergraduate life. New friendships and relationships burn bright. Some last a lifetime, others fade almost as soon as they started. For most, university is a joyful adventure of discovery, but for some it is a voyage that is stressful, traumatic and dark.

I meet my own personal students in small groups in the first week. As best I can, I offer advice on how to navigate this formative moment. A few days later in the lecture theatre, I look out at a sea of 150 people and recognise some of those same faces as I launch into an introduction to the geographical foundations that made the modern world. A few weeks later, I give feedback on their first essays and discuss their work, and I see the early signs of how students can think critically and creatively about the world around them as they take on new ideas. A few months later, on their first field trip to medieval York, some of the jigsaw pieces begin to fit together. Over tea and scones outside the formal confines of the college, I chat with them and hear about their observations in the field. The next year on international fieldwork in Lisbon, where it is now coffee and custard tarts, I see them grow in independence and become more sophisticated as researchers as they connect theories to their own data. In their final year, I supervise their dissertations, mentor them through blending together their own ideas, their interviews or other fieldwork, and their reflections on established theories, to make a new contribution to knowledge. They finish their degrees producing something truly of their own.

Throughout a degree journey, a student's progress is punctuated by grading. Scores show how well they are doing, and unsettling comparisons are inevitable. Most often I encounter this when students complain about marks, arguing that they feel the grading was too harsh in comparison to either work marked by another lecturer, or to the score given to another class member. Anxiety around academic performance is a major factor in the crises of well-being and mental ill health that increasingly stains the student experience.[87] To help alleviate the tension around grades, I tell frustrated students to meet with the marker so they can understand how and why the score was given. Looking at the work in isolation and understanding its merits and shortcomings from the very person who marked it will always shed more light on the result. This is always more helpful than trying to compare an assignment to other work with different parameters.

I face a lot of grievances over marking, and as the Deputy Head of Department I have had to deal with complaints from both students and staff. Previously it was my responsibility to oversee the results of the 250 students studying towards Master's degrees. I would organise second marking and run statistical tests to find if any markers were out of step and being too harsh or lenient in their grading. I discussed the outliers and referred concerning cases to external examiners. Most of this work was a huge exercise in comparison, and I trawled through never-ending Excel spreadsheets looking for unusual patterns. Working alongside my academic and administrative colleagues, I'm confident it was carried out to the highest standards. And yet maybe UK higher education ploughs too much energy into assessment. Has the enervating focus on attainment gone too far and is it contributing to the widely reported crisis in student well-being? In tandem, is a market-based results-driven system blunting young people's opportunity to use university as a time to take risks and explore new ideas?[88] Have students become fearful of failure and the chance of missing out on certain graduate career paths? A recent encounter with a student left me wondering about these questions.

After a small group tutorial where we discussed a new research project, one undergraduate, Juliet, stayed behind to talk to me. We began chatting about her plans to investigate an alternative housing community of self-builders in South London. I foresaw that the conversation was heading towards her asking what she had to do to get an A grade. So, I began to discuss what approach would be best to target a higher mark, then something unexpected happened. Juliet interrupted me. She politely stated she was not interested in attaining a first-class degree. She wanted to know how to grab this opportunity. She wanted to know what risks she could take. She wanted to challenge herself. Ultimately, she wanted to get the most out of the degree experience. If she achieved a high grade that would be a great collateral benefit, but the goal was not about measuring her performance on a scale, but rather satisfying her own curiosity and learning for herself. After this conversation I was quite taken aback. It left such a strong impression on me. Juliet was right. It is common for students and staff to lose sight of what a university education is really about. A single target of high grades has reduced the degree to something akin to a driving test, where all that matters is leaving with the right certificate so you can make your way on the road to a successful career.

The examples here reflect my experiences in England. Most education systems around the world are structured around an imperfect meritocracy. School assessment enables the comparison of children and young adults to measure worse, average or better achievement. Students are reduced to grades: 'she has straight As', 'his GPA is 3.70', 'they only got a 2:2'. These indicators allow employers to compare job candidates or parents to differentiate between their children or gloat to the neighbours about high achievers. In later life these once all import measures fade in significance. Many adults shy away from comparing old educational records as they feel they do not accurately represent who they truly are, their past circumstances, achievements and skills, or even their intellect. They caveat their performance by referencing their poor school, unsupportive parents or flawed assessment criteria. They contextualise their record, because in isolation, educational results are far from a perfect means of comparing intellect.

Recognising the sometimes false meritocracy of formal education is not only common sense, but it can also improve learning outcomes. Most medical degrees taught in the UK and the USA have a simple pass/fail classification. That nurtures a greater sense of teamwork and collaboration among students, which is vital in medicine, while reducing unhelpful competitiveness and comparisons between students.[89] It also does away with the problem of having low-ranked graduates. Nobody wants to be treated by a D grade doctor, even though the stringent testing of medical schools will ensure all who pass meet the required standard to practise! Across all Swedish universities they go as far as to not measure overall performance. Students do not graduate with a grade and are not ranked against classmates.[90] A degree is a pass/fail qualification. A Swedish colleague explained to me how this encourages students to take risks, experiment and be more liberal and creative in their learning, while the presence of a fail category makes sure that students still demonstrate competence in the discipline overall. I know my students are clever and able as they have received good school grades before university. Abolishing much of the assessment would liberate them to really learn and develop new skills, boosting their abilities to think critically, problem solve, experiment and present arguments. Currently, the myopic focus on results means students are unwilling to take risks and are crippled by a fear of failure. Some are so consumed by anxiety around performance that they turn to misconduct. My hardest professional moments have been when I have sat on committees that have expelled students who have cheated by sourcing coursework answers from third parties and passing this work off as their own. The advent of so-called Artificial Intelligence like ChatGPT has further eroded the value of traditional coursework essays as they become easier to cheat, yet the growth of language model-based chatbots cements the need for graduates who can use technology appropriately and think critically and creatively about the world in ways in which a machine can never replicate. A redirection of university education away from producing machine-like students that churn out bland assessments would be a step towards a more progressive and enlightened society.

Grading

J. K. Rowling, Bear Grylls, King Charles III – one of the most successful authors of the last three decades, a TV adventurer who has climbed Mount Everest and the monarch. What do each of these famous faces have in common? They all graduated with a 2:2 degree. An unremarkable end to their university educations, but not one that held them back, given their wider skills and abilities, or the circumstances of their birth. The 'Desmond' degree, named for Archbishop Desmond Tutu ('Two-two'), increasingly signifies low, below-par achievement. Britain's arcane system of ranking degrees has four tiers: First Class (1st), Upper Second Class (2:1), Lower Second Class (2:2) and Third Class (3rd), as well as the Fail classification. In recent years, graduating with a two-two, or worse a third class, has become paramount to failure for most students. The value of those degrees has been eroded in concert with quite dazzling grade inflation across the sector.

Between 2010–11 and 2021–22, the proportion of students awarded first-class degrees in England rose from 16 per cent to 32 per cent and the proportion of those gaining either a first or a 2:1 climbed from 67 per cent to 78 per cent.[91] The Desmonds, thirds and fails have become increasingly rare beasts. With four in five graduates leaving university with either a first or a 2:1, the Office for Students (OfS), the higher education regulator for England, cautioned inflation was a 'significant and pressing issue' that threatened to erode public confidence and questioned if universities were using their awarding powers responsibly. Some of the high numbers of firsts are awarded at the country's most illustrious seats of learning including Imperial College London (48.5 per cent) and University College London (47 per cent), which increasingly attract great students from around the world, but there have also been major increases at less established institutions. At Anglia Ruskin, the proportion of firsts jumped from 14.5 per cent in 2010–11 to 36.7 per cent eight years later; Bradford's rose from 10.8 per cent to 35.1 per cent, and Kingston's climbed from 14.6 per cent to 33.6 per cent over the same period.[92]

How can this be explained? Is it a) an explosion in attainment by new brighter, dedicated students that are taught more effectively by better staff in improved institutions? Are better approaches to study and superior teaching leading Gen Z to out-achieve previous generations en masse? Or is it b) have university grading standards slipped off a cliff edge? To take the more generous perspective first, it is certainly true that university life has become more professional. Students take a greater interest in performance and institutions place an enhanced emphasis on delivering great teaching. New online technologies have further facilitated study, yet has student work really improved that much in such a short period? It is virtually impossible to prove empirically either way if coursework or exam answers are better or worse (due to the comparator being the grades themselves), but from the inside it does not look like there has been a revolution in the calibre of students' outputs. In contrast, I often hear the opposite. In my experience, lecturers from a variety of institutions and disciplines have bemoaned the lack of time students spend on reading, their poor writing, their lack of technical skills, or their underdeveloped creativity. So maybe the explanation does lie with a change in the approach to grading? The OfS has raised concerns about standards and highlighted that 'degrees must stand the test of time', not least to enable comparison over time: '[i]t is essential that degree classifications are meaningful for students and employers.'[93] Given the tremendous grade inflation it is unrealistic to argue that a first-class degree awarded today is 100 per cent comparable to that of a student who graduated just a decade earlier.

What is driving this inflation and why would markers and institutions let grades increase year on year? At the level of the individual lecturer, faced with mounting workloads and pressures to deliver across different domains – teaching, research and administrative service – grading has become one area where it is easy to cut corners. Not by giving less written comment and feedback – that is an obvious way to game the system that is easily picked up – but rather through being generous with marks. A subtle recalibration upwards has multiple benefits for an overworked faculty. It makes students happier, it discourages complaints, it improves module feedback, and it reduces the number of resits to re-mark. At the level of institutions there can be a culture shift that uplifts students' grades: rewritten marking criteria, preponderance rules that reduce the weighting of low marks, and messages from the top which encourage staff to make their students satisfied with their learning experience and to give them better degree titles to boost their prospects in the job market. This final point, the desire to improve satisfaction, has become a primary goal for university managers as high satisfaction elevates their institution's position in comparative league tables.

Universities are ultimately defined by their people not their league table position. This chapter bridges between people and places. At this juncture the argument moves from a discussion of students, a people-centric comparison, to a focus on the ways in which universities are compared, a place-based comparison. Both people and places need to be understood relationally rather than being compared as isolated units. Merit is determined by their extrinsic values, the relationships of students to other learners, and the wider context of higher education. The debate around grading has illustrated that marks are viewed as relational – an A grade is not like a reading of 100 degrees centigrade on a thermometer; it does not have the same objective empirical truth. Boiling point is the same in 2024 as it was in 2023 or 2004 or any other moment in history, but an A grade is not. Academic performance is contextualised. It depends on the quality of the education received and is relative to the wider achievements of the cohort. Is a B grade from a pupil at Eton equivalent to a B from a student at a poorly resourced inner city comprehensive? Basic comparisons of learners shorn of context are of little value. Yet the same can be said of places. To understand if somewhere is a successful school or university we need to look far beyond metrics to the relationships of the institution with wider society. We need to situate that place within the education landscape, but that topography is poorly mapped.[94] This is a territory where a set of distorted metrics – student satisfaction surveys, research excellence frameworks and league tables – are the crooked altimeters of success and failure.

Surveys

Prospective students, academics, employers and the government compare universities using league tables. One of the most

persuasive is that produced by the NSS (National Student Survey).
Every final-year student is invited to score their satisfaction with
the degree experience across categories such as 'assessment and
feedback' and 'learning community'. Each university and every
teaching discipline are ranked by student satisfaction, or to drop
the veil of conceit 'customer satisfaction'. A high placing is
something to gloat about and is used to promote the university
and draw in more applicants. Low achievement is a different story.
I have been in plenty of meetings with senior managers who are
themselves far removed from the day-to-day realities of teaching,
who vent their displeasure through finger pointing, raised voices
and worse. Nothing gets them angrier than a poor NSS result.
As universities have become increasingly market-orientated and
more students mean a greater revenue, recruitment has become
a vital competition. The NSS is one of the few metrics available
for prospective students to compare universities, so it has grown
in influence, but is it helpful and accurate?

There are plenty of critics of the NSS[95] because it is a
crude quantitative score that groups together diverse institutions
working across different geographical, social, cultural and
disciplinary fields. The measure is very sensitive with the 'best'
and 'worst' institutions often separated by a few percentage points
and therefore a handful of dissatisfied students in a year group of
a hundred can make a big difference to the ranking. There is a
tendency for arts courses to receive lower satisfaction scores that
other disciplines. This may be because arts students are trained
to be more critical of this type of evaluation than their fellow
students working towards degrees in more positivist science.
This has the effect that universities with many arts courses tend
to rank lower. This comparison is not particularly useful for
prospective students who want to compare universities, as they
will be unaware that the rank could be influenced by their blend
of arts and science teaching, and they are better off comparing
individual degrees rather than whole institutions.[96]

The above criticism takes for granted that the survey works,
but there are many problems with its methodology. The NSS is
conducted at the mid-point of the final year, at a time of high

stress for students, and not after the degree has been completed. It is like asking you to rate a restaurant when your dessert has arrived, but before you've tasted the last course or seen the bill! Moreover, there is a sense of self-fulfilling prophecy with students at the most elite institutions, especially Cambridge and Oxford, eager to reconfirm these places as the best. Additionally, the survey in general finds campus universities inherently more 'satisfying' as they have a stronger sense of community, but the counterpoint is that urban city-centre universities cannot really be compared as their students are invariably more dispersed and involved with a wider range of social and cultural communities – family, employment, nightlife, religion, sporting etc. – that are not centred on the university. More concerning than these flaws is the material impact the NSS has on the actual student experience.

Heads of department host parties and other feel-good experiences for final-year students on the eve of the NSS opening. It sounds farcical, but there have been controversial incidents where students have been plied with free drinks before being directed to computer rooms with the surveys loaded up ready to go. The OfS has voiced concerns about institutions gaming the system.[97] This has not stopped universities organising one-off events that draw attention away from delivering educational excellence in the name of promoting a better student experience that will be remembered as they complete the NSS. Teaching gets reorganised. Dissertation timelines, exam dates, teaching activities and important assessment deadlines are moved around the academic calendar to accommodate the survey. More generally, once the NSS period has closed, attention pivots away from the final-year student at the very moment when they are approaching what should be the climax of a three-year journey.

In my discipline of geography, there has been a mini arms race between departments to offer the most exotic destinations – Cuba to explore street festivals in Havana, South Africa for football and vineyards, even all the way to New Zealand to see alpine environments. The rationale being that intercontinental field trips, especially in the final year, will give students a once-in-a-lifetime experience and some happy memories before they start ticking the NSS boxes. Unfortunately, these trips don't always happen at the right stage of the degree. Neither are the locations consistently selected because they fit within the wider curricula offered, nor do these far-flung places necessarily present opportunities for field learning that could not be found in the UK or Europe in destinations that are more affordable and result in less carbon-emitting long-haul flights. But what these destinations do have is a potential wow factor.

A minority of students have voiced their discontent concerning the oversized influence of the survey on their education. In 2017, a national boycott was instigated with support from the National Union of Students which was concerned that the NSS would provide the evidence to allow high-scoring English universities to increase their tuition fees. Across the sector there are deep-seated concerns about whether students should be framed as consumers and to what extent market forces should penetrate university life.[98] The NSS is, after all, an opinion survey and a glorified version of the sort of thing you get emailed after making an online purchase, staying in a hotel, or speaking to a call centre. The culture of rating and reviewing is omnipresent, but it doesn't take a statistician to be sceptical of the data produced through some of these surveys. Yet, what is less questionable is the way in which this prominent emphasis on opinion and feedback, not just via the NSS but throughout a degree, can guide students to think of themselves as customers buying an education. Meanwhile the OfS has highlighted how some lecturers feel the NSS 'places undue pressure on staff, subjecting them to greater and unwarranted surveillance and making competitive but specious comparisons between courses'.

Overall, though, what is most damaging is how the NSS has a corrosive effect on academic standards as the need to deliver 'satisfying' teaching invariably leads to immense pressure on markers to award high grades and satisfy students' own expectations of their education. I think many academics would favour dropping the NSS because of the distorting impact this survey has on learning and grades. Many students are also savvy to the powerful impact of their responses and use it to punish or reward their department. It is an open secret that nearly every manager who wants to succeed in the higher education hierarchy tries to game the NSS outcome or other metrics to showcase their leadership acumen. As one former Dean at King's who was sensitive to the corrosive effects of comparisons pointed out to me, this is a good example of Goodhart's Law: when a specific goal like a high NSS score becomes the over-arching target, people will tend to optimise for that objective regardless of the consequences. The NSS is a bullshit comparison that takes energy away from what really makes universities great.

Rankings

The NSS is far from the only influential ranking that shapes the working life of academics across England. Alongside discussion of the NSS in staff meetings, teaching allocations, job panels and promotion applications, there is a sister research metric that generates even more debate and carries even further significance for individual academics' professional progression: this is the Research Excellence Framework or REF. Simply put, the REF can make and break careers. Periodically, every six to eight years, the research outputs of the entire UK higher education sector are audited through the REF process. Every active scholar must submit their best work for evaluation. Articles, books and other outputs are ranked on a scale of one to four stars by a panel of academics to determine the best university departments. The scores of individual papers are never revealed, only the collective mark. I know several panel members and they complain that comparing the work is a long and arduous task. Four-star work is classed as world-leading in terms of originality, significance and rigour and is incredibly valuable. Elite universities try to return as many four-star outputs as possible. The promise of delivering work that will be recognised as worthy of four golden stars can shape staff recruitment, change research agendas, as well as inhibiting collaboration and wrecking the balance between teaching and research.

When I was entering the academic job market towards the end of my PhD in 2011, I was fortunate to be arriving at a moment when many universities wanted to recruit early-career staff with excellent research ahead of the 2013 REF. I had strong publications in leading journals and a competitive CV and got a great job. After 2013, some institutions restricted their staff recruitment as they had overspent in the run-up to REF to boost their rosters for the audit date. In the following years, I saw many other PhD graduates with better publication records than me struggle to find permanent roles because universities were not investing in the same way. The jobs available for early-career scholars today tend to be primarily teaching fellowships rather than the traditional lecturing posts that blend teaching and research. This means teaching is now increasingly done by colleagues that have less time to be research active. For students this takes higher education further away from cutting-edge research. The distortion of university employment doesn't just happen with junior posts, but at the most senior levels where competition for superstar professors has seen wages rocket for a lucky few.

There has been some incredibly short-term decision making by institutions wanting to boost their REF rankings. Like football clubs blowing their budgets on a Messi or a Ronaldo during a transfer window, universities dangle the carrot of huge salaries and low teaching loads to draw in the hottest academic talent on the eve of the audit date. However, unlike the star footballers who add value to their new teams through their performance on the pitch, academics arrive carrying with them their body of work and can transfer their recent four-star outputs to their new institutions. This can mean bringing in established professors in the autumn of their careers, whose best work is behind them to give a department a sprinkling of stardust. The impacts are demoralising for long-serving staff. Rather than building from within, for richer universities it has become easier to hire in those with a record of excellence. The new star man hoovers up the acclaim, and here I say man deliberately as in academia it is most often the male, pale and stale that prosper. Across academia there are big disparities in pay and progression. In 2021, there were only thirty-five black female professors in UK higher education compared to 12,860 white males.[99]

In the years before the REF audit date, academic conferences are dominated by a rumour mill of which leading professor is going where. While for the individuals at the top of the tree this is great, the losers in this huge exercise in comparison are the junior colleagues that have to take on more administrative and teaching responsibilities and help recruit the students that bring in the tuition fees that pay the big-name academics. Early-career lecturers have less time for research, which stifles their careers, while also seeing their opportunities for pay progression limited as salary budgets are eaten up by a handful of alpha males. There is a further distortion as much great research is collaborative and built on teamwork, yet rather than the new star man energising the team around them, under REF, academics are perversely disincentivised to collaborate with colleagues in their own department. Multi-authored work can only be attributed to one staff member in a single university. In contrast, work co-written with collaborators at other institutions can be submitted by multiple universities. This can encourage academics to work with outsiders and reap the collective benefits of great research rather than mentoring early-career colleagues in their home institution and risk fighting with them for the right to submit a co-produced book or journal article for the next REF as 'their' work. This might sound far-fetched, but I have witnessed professional relationships being wrecked over REF. This includes heated face-to-face arguments among senior professors and even once close friends no longer speaking to one another and reduced to legalistic negotiating via email over who is the lead author on collaborative work. This is part of a wider, sometimes toxic, culture that enables bullies to thrive among the professoriate of Britain's top universities.[100]

Ultimately everyone loses out with the REF. The micro-politics of arguing over authorship can suck the joy out of departments, moments of fevered REF recruitment have long-running consequences, and further a rush to finish research projects and dash out results before the audit date all contribute to corroding the type of world-class research environments the REF process was intended to stimulate. Worst of all, people lose their jobs because of one poor cycle, even while performing well in teaching and administration. Students pay a great price as university managers use huge fee incomes to strengthen their REF return rather than thinking about how new staff recruits can fit within or enhance the teaching criteria. Instead of doing what is best for students, thinking forward to new research agendas, or trying to manage universities in a sustainable way, there is an obsession with boosting a comparative ranking in yet another example of Goodhart's Law.

Challenging the League Tables

Comparisons are taking on an ever-greater significance in determining the vibrancy of universities. At a global scale, the *Times Higher Education* magazine – which goes by the confusing acronym THE – publishes myriad rankings, including not only World University Rankings, but Young University Rankings and World Reputation Rankings. Other global comparisons are compiled by U.S. News and QS. Universities that are completely different to one another and perform diverse teaching and research functions across incomparable disciplines, and economic and social contexts are continually ranked against one another. Each aspires to world-class status.

In the UK, there is a flourishing mini-publishing industry in comparing universities reflecting the British obsession with reputation, status and ultimately class. Newspapers including *The Times* and the *Guardian* as well as the Complete University Guide publish institutional ratings on different variables including subject level list. Occasionally, in the university lecturer's favourite newspaper, the *Guardian*, or THE op-eds decry the spread of marketisation in the university sector and the counter-productive and demoralising effect of target setting, comparisons and metrics.[101] It is important to shine a light on this contradictory editorial stance as these same media outlets know all too well that rankings are avidly consumed by prospective students and their parents and drive considerable traffic to their websites.

One commonality across these comparisons is that institutions fall into a predetermined order of precedence. It is difficult to find a league table that is not topped by Cambridge or Oxford, or at least places them near the summit. One factor to explain this is the notion of a self-fulfilling prophecy. Subjective indicators based on opinions tend to reproduce old rankings. Here the reality that many of the leading academics who score institutions for comparisons are alumni of Cambridge or Oxford and they reflect positively on their undergraduate experiences from decades back and reinforce the status of their alma maters. These same dons may not be as vested in becoming familiar with new innovations and changes in other less-established institutions.

Oxbridge produces world-class research and provides excellent teaching – that is not in doubt; but also these outcomes are to be expected. Their colleges recruit the brightest students from overwhelmingly privileged backgrounds and have economic resources that dwarf research facilities elsewhere. Might it be that other universities are doing a 'better' job? Maybe institutions that recruit more students from disadvantaged backgrounds and help propel them towards new intellectual horizons and job prospects – futures their parents' generation could only have dreamed of – are doing more educational good with less financial resources and are thus more impressive? Perhaps institutions like Birkbeck that provide opportunities to mature students that lead to life-changing outcomes should be lauded? Maybe less fashionable institutions that champion new ideas and emerging disciplines, like Birmingham did with its revolutionary Centre for Contemporary Cultural Studies, need more accolades and should be celebrated for their research heritage? Taking a holistic view of universities can show that great achievements are not always found in the most obviously successful places.

Beyond high rankings for Oxbridge, league tables are inconsistent. For example, in the most up to date UK rankings, my institution, King's College London, came ninth in the *Daily Mail*'s league table, 18th in *The Times*'s index, 24th in the

Complete University Guide and was ranked 29th by the *Guardian*. The reason for this variability is that there is no agreement on what to measure or how it should be measured. What makes a good or a bad university? How do you balance different attributes such as: entry standards, satisfaction, research quality and graduate prospects? Different publishers weight these factors in various ways. The data is also 'noisy' and year on year there is huge variation. King's has jumped around, moving up and down the rankings by tens of places. From 2020 to 2023 in the *Guardian*'s table, King's leapt from 63rd to 29th. In one year alone it moved twenty-one places! I know full well that there was no fundamental change that would account for this huge improvement in performance, nor a mass deterioration in the performance of other universities. The year-on-year variation in the tables makes them meaningless for judging short-term trends.

Given King's' rankings ranged from ninth to 29th best university in the UK, it would be fair to assume that it would be nowhere near the top of global rankings. But in 2023 THE ranked it 35th *in the world* (and sixth in the UK), QS 37th (seventh in the UK) and in U.S. News 33rd (fifth in the UK). How can a university with an unremarkable national status do so well internationally? Clearly these global rankings were using a very different methodology to the UK-centric comparisons. Conveniently for King's, the institution can cherry-pick the best of these global rankings to use in promotional materials. But are such comparisons at all helpful?

The problem with all these statistical compilations is that they try and rank multidimensional data. Different variables – research, teaching, graduate prospects – taken from sources like the NSS and REF are collapsed into a simplistic ranking. Universities do not perform consistently across these domains, so if you change the importance of, say, teaching versus research, a new ranking is produced. Ultimately you just cannot rank multidimensional data, as Richard Harris, a Professor of Quantitative Social Geography states: 'Sadly, that doesn't stop people from trying! And they can do so in lots of different ways with lots of different data, which helps explain why there has been a proliferation of such rankings and also how university publicity can select and promote only those that rank them highest!'[102] He continues to argue that there is no foolproof way to compare and rank universities and more and more rankings never resolves the problem, 'it just reveals the arbitrariness of each one.' His argument is not against the total use of comparisons, but Harris is concerned that poor methods of comparison lead universities to try and game the metrics to boost their reputations. Attributes like 'excellence' or 'success' or 'worst' and 'failing' are often amorphous and reflect value judgements. Comparative exercises seek to convert these subjectivities into objective facts, which they are not; they are statistical constructs.

Despite being artificial, these comparative statistics really do matter. Being top of the league is great. Coming bottom is failure. Even if the lowest-scoring institution is delivering good teaching, high-quality research and contributing to the surrounding community in its own right: it is a failure by comparison. However, like the adults who rightly caveat their old educational records, universities that do poorly in comparison may do so for good reasons. Perhaps they recruit disadvantaged students, teach challenging subjects or face problems of local geography. This relationality is vital but is divorced from the metrics which produce simple numerical values that look like robust evidence.

In contrast to the ceaseless trend towards matching performance against metrics that have proliferated across the higher education sector in the UK, one of the leading institutions in Holland voluntarily withdrew from the global comparisons. Utrecht University, which previously ranked highly at 66th in the world, had the self-confidence to disengage from the 2023 THE World ranking by not providing any data to the British magazine. The rankings place 'too much emphasis on scoring and competition', while Utrecht University says it considers collaboration and openness of scientific research to be more important. They further highlighted the fallacy of reducing the complexity of a university to a simple comparator as it is 'virtually impossible to capture the quality of an entire university with all the different courses and disciplines in one figure'.[103]

Back in the UK, the primacy of comparison has gone hand in glove with the marketisation of universities. A former public good has morphed into a pseudo-private sector. As students have become burdened by tens of thousands of pounds of debt, a false market in tertiary education has developed. Universities compete for young people, lavishing resources on recruitment to boost their income in a zero-sum gain for education. For instance, in art and design subjects, many lower-profile institutions have seen their student numbers fall, whereas successful departments at the top of the league tables have grown rapidly. In practical, creative disciplines, staff-to-student ratios are vitally important, but these can now be worse in the highest-ranking arts institutions that have hoovered up more and more top-grade students without hiring staff at the same rate. Perversely, those students studying in a smaller, 'less successful' department can gain more studio time, further access to resources and more teaching hours. While they might not be at the top of the rankings, these institutions currently offer among the best educational experiences in the studio where it matters most, despite their low league table rankings.

Institutional attention has pivoted away from providing a high-quality learning for today's students and fixated upon getting more debt-incumbent applicants into their halls of residence tomorrow. Meanwhile, academics are tasked with gaming the various research and teaching metrics that register in league tables to the detriment of their wider role as educators and researchers. At the top of these target-driven institutions are a new elite class of senior managers earning eye-watering salaries from student fees and fixated on making creative comparisons to justify their authority and remuneration. In an infamous exchange, the Deputy Vice-Chancellor of the University of Sheffield, Professor Gill Valentine, when speaking to a group of archaeology students as their department was threatened with closure, reportedly made the following outrageous comparison that reduced students to commodities akin to supermarket goods. When Valentine was asked if entry requirements could be lowered to bring in more undergraduates, she replied: 'We need to protect our brand. If you shop at Marks & Spencers [*sic*], and then Marks & Spencers brings in Aldi-level products, then people won't want to shop with you anymore.' This left a student who attended the meeting feeling 'incredibly unwanted and unimportant – we are no more valuable than our tuition fees and our grades . . . The university does not care about us once we are here.'[104]

I am far from being alone in raising concerns about the organisation of the higher education sector, but frequently the arguments that gain most traction pick out two challenges: that there is a problem of too many people going to university and attending low-quality courses. And that there is a mental health crisis spreading through a vulnerable and unsupported student body.

Lying beneath the first challenge is the perception that some degrees are not worth having because they are awarded by low-ranked universities. Relentless comparison has made failing institutions, even if they are delivering a good education, because they are at the bottom of a hierarchy. The 'bad' university has been produced both by being represented as doing poorly versus other places and through the market forces that have penetrated deep into the higher education sector. The utilitarian argument made by, among others, David Goodhart in *The Road to Somewhere*[105] is that there is a 'bloated cognitive class' of overqualified graduates in low-skilled jobs. This deeply problematic thesis has been nurtured by the argument that large numbers of people are graduating from these 'failing' institutions. Here I fundamentally take the opposite view. It is not a failure of UK universities that, for example, a philosophy graduate from a low-ranking university is managing a bar, but rather a great social success that a bar manager had the opportunity to study philosophy for three years in a new university. The way in which they and the courses they graduate from are considered somehow a failure is a political and cultural problem that those of us who care about the fundamental right to a university education need to overcome.

Secondly, with regard to the wide-ranging issue of the crises of well-being, I certainly do not have all the answers. Many of the pressures acting upon young people are societal and extend far beyond the university experience and, for instance, have been darkened by the shadow of Covid. Yet I do know that comparative exercises like the NSS are part of the problem. Rather than increasing satisfaction, the NSS is pouring petrol on the fire and heating the pressure-cooker environment students find themselves in. I have witnessed over the last decade that the rising prominence of mental health issues have coincided with grade inflation, the growth of the NSS and the wider culture of rankings. Correlation is not an indicator of causality, but accelerating market forces, rising student fees, growing pressure to perform and increased expectation to achieve high grades heap further stress on students and staff. It bakes anxiety into the university experience, while eroding the capabilities of educators to help resolve the issues of their students.

One of the most horrific examples of the power of marketisation in universities is the tragic story of Stefan Grimm, a Professor of Toxicology at Imperial College London's Faculty of Medicine. Grimm had been told that he was 'struggling to fulfil the metrics' as he had not been bringing in the £200,000 a year of research funding expected of a professor in his position and was facing a performance review.[106] He took his own life by asphyxiation. An email attributed to Grimm at the time of his death recounts being treated 'like shit' by the university and points the finger clearly at the hyper-competitive culture: 'What these guys don't know is that they destroy lives. Well, they certainly destroyed mine . . . This is not a university anymore but a business with very few up in the hierarchy . . . profiteering and the rest of us are milked for money'.[107] In response to the tragedy, Imperial wrote that 'Professor Grimm's work was not under formal review' and that they had followed standard practices of 'informal and formal performance management'.[108]

Sadly, Grimm's story and his experience of the crushing effects of marketisation are not unique to the universities, but extend throughout schools and colleges in England, and other heavily competitive education sectors around the world. In English schools, the Ofsted inspection regime has become a constant trauma for school leaders. Chief inspector, Amanda Spielman, has admitted that the system creates a 'culture of fear'.[109] Through periodic visits, inspectors assess school performance and ultimately rate all schools in England as one of four grades: Outstanding, Good, Requires Improvement and Inadequate. Inspectors focus on four key areas: the quality of education, behaviour and attitudes, personal development, and leadership and management, with less focus on the wider relational context in which the school is situated such as local conditions of poverty and the onward trajectories of school leavers. Ofsted has been condemned for reducing all the multifactored characteristics of schools to a single one-word comparator. Former Education Secretary Lord Blunkett argued that 'simplistic judgements turned into one or two-word outcome measures are no longer meaningful in a post-Covid world of complex elements building a meaningful picture of how a school is performing'.[110] Another previous Education Secretary, Lord Baker, highlighted one such element: 'destination data' that he feels must be incorporated into the evaluation of schools to produce more meaningful comparisons. 'Destination data is a key judgement for a school because, at the end of the day, it's important to know what happens to them after leaving state education.'[111] Although these former ministers were not against the principle of metricising school performance, both wanted to fix a broken comparative system.

The arbitrariness of the grading influences the behaviours of schools which do what they can to game the inspectors' reports, and sometimes lose focus on addressing the needs of their pupils, in another example of Goodhart's Law, just like the corrosive influence of the NSS and REF in universities.[112] Moving upwards through the grades can bring great rewards for head teachers and the wider communities, so there is tremendous pressure to succeed. Local house prices are incredibly sensitive to their proximity to Outstanding schools, so home-owning local parents pay special attention to reports. Sadly, when a school is judged to fall down the grades, the impacts may be disastrous. Ruth Perry was the head teacher of Caversham Primary School in Berkshire, who took her own life while under huge mental pressure when her school was downgraded from Outstanding to Inadequate.[113] These bullshit comparisons must stop.

CHAPTER 6

Is Lisbon the New Barcelona?

How global competition erodes local culture

Welcome to Lisbon

A rich egg-yolk yellow custard, slightly charred with mottled patches of darkest brown, surrounded by a rim of buttery pastry, flaky, crisp and golden. The tart's base impossibly thin, like a few leaves of tracing paper. The just-set filling perhaps dusted with cinnamon. *Pastéis de nata* are an obsession throughout Portugal. Waiting in line in one of Lisbon's downtown art deco cafes, I often find myself in eager anticipation, mildly frustrated as the customer ahead compares *natas*, jabs a finger at the glass-fronted cabinet, chooses the one which they think has the best colouring, before changing their mind on closer inspection. Once they make their final selection, I quickly pick one and greedily enjoy its sweetness alongside a bitter strong espresso. If you want the best custard tart in the world, though, you must leave the city centre and ride the 15E tram out to Belém. But then it won't be a *pastél de nata*, rather something more special: a *pastél de Belém*.

The *pastéis de Belém* have been made at the bakery-cafe of the same name for more than 150 years. They are, though, based on a much older, secret recipe from the neighbouring Jerónimos

Monastery. This late Gothic architectural marvel is one of the most important buildings from the period five centuries ago when Lisbon was the centre of the powerful global Portuguese Empire. It no longer houses the Order of Saint Jerome and is now preserved as a UNESCO World Heritage Site. The story goes that tarts were made here as the monks found themselves with an abundance of egg yolks. Throughout Catholic Portugal, convents and monasteries used many egg whites for starching religious habits. Surplus yolks became the ingredients for sweet cakes and pastries. After the dissolution of many religious orders in the nineteenth century, the baking tradition continued. Across the country, every neighbourhood bakery has displays of heavenly golden goods; *bolas de Berlim* (custard-filled doughnuts), sweet *pão de Deus* (God's bread) and dainty seashell-shaped *ovos moles* (soft eggs) as well as *pastéis de nata* – all are enriched with bright yellow egg yolk. In Belém, in 1837, the monks sold their carefully guarded *nata* recipe to a nearby sugar refinery, and that then became Portugal's most famous bakery. Today the *Pastéis de Belém* shop attracts millions of tourists a year.

Alongside *pastéis de nata*, visitors from around the world flock to Lisbon for nightlife, tram rides, sardines, neoclassical architecture and the reliable sunshine of a near subtropical climate. The most popular sights include: Bairro Alto, the quarter of the high city made up of labyrinthine narrow lanes packed with bars, where every summer night is a street party. The charming number 28 tramline that has vintage cars the same bold buttercup yellow as the custard tarts. These timeless tramcars rattle through cobbled streets, screech down inclines and arrive in the grand open squares of the downtown. Here, restaurants aplenty serve simple fresh grilled seafood in between the ornate, picturesque unity of elegant shops, town houses and churches of the imperial era. Lisbon has the graceful majesty and cultural magnetism to rival any grand European city.

Beyond the scope of the typical tourist gaze, some of my favourite highlights are the eastern Marvila district where creativity and industrial heritage collide. Old semi-derelict riverside warehouses are covered in lurid cartoon street art. Some are repurposed into cafes and second-hand stores. Also in the east is a former convent that now houses the National Tile Museum, an unrivalled celebration of craft, colour and pattern, with a glorious courtyard garden cafe. Portuguese *Azulejo*, tin-glazed ceramic squares and other shapes, cover the nuns' cloisters and cells showcasing harlequin tile designs. Bold colour work, new and old, adorn facades throughout Lisbon. There is so much for the eye to see. After drifting leisurely through the city, simply taking a moment with a cold *imperial* – a slender glass of draught beer – in one of the many magnificent *miradouros* (viewpoints), watching the swallows soaring overhead, riding the uncertain eddies of air rising from the sun-baked paving stones, is enough to warm my heart.

Custard tarts and Gothic architecture feature prominently in international tourism campaigns as Lisbon competes with rival cities such as Barcelona, Berlin and Prague to be the European city break destination par excellence. Urban policy has been increasingly orientated towards a global audience as Lisbon, through the iconic landscape of Belém, is compared against these other European cities and their respective highlights such as La Rambla, the Brandenburg Gate and the Charles Bridge. New initiatives seek to improve and package aspects of the city as a great short-term destination, rather than Lisbon's leaders focusing on what makes for a great place to live for its citizens across all neighbourhoods, be they central or peripheral, rich or poor. This global vision, which revolves around comparing Lisbon to other world cities, has transformed urban life in the last decade and a half.

Globalising Tourism

Be it for the most famous guidebook attractions, or the more obscure gems, Lisbon has certainly baited the tourist hook and lured a huge number of visitors. International tourists have nearly tripled since the turn of the century with around six million arrivals a year.[114] Visitors come from neighbouring Spain, and Portugal has long been popular with the Brits, French and Germans, but increasingly it is Chinese and visitors from the United States which are among the biggest groups in the capital.[115] Lisbon has not just grown in popularity, it has an elevated status. Across the continent, cities compete for tourist euros and Lisbon is increasingly compared very favourably to its rivals. Lisbon has been 'the European city break par excellence for some time now; the new Barcelona, if you will' according to the *Independent.*[116] Portugal's capital won the 'World's Leading City Break Destination' in the 2017 World Travel Awards. It is further compared to its regional neighbours and showered with praise as 'Europe's best work-and-play capital' for international business travellers by the BBC[117] and 'the coolest capital city' by CNN.[118] Whether or not Lisbon is a 'better city break' than Barcelona, or the 'best' cultural capital or place for business trips is entirely subjective, and how these new opinions are formed is important to unpick.

Global comparisons are reshaping urban life and driving forward gentrification. Lisbon is becoming increasingly *great* in comparison to other European cities as a place to visit, but for residents this is having a toxic effect. The city has wholeheartedly embraced globalisation. Visitors arrive on easyJet, travel by Uber, stay in Airbnb apartments and consult the same handful of websites or guidebooks for travel tips. One of the publishers of the old-style guides has been particularly active in curating new experiences of the city. The Mercado da Ribeira, Lisbon's main market hall, has been leased by the international media company Time Out, previously known for cultural listings and books. This is the starting point for a new model of tourism with global ambitions. Since 2014, the renamed Time Out Market has been populated by twenty-six restaurants, eight bars, a dozen shops and a high-end music venue. Concessions serve gourmet food curated by Time Out's writers. Many are outlets of successful local restaurants or famous chefs. Stalls offer bijou versions of Portuguese classics like slated cod, *bifana* (pork sandwich) alongside *pastéis de nata* as well as popular international dishes: 'the best hamburger, the best sushi'. Lisbon is the first outpost in an emerging global geography: Time Out Markets have since opened in Boston, Miami and New York with plans for Chicago, Dubai, London, Montreal and Prague. Time Out is then part of a mosaic of international firms – budget airlines, Airbnb, Uber – that neatly package comparable short-term experiences of unfamiliar cities making life easy for tourists.

This is not the same type of formal 'package' that from the 1970s to 2000s dominated the short-haul sector when companies like TUI and Thomas Cook transported millions of northern Europeans to the resorts and beaches of the destinations in southern Europe. Package holidays helped make the Algarve in Portugal and the Costa del Sol in Spain and are still an important force in shaping the tourism market, but the new global online firms are more flexible and responsive to change. They make it ever so easy for a prospective tourist to open their laptop and click together a mini break, with minimal effort. The experiences they promote tend to be homogeneous and expose one of the contradictions of globalisation; as connectivity has increased, opportunities to experience new countries has expanded, yet our engagement with different places has narrowed. City breaks are becoming more similar to one another.

The prevalence of Airbnb lets and the familiar experience they serve up illustrates how globalisation can scrub away at local identity. Airbnb dominates short-term rental across global tourist cities and gives great choice, but the most popular apartments tend to offer a common user experience. Guests consume the same familiar interior aesthetics in their holiday lets. The apartments that top the search algorithms share a common look, be they in Belém, Brooklyn, Bilbao or Budapest. Each is strangely similar. Airbnb's Instagrammable vernacular runs to reproductions of mid-century-style furniture against a backdrop of clean white walls, grey sofas, low-maintenance succulent house plants, some carefully selected coffee table books with a nod to the local culture, the occasional bold feature wall, and perhaps most emblematic of the globalised aesthetic, some empty words or phrase: 'Coffee', 'Hugs', 'Live, Love, Laugh' or 'It's Gin O'Clock!' Close the curtains and you could be anywhere. So why is the globalisation of tourism a concern? What is the problem with different cities offering comparable experiences, be that Time Out markets or boilerplate Airbnb lets? As lessons from Barcelona and the emerging experiences of Lisbon illustrate, the reorientation of urban life towards foreign visitors and the boom in the housing markets can have devastating social and financial impacts on local residents.

Internationally Attractive

Lisbon's success as a tourist destination is a result of urban policy aimed squarely at an international audience. The city has been assertive in competing for investment, visitors and wealthy migrants, not with other parts of Portugal, but with other global cities such as Barcelona, Berlin, Dublin and Prague. The tourism board, airlines, international leisure chains and some forward-thinking local entrepreneurs have led this change. It has become a place of consumption for affluent people that are globally mobile and have a disposable income, rather than somewhere to live for the average Portuguese citizen who have been priced out of the downtown. Shops, restaurants and hotels in the city centre want to attract foreign dollars, pounds, yen and yuan as well as wads of northern Europeans' euros instead of the modest spending power of local people. This goes well beyond promoting tourism and Lisbon attracts not just short-term tourists, but a growing number of outsiders who stay for longer and choose to make it their home for a few months, a few years or for the rest of their lives: including international exchange students, footloose tech entrepreneurs coming for a 'workation' (working in a holiday location) or setting up a new life, and affluent foreign retirees. The arrival of these groups reinforces the notion that Lisbon is a vibrant, successful global city. Somewhere that is considered alongside other world-class destinations for leisure or a fresh start in the sun. Here there is a clear parallel to the long-standing experience of Barcelona where spiralling rents have pushed locals out of the city.[119]

The city council and national policymakers have purposefully worked to boost Lisbon's international reputation in comparison to other cities like the Catalan capital. The Portuguese government initially used high-profile one-off events to build a new profile for the capital city at the turn of the twentieth century. It bid against rival cities to boost its status. One of the first mega-events was when Lisbon became the European Capital of Culture in 1994, then the 1998 World Expo, and the finals of the 2004 European Football Championships. Those three cultural events, alongside many others, drove change and attracted a new type of visitor to Portugal. The nation had long been popular with budget travellers, but whereas the Algarve was a destination for cheap package holidays, these global events catalysed the development of new mid-market and high-end hotels, better restaurants, conference venues and fresh attractions, and provided a stimulus for investment in transport. They drew in millions of new visitors that spent much more in the capital. Lisbon became more prominent in airline schedules, tourist brochures and travel reviews as well as on global conference circuits. The latter got an important boost in 2016 as Lisbon permanently replaced Dublin as the host of the annual Web Summit, which is the premier tech conference in the world.

The Web Summit began in Dublin in 2009 and soon attracted tech's big names, from Twitter founder Jack Dorsey to Tesla's Elon Musk. Local stars were drawn to the Irish event. U2 frontman Bono attended in 2011 and even hosted a Dublin pub crawl for a select group of Silicon Valley leaders. Given its high profile and its unique status as a platform for accelerating globalisation, it was something of a coup for Lisbon to poach the event. The Portuguese capital won out following competition from Amsterdam and London.[120] Making the announcement in 2015, founder Paddy Cosgrave argued: 'Our attendees expect the best. Lisbon is a great city with a thriving startup community. What's more, it has great transport and hotel infrastructure and a state-of-the-art venue with capacity for more than 80,000 attendees.'[121] Clearly for him, Lisbon offered everything and since the move the summit has gone from strength to strength. Seventy thousand people from hundreds of countries come to hear speakers which have included Edward Snowden, Tony Blair,

Eric Cantona, Brad Smith, Microsoft president and CEO, and Tim Berners-Lee, inventor of the internet. Despite the range of presentations, this is not an event for everyone as the standard tickets for the four-day event is €995 per person.

The high cost of entry does not deter the global tech crowd. Since 2016, hundreds of thousands of summit attendees have arrived from western Europe and North America with their carry-on bags, laptops and their bank accounts full of bitcoins. Some of these footloose, tech-savvy, digital nomads have begun to settle in Lisbon, attracted by the lifestyle and low living costs. These rich young professionals tend to be relatively isolated from the wider city population. They socialise in groups that are overwhelmingly English-speaking. They spend their money on a range of new service industries: co-working spaces, exclusive gyms, serviced flats let by global estate agents such as RE/MAX and Savills, ride-hailing apps like Uber, as well as their food deliveries arm Uber Eats and their rival couriers Glovo, or perhaps entertaining visitors at Time Out Market. These services tend not to cater to local people due to their cost and are targeted towards serving a globalised clientele rather than fitting into the rhythms of Portuguese life. Expats like three-euro flat whites with overpriced spelt granola rather than fifty-cent bitter espressos alongside a cheap *bifana*.

Laptop-based entrepreneurs have become emblematic of Lisbon's gentrification and the businesses they patronise capture prime real estate, while their accommodation choices are intensely clustered in the city centre, driving up residential rents. Some of the new sons and daughters of Silicon Valley have even purchased apartments – homes on the premier avenues that seemed ridiculously cheap in comparison to Dublin, London or San Francisco. With each contactless payment they are nudging urban life away from providing for local people and towards meeting the needs of a global elite.

Alongside those headline-grabbing events that attracted the digital nomads, there have been wider and sustained attempts by local government to make the city more attractive to foreign spending power through reimagining long-standing traditions.

Starting in 2003, the city council launched a bid to find a new brand for the month-long Catholic *Festas Populares*. This centuries-old tradition revolved around the celebration of Santo António, the semi-official patron state of Lisbon, on 12 and 13 June. These were once modest festivals for local people that centred on churches, neighbourhoods and the theme of love, and included a feast of sardines. Jorge Silva, a graphic designer, responded to the council's competition and had the idea of using the symbol of a sardine to promote the whole city and in doing so commodified these summer holidays. They are now more of a sardine festival. Ever since, throughout the warm months, sardine-shaped signs adorn shops and restaurants, sardine-shaped gifts – porcelain sardines, sardine T-shirts, chocolate sardines and, of course, tinned sardines – make their way into tourist suitcases. Out on the streets, grilled sardines are consumed in huge numbers. Thirty-five million sardines – or thirteen every second – across Portugal during the month of June.[122] During the *Festas*, tourists and locals alike flock to the streets and eat, with their hands, the grilled sardines. They stand, chatting and revelling in the *rua*, while dealing with the messy flesh of oily fish. And while this ritual predates 2003, it has grown in scale and been commercialised, including through a key sponsorship with the major brewer Sagres. The *Festas* and the sardines have become a means by which Lisbon imagines itself as a city of enchantment, somewhere exciting and different for the tourist, more relaxed and exotic than other European cities. But this is also something of an invented tradition designed to make the streets vibrant and attractive, and one that is dislocated from its local roots in Catholic culture.

There are other strategic attempts to make Lisbon attractive and easy for foreigners to consume. A clear example of the outward, global-facing strategy was the city government's 2015 plan for tourism prepared by the German firm Roland Berger strategy consultants. Roland Berger identified young international city-breakers as a key market for central Lisbon. In so doing they proposed to segment the city into three marketable, territorialised packages: Bairro Alto was part of *'Lisboa Jovem'* ('Young Lisbon'), the downtown *'Baixa Chiado'* ('Trendy Lisbon') and the medieval areas around the castle including Alfama, *'Lisboa com história'* ('Lisbon with History').[123] These are not mere marketing strategies but have had real impacts. Today, it is almost as likely that you will hear English as Portuguese spoken in any cafe across these districts.

The changes to Lisbon are most apparent at night when the city becomes orientated towards students, local middle classes, European tourists and wealthy foreign residents. The glut of new arrivals which flow through the city alter its texture, purpose and meaning. Key areas become designated for certain groups with few alternative marginal spaces that break down social barriers. Some areas are seemingly for outsiders first and locals second. One prominent street, Rua Nova do Carvalho, was painted bright pink in 2013 and is now known as Rua da Rosa or 'Pink Street' as part of a so-called clean-up of Lisbon's red-light district. While there may have been some improvements associated with this change, as a very distinctive and popular tourist spot it brings revelry, noise and disruption to local people, while likely displacing the vulnerable commercial sex workers to less visible but potentially more dangerous locations. More widely it is symbolic of how some pockets of Lisbon feel more like a theme park than a liveable city. A further example is Bairro Alto. This area especially appeals to both Portuguese and international university students. Erasmus student organisations use specific bars and street corners to manage and promote drinking and partying in the streets. Long-term residents of Bairro Alto have been at the sharp end of Lisbon's transformation and are among those who have seen their quality of life decline at the same time as Lisbon has been internationally celebrated as a cool party city.

Students have become the most significant group in the city's rental housing market and have driven up property prices. Local academics such as Jordi Nofre are among those who identify the influx of international study abroad as well as full-time students at Lisbon's universities as being part of the 'broader public and private-led strategy of internationalisation of the city'[124] and believe 'studentification' alongside the linked process of touristification and gentrification have had negative impacts for the residents of Lisbon. The outward-facing programme of development and the constant flow of visitors and new arrivals have begun to erode some communities. When I speak to locals, although there is disquiet about the large numbers, outsiders are normally welcomed. Rather the number one problem is that it is the increasing unaffordability of the city that people are most angry about. This has driven down the quality of life. Not everyone is unhappy, and some locals have grown successful businesses in leisure and tourism or seen the value of their property transformed and become rich. Overall, gentrification has transformed the characteristics of central historical neighbourhoods, making them unaffordable for the urban poor. Opposition groups have attacked the state as they feel the government has gone too far and put global status ahead of serving the needs of Lisbon's citizens.

Terramotourism: 'A Tourism Earthquake'

Whenever I'm on holiday and I stroll past an estate agent's window I can't help myself. I stop, browse and start daydreaming. I do the mental arithmetic, try to work out exchange rates, calculate what I could afford. I catch myself imagining a fresh start in a new country. When in Lisbon I think about the sun, the relaxed lifestyle, the huge apartment I could afford for the price of a small London flat. How would I furnish my elegant city pad? Maybe with furniture from the flea markets, definitely with some unique tile work. It is an enticing prospect. For me this is a recurring fantasy. I've been visiting Portugal at least once a year since 2007. I've lived in Lisbon, as well as leading undergraduate field trips to teach my geography students about urban inequality. I've seen first-hand the exponential growth in house prices. Plenty of acquaintances have heard me say I wish I'd got on to the property ladder before the boom, but even now it still seems very attractive and affordable. And that's the point. For outsiders, the city has been too tempting for too long.

The emergence of low-cost flights and new online platforms for accommodation booking, like Airbnb, over the last two decades were the new connective tissues that linked Lisbon to the UK, US, Germany and elsewhere. City breaks advertised the low cost of apartments to foreign buyers with more financial muscle and invited local property speculators to stretch and buy up as many homes as possible and turn them into holiday lets. Central Lisbon is one of those places where the new technologies of globalisation hit the ground and had real-world effects, as tourism pumped up the value of housing.

It is not just global firms, but government policy that has ushered in new affluent migration which has further stimulated property markets. A controversial 'golden visa' system was symbolic of this process. This special visa programme granted residency to people who invested in properties worth at least €500,000 or created ten jobs and attracted affluent migrants from Brazil, Russia, China and South Africa. Government policy helped make central Lisbon a global property hotspot. The 'golden visa' for real estate investment closed in October 2023 after a local backlash against rising house prices. They are still popular options for immigration. Portugal's D7 retirement visa offers a route to permanent Portuguese residency and is aimed at non-EU/EEA citizens who have a regular passive income, such as a pension, that is equivariant to 100 per cent of Portugal's minimum wage (€9,120 per year).[125] There is also the entrepreneurial D2 'digital nomad' visa for remote workers that earn four times the national minimum wage, who can extend their stay for up to five years.[126] Both of these visa schemes attract globalised, affluent migrants to move to Lisbon and provide continued routes for immigration following the closure of the headline-grabbing and divisive 'golden visa' programme.[127]

Globalisation does not just bring the rich to Lisbon. In parallel, impoverished migrants – which also includes Brazilians and Chinese, as well as Eastern Europeans, Lusophone Africans and South Asians – arrive in Lisbon to work in the secondary labour market, sometimes undocumented. They are over-represented in the least attractive, low skilled and insecure jobs, including the service sector roles that prop up tourism such as food couriers, cleaners, kitchen hands and street hawkers.[128] Their arrival, and the lack of labour regulation, creates downward pressure on wages. This hidden underside of globalisation makes employment in the otherwise booming leisure sector less attractive to working-class Portuguese. When locals lose out to new arrivals, they are further displaced from economic life in the city centre and tensions emerge between different cultural groups.

To understand the damage done by Lisbon's overenthusiastic embrace of urban change, we must shift from a global to a local perspective to appreciate the impacts of globalisation on the city's inhabitants. One of the areas most touched is the maze of narrow cobbled streets with Moorish and Jewish influences that forms Alfama, the historic quarter around the medieval castle. Seemingly every other apartment, sometimes entire blocks, in Alfama are rented out on Airbnb. Again, state policy has facilitated the property boom to the detriment of local people. A centre-right government implemented a new lease law in 2012 that made it easier to evict long-term tenants. Many Alfama tenants have been evicted as new investors have purchased prime real estate.[129] Rents have risen to an average of €1,000 a month for a two-bed apartment, well above the national minimum wage and approaching the average Lisbon pre-tax salary of €1,472 a month.[130] Yet in hotspots like Alfama, fewer and fewer homes are available. A €1,000 a month rental can be let for at least €100 a night on Airbnb, much more during peak seasons and at times of high demand like the Web Summit. A rational business person would be quick to turf out the long-term tenants and embrace the tourist trade.

Lisbon only has around half a million inhabitants. Across the city, but concentrated in the centre, there are more than 20,000 tourist flats for let, in addition to tens of thousands of hotel rooms, holiday homes and other temporary accommodation. Sale prices increased 137 per cent between 2015 and 2023 and rents increased 37 per cent in a single year between 2022 and 2023.[131] The socio-economic transformation has spread out from the historic urban core. Exclusionary developments including *condomínios fechados* (enclosed condominiums), luxury apartments, student flats and other short-term lets predominate.[132] A-list celebrities including Madonna and Michael Fassbender are among those who have snapped up property. In many cases these properties are not homes, but at best second homes occupied for part of the year. Sometimes they are just investment opportunities left empty, a mere asset on the spreadsheet. Their new owners link Lisbon to global networks of capital and mobility and displace the working classes from historically mixed neighbourhoods.

The correlation between low wages and high rents, a surge in visitors, the wider transformation of the city's economy and the new geographies of exclusion, displacement and labour have ripped up the social fabric. Some speak of a *terramotourism* – 'a tourism earthquake' – in a word play that echoes the 1755 natural disaster that devastated the city Alfama is the ground zero. Defiant locals have painted anti-gentrification murals and drape banners between windows over the street. Elsewhere, former residents of inner-city Mouraria and Magdalena districts, interviewed in one of my projects,[133] left their neighbourhoods because of noise from adjacent flats, too much tourism and the density of housing. Transformations have not been accepted passively by Lisbon's residents. Housing movements (such as *Habita*), political parties (such as the *Bloco de Esquerda* and the *Partido Comunista Português*) and social movements have sought to counter the hegemonic narrative promoting tourism and urban regeneration. Thousands took to the streets in repeated protests in anti-gentrification demonstrations aimed at the local government, and some placards simply read: *A casa a quem a habita* – 'A home is somewhere you live'.

Distinction not Comparison

Lisbon has been promoted as among the best cities in Europe by a proud national government. They want it to rank alongside the greats. Somewhere to compare to Amsterdam or Dublin or even much larger Paris or London. Luís Mendes, an urban geographer working in Lisbon, identifies tourism – and particularly the idea that Lisbon needs to 'compete' with other cities – as crucial factors in the process of gentrification, which he further argues have been so damaging for local people.[134] Critics who share his view have been drowned out, as on its own terms, Lisbon has been a winner in the competition for greatness and has gained many accolades. The vitality of central Lisbon's tourist economy led to it being crowned the 2015 'European Entrepreneurial Region of the Year'. Two more Portuguese scholars, André Carmo and Ana Estevens, directly connect this 'entrepreneuralism' with the restructuring of urban space and deplore that 'today, Lisbon is a city of paradoxes and contradictions, along with other European cities. Arguably, a city that is made for capital, not for people.'[□] Vitally, this change is part of a global map and hotspots including Berlin, Barcelona and Prague, with which Lisbon is competing, and crucially *compared*, are also being spoilt by gentrification.

Is Lisbon the new Barcelona? In terms of the global buzz, the growth in tourism, the influx of affluent migrants and the spiralling rents, there are clear and obvious parallels. It is a could-be-true comparison as they are kind of the same. Yet there are also irreconcilable differences between the two great Iberian cities that this sort of offhand comparison elides. In national politics they could not be further apart. Lisbon is the beating heart and administrative centre of a unified nation state, somewhere that encapsulates Portugal and its historic empire. Barcelona is the largest city of Catalonia, an autonomous community where many want to leave the Spanish state, with regular mass protests against the federal government. There are many more fundamental differences in these two brilliantly unique places. But what makes '*Is Lisbon the new Barcelona?*' a bullshit comparison is not the differences in cultural geography, but the premise of the question. Implicit in the superstition is the notion that centuries-old Lisbon has newly become attractive to outsiders, somewhere that can be consumed, enjoyed, exploited and forgotten as attention pivots to the next fashionable city.

In a race to be the best destination for tourism and international investors, city leaders neglect the needs of citizens. In Berlin there have been tensions between new foreign residents and locals, as digital nomads have flocked to the cool eastern German city displacing local residents. In Prague, conflicts erupt as tour groups overwhelm parts of the historic city. In Barcelona, the impacts of

Airbnb and tourist-led gentrification have been characterised as 'collective displacement': no less than a loss of residential life.[136] Cities learn from one another, as they compete to be 'the next Berlin', 'better than Barcelona', or perhaps 'the new Lisbon', but key decision makers all too frequently look to what elevates their global reputations, rather than heeding the needs of their people, especially the urban poor. Cities get reduced to being the best globalised destination which has the greatest of a known set of attributes: widest range of Airbnb accommodation, best ranked bars, easiest flights and so on. Governments get attracted to lure in new investment which inflates property prices, giving the illusion of an economic success story. In parallel, rather than fostering unique and interesting local cultures that are celebrated in and of themselves, there is an overwhelming tendency to simplify and homogenise the urban experience and make it more accessible and easier to consume for the tourist.

International travel awards, corporate accolades and other subjective urban comparisons may be useful for a business leader deciding to host their conference in Lisbon or Dublin and wanting the 'best' meeting facilities, or for a city break tourist looking for somewhere that provides a similar experience to Berlin, or for the retired professional looking to buy a second home in the sun in Barcelona or somewhere which gives them more real estate for their euros. But for the Portuguese, Irish, German or Catalan urban residents, such international comparisons are meaningless. For them it is not important that their city tops a global popularity competition, but rather that it provides the best possible home. Great healthcare, good schools and affordable homes, these are the types of qualities that matter to residents but mean little to short-term visitors. Most people can't readily move somewhere 'better'; leaving behind work, families and friends is even less realistic than my daydream of moving to Lisbon.

In striving to make their cities globally attractive, urban leaders can make them less liveable. They can naively follow the examples of other places that have embraced unbridled globalisation. Inward investment can drive up property prices making homes unaffordable, rebranding districts can erode their historic qualities, and changing traditions can undermine local culture. Attracting global brands can make the city homogeneous and overshadow its distinctive properties. Across the road from *Pastéis de Belém* is a McDonald's. It is sad to see tourists tucking into the soft bun and salty patty of a flavourless Big Mac that you can find anywhere on the planet, rather than enjoying the distinctive crisp pastry and glorious sweetness of a world-class custard tart. Throughout the city, Lisbon's famous old cafes must compete with new venues that primarily cater for outsiders.

This is not an argument against you taking a city break, going to a conference or buying a second home. Lisbon and other popular tourist cities need visitors to contribute to their economies. Everyone should have the opportunity to travel, study, work and live overseas. And whenever you visit somewhere, try to support local business, take the time to venture off the beaten track and get a rich, local perspective not a shallow, global view of a city. So rather than being a blunt anti-globalisation argument, this is a call directed at political leaders to always think first and foremost about making their cities liveable for local people. International comparisons give primacy to a global audience and override the needs of residents. Visitors can be part of the picture but should not erode urban life. The policies national governments and city councils set frame outsiders' experiences, and they can temper the excesses of gentrification and avoid the horrors of a *terramotourism*. Europe's great cities have so much to offer their citizens and outsiders alike, and there is a balance to be had between maintaining what makes them special and welcoming new arrivals. And this importantly means both those that have plenty of money to spend and people from disadvantaged parts looking to study, work for a period of time or make a new start. These are the attributes that would make for a truly great city, but the mosaic of different qualities is contingent on unique combinations of local factors that are nearly impossible to compare.

CHAPTER 7

A Success Story for Africa?

How international comparison hid a failed state

Colonialism and Conflict

The Portuguese Empire was once the most expansive the world had ever seen. At its height in the seventeenth century, it stretched from the edge of Europe to the Atlantic islands of Madeira and the Azores, over to the Amazon basin of Brazil, across the equator to the Gulf of Guinea, round maritime trading posts fringing the southern half of Africa to Asian enclaves spanning from Goa in India to Timor in the Indonesian archipelago and Macau on the far eastern coast of China. Colonial capitalism and the trade in slaves, spices and sugar enriched Lisbon and bankrolled the development of Belém in the city's original golden age. Over the next four centuries the empire would gradually fall apart as European rivals challenged Portugal's trading networks and colonised peoples exerted their independence. António de Oliveira Salazar, who ruled as a virtual dictator from 1932 to 1968, tried to reinvigorate the empire in the mid-twentieth century. Salazar believed colonies must 'produce raw materials to sell to the motherland in exchange for manufactured goods'.[137] Like his British contemporary, Winston Churchill, he was an avid imperialist, and was voted the greatest ever national icon in the 2007 televised Portuguese competition.

Portugal was among the poorest countries in Europe in the twentieth century, but still benefitted from the remaining parts of its colonial empire. One of the major industries of Lisbon and Porto was clothing manufacturing. Cheap Angolan and Mozambican cotton provided 82 per cent of inputs for the sector in the 1960s, which employed a third of the industrial labour force and accounted for a fifth of Portuguese exports.[138] Meanwhile, in Mozambique cotton was known as the 'mother of poverty'.[139] Peasant farmers were forced to grow cotton and were paid pitifully low prices, their food consumption fell, and famines were common. They were harassed by colonial police to maintain cotton production, and rebels were exiled to São Tomé on the other side of Africa, never to see their homeland or families again.

Salazar's *Estado Novo* regime fought bitter wars in the 1960s and 1970s in a vain attempt to hold on to their five African colonies. Many Africans and Portuguese needlessly died. Angola, Cape Verde, Guinea-Bissau, Mozambique and São Tomé and Príncipe gained their independence in 1975 after the prolonged and bloody overseas conflicts catalysed an uprising on the streets of Lisbon that led the army to overthrow the *Estado Novo* in the near bloodless Carnation Revolution. Into the twenty-first century, all these new Lusophone African nations were beset by development challenges and faced widespread poverty. Mozambique was among the absolute poorest countries in the world.

In Mozambique it is best to travel by car. You wouldn't take a bus, unless of course you are poor like nearly all Mozambicans and have no choice other than to walk. The *Chapas* – which literally translates from Portuguese as 'sheets of metal' – are dangerous, overcrowded, slow and desperately uncomfortable minibuses. Rail is not really an option as there are only three lines. Train travel has deteriorated since the days of colonialism. Parts of the old coastal railroad have only recently been cleared of mines left from the sixteen-year civil war that finished in 1992. After the independence fight against Portugal, conflict reignited between Mozambicans that had fought on the side of the Europeans, and Frelimo, the new Marxist dominated government. The Renamo opponents were backed by the apartheid regime in neighbouring South Africa and received tacit support from the US, which during the Cold War wanted to destabilise the new independent, black-ruled socialist country. This conflict resulted in more than a million deaths.[140]

The central train station in the capital, Maputo, survived the war. This terminus is a grand Beaux-Arts structure built by the Portuguese and South Africans at the turn of the twentieth century. It is now more of a cultural icon than a transport hub. *Newsweek* recognised it as one of the ten most beautiful in the world. The domed façade formed a backdrop for the Sierra Leonean-set thriller *Blood Diamond* starring Leonardo DiCaprio. Inside, a colonial-era bar serves up ice-cold cocktails and live Afro jazz between the empty platforms on warm evenings to an elite and cosmopolitan crowd.

The other option for journeys in a country more than twice the size of Germany is the national airline LAM – *Linhas Aéreas de Moçambique* – or often 'Late and Maybe' among English speakers. LAM has a reputation for tardiness and sadly suffered a fatal crash in 2013. All twenty-seven passengers and six crew were killed.

Travel by car is enervating, especially if you are in one registered over the border in South Africa or if you are white. Police checkpoints are a feature of everyday life. Foreign motorists are the preferred target. A typical encounter starts with some cones and a police pick-up truck parked to narrow the carriageway and form a control point. Men in police *kepis* (French-style peaked caps) wave through the slow-moving line of battered cars, trucks and *Chapas* waiting for the right quarry. One officer has an AK-47 nonchalantly slung over the shoulder. Others are resting in the shade, escaping the tropical heat. You creep forward in the line trying not to catch their eye. Edging closer to the open road. Almost there. Then a hand waves you over. A policeman saunters up to the car. You shut the engine off and wind the window down. The requests follow: driver's licence, passport, registration, insurance, two red warning triangles, two yellow reflective vests. After thirty minutes of checking, all are in order. Passing this hurdle, the policeman starts inspecting the vehicle. Moving round to the back of the car to begin testing the lights one by one, he stops. Something has caught his attention, a small crack in the passenger side wing mirror. Still seated in the driver's seat, you glance his refection in the same mirror and catch a glint in his eye. For a split second a smile passes his face as the party mask of professionalism slips.

The policeman returns to the driver's side window. He deems the vehicle unsafe. You try a half-hearted argument that you can see rearwards fine in the barely cracked mirror: *this is nothing, Officer*. Certainly not compared to the passing *Chapas*. One is carrying twice the passengers they were designed for, nearside rear lights all smashed, and thick black smoke bellowing out of the exhaust. That *Chapa* is not the concern. This car is unsafe. You need to pay a fine – 10,000 meticals (£125). Normally, payment should be made at the station, *but maybe a solution can be found*. If you pledge to get it fixed, he can use his discretion. But could you do a favour? The police truck is low on fuel and the force needs money for petrol, can you help out?

So, this is how the bribe works. To save face all round, there is a charade of public service. Everyone knows where the money is really destined. Shuffling uneasily on the sweat-soaked driver's seat as the car bakes with the air conditioning off, you fumble for your wallet. With a clammy hand in the pocket you feel for a few notes. Less than ten thousand, you try to gauge the right amount, not too little, not too much. At the same time suppressing the curdling bile in the pit of your stomach and burying the rising thought that any amount lost will be preferable to a trip to the police station. You still haven't got the money out. As you hesitate, his comrade shifts the weight of the assault rifle slung on his shoulder. Is it an intimidating micro-gesture or is he just getting comfortable after hours on his feet? You add another note to the small wad and pass it over. The first policeman nods and waves you off. You drive on, cursing under your breath. Full of regret and relief.

A police shakedown like that is frustrating and disquieting even for experienced foreign drivers. When tensions are high on the city streets during oven-hot nights, it can be downright terrifying. This type of petty harassment is the outsiders' experience of Mozambique, but is indicative of wholesale police gross malpractice. The vast majority of Mozambicans are among the world's poorest people. For them vehicle ownership is an impossible dream. Most encounters with the police do not take place through a car window or the prism of white privilege. Few Mozambicans will ever face these, often racially charged, roadside confrontations, but they are victims of other wide-ranging police abuses that are potentially more deadly. For the poor there is no recourse to a handful of Meticals to smooth away the problems created by an unaccountable and often violent police force. Extortion, brutality, voter intimidation, human rights abuses and corruption are all among the charges against the *Polícia da República da Moçambique* made in the international media and by independent observers.[141] Policing is an area of state failure, but how is Mozambique faring more widely? Overall, after overcoming centuries of Portuguese colonialism and decades of warfare, is it a successful or a failing country?

Prosperity or Poverty?

Mozambique is not well known internationally, but until recently if you knew anything about this country of 30 million, you would most likely have heard that it was a comparative success story, an African country on the rise. The negative experiences of transport and policing does not chime with its international reputation. For thirty years, since the end of the civil war, it has been singled out as a success story in comparison to the rest of sub-Saharan Africa. A model for the rest of the continent. Mozambique moved from late-twentieth-century warfare into a new millennium of peace, stability and rapid economic growth. Positive comparisons were made in contrast to conflict-scarred Liberia, corrupt Guinea-Bissau and to Angola, which had squandered rich natural gas resources.[142] The former Secretary-General of the United Nations,

Kofi Annan, hailed 'Mozambique's continuing success story and the climate of trust it has generated [which] is the best possible antidote to the sceptics and cynics about Africa' when he visited in 2002. Fourteen years later, Annan's successor, Ban Ki-moon, visited and stated it was an 'important success story for the global community'. Throughout the 2000s and 2010s, Mozambique's annual growth averaged 6.5 per cent a year; a phenomenal period of sustained economic expansion, more than double the global average of 2.9 per cent.[143] In 2010, the *Guardian* said it was 'Boom time for Mozambique' and the same year the BBC reported that the World Bank and International Monetary Fund (IMF) regarded Mozambique as a success story.[144] The IMF reinforced this message by choosing to host a 2014 conference in Maputo unambiguously titled 'Africa rising: Building to the future'.

The bold supportive political statements, stellar economic trajectory and glowing media stories should have been borne out in international development indicators, which measure countries' successes and failures. It would be expected that Mozambique had done better in comparison to its African neighbours and be on the road towards middle-income status. However, this was far from the case. The United Nations' own comparative metric, the Human Development Index, a well-respected measure of social progress, indicated Mozambique has been a failure. In 2010, life expectancy was 48.4 years, gross national income per capita was only $854, and on average, children only received one year of schooling.[145] Mozambique's was 165th out of 169 states, stuck at the bottom of the league table, as it had been for two decades. Mozambique was below conflict-ravaged Sudan and Afghanistan in the UN statistics. I have seen first-hand the impoverishment experienced by most Mozambicans. Across years of fieldwork, I spent countless hours hearing stories of hunger and indebtedness, of children who missed school, of healthcare failures, corruption and police brutality. Poverty was a fact of life in the middle of Mozambique's celebrated boom period.

How do we explain this paradox? Why did two Secretary-Generals of the United Nations make such erroneous comparisons between Mozambique and the rest of Africa? Why did they and many other international commentators celebrate a failing state with a population trapped in poverty? What was behind this bullshit comparison?

A Donor Darling

Mozambique was a *donor darling*. Providers of development aid – international agencies like USAID and UK Aid – decide which countries to assist. Rich nations may support poorer countries for preferential reasons such as their geopolitical importance, shared cultural or religious values, a historical relationship, or to steer their politics and ideological alignment. This results in imbalances as donors tend to herd in popular places and some *darlings* accumulate more and more funding; meanwhile other poor countries become *aid orphans* that no one wants to support, like the Central African Republic and Gambia. This concentration of funding had a variety of interconnected causes and effects in Mozambique and the reasons behind this explained the persistent favourable, but deeply misleading, comparisons to the rest of Africa.

Maputo became a major destination for donor agencies once the civil war ended. Aid supported reconciliation and reconstruction, helped mend a broken society, and institutionalised the role of foreign powers in influencing government policy. A total of \$47.8 billion of donor support flowed into Mozambique between 1992 and 2018.[116] At first, aid helped build peace, but this was not pure altruism as the dollars increasingly came with strings attached. The rich nations had an economic worldview they wanted to promote. The ruling socialist Frelimo party – that has won every election since independence – had to follow policy prescriptions that meant abandoning its Marxist ideology and embracing free-market principles. The leadership have done so with great enthusiasm. They became the architects of a new liberal economy. Frelimo reduced state intervention in business to encourage foreign investment and foster a competitive economy. The moves brought inward investment, and spurred economic growth, but delivered little meaningful progress for most Mozambicans.

Brazil's mining giant Vale, another major ore company, London-listed Rio Tinto, and oil and gas firms, including Italy's Eni and US firm Anadarko, are among the many major investors in Mozambique. Increasingly, Chinese firms are also buying up Mozambique's natural resources, especially hardwood timber. The most iconic source of foreign money is Mozal, an aluminium processing facility near Maputo which in the mid-2010s employed fewer than 2,000 workers but accounted for 40 per cent of Mozambican exports. What most foreign businesses had in common was a specialisation in natural resource extraction and processing, which produced limited employment opportunities or wider benefits for society. But a few Mozambicans grew very rich. Frelimo's leaders carved out money-making opportunities working as intermediaries between the local and global economies.[147] The prime example was Armando Guebuza, who was president of Mozambique from 2005 to 2015. Guebuza had been a general in the civil war, but this former socialist revolutionary became one of the wealthiest people in Mozambique, nicknamed 'Mr Gue-Business'. He grew enterprises in the 1990s and held stakes in a bank, a brewery and the phone company Vodacom (part-owned by South Africa's Telkom and Britain's Vodafone).[148] Guebuza's shift from liberation leader to internationally networked tycoon embodies the integral relationship between foreign business and government in Mozambique.

Mozambique has been a real darling of the global business and donor community. The WTO was especially pleased with its financial policies in the 2000s and 2010s that were among the most progressively liberal in Africa and argued that 'trade liberalisation and economic reform have shown significant signs of success in Mozambique'.[149] They heaped praise on the nation. It was favourably compared to less ideologically committed neighbours because it dutifully followed the economic policy prescriptions championed by America and Europe, and was widely supported at the UN. Many globally influential right-leaning economists and politicians believe that an unshackled free market economy is the key to prosperity. They sank a lot of money and effort into supporting this idea and wanted a reformed post-socialist Mozambique to be an example for other African nations to follow, even if the evidence got in the way of this fantasy.

When Mozambique was heralded as a model for development, the audience wasn't ordinary Mozambicans; they were aware of their poverty in relation not just to the rich nations of Europe and America, but also more affluent African nations such as South Africa. Nor was it primarily the Frelimo government; they were not naïve to the development impasse, but the supportive statements reinforced their close relationship with donors. Rather the audience was other African leaders, the could-be-true story of Mozambique's 'success' was meant to spread the economic liberal model to other states. By promoting Mozambique, the UN and the major donor countries were trying to steer other African nations down the same neoliberal development path.

Living the Good Life

There was then a strong ideological basis to the false comparison, but there was also a personal side that is harder to evidence. While I lived in Maputo, I saw first-hand how the positive experience of many influential ex-pats informed their opinion of Mozambique and believe this is part of the explanation for the stickiness of the 'success' label. It was a wonderful place to live when I did my PhD research, and even a modest foreign salary bought you a luxurious lifestyle. I continued to visit through the early 2010s, when I began working as a geography lecturer at King's College and enjoyed my field research, but I got increasingly concerned about the risks of working in Mozambique. I'd written about corruption in the custom services, where there have been assassinations of investigators and after this work was published, I became fearful for my own safety.[150] The wider dangers of living and working in Mozambique further made me question the security situation. I'd been mugged at knife point and lost a friend in a car accident. So I decided not to return despite my deep affection for the country and moved on to research in equally poor Sierra Leone. My own concerns were sadly a harbinger of a wider breakdown in security that Mozambicans cannot escape and that have shattered the myth of the success story.

Maputo has long been a popular overseas posting. When working in the vibrant subtropical coastal city, I knew UN agency staff, diplomats, private consultants and aid workers from major international NGOs. Many were veterans of work around the world. I met foreign officials at open-air receptions in tropical gardens hosted by embassies, dined with economists in beachfront restaurants sharing platters of giant king prawns, and partied with international volunteers at the train station cocktail bar. Virtually without exception they loved the lifestyle and viewed it as a great place to enjoy the ex-pat experience in comparison to most other very low-income countries, like Afghanistan, the DRC and the Central African Republic. Life was easy. Even disruptions like the police checkpoints could be circumvented by holders of diplomatic passports from foreign missions or those ex-pats happy to dip their hands straight in their pockets with a quick bribe to avoid a major hold-up. Maputo was a place people wanted to live, and everyone in the sector had a vested interest in maintaining the story that the donor programmes were a success, that economic liberalisation worked, and that Mozambique was on the rise.[151] This story was a fiction with many foreign authors.

The *Jardim dos Professores* or Teachers' Gardens is a small park in the affluent centre of Maputo. Its desirable elevated location has fresh sea breezes and views out towards the Indian Ocean. Unlike most parks in Mozambique, the gardens are beautifully maintained. Security guards patrol the grounds and while it is nominally a public space, in reality it is an enclave for the local elite and ex-pats. A modern bourgeoisie cafe, *Campo das Acácias* (The Acacia Field), serves bitter espressos and sweet *Pastéis de nata* that are almost equal to those of Lisbon. The European pricing of the food and drink pays for the guards and upkeep of the gardens, as the wider park has been virtually privatised by the cafe owners. I met an acquaintance there to discuss work and he brought with him a senior Scandinavian diplomat; he was every inch the eloquent and educated patrician. Conversation turned to poverty levels in Mozambique. Our perceptions were completely different. Whereas my field research and data analysis had led me to believe impoverishment remained stubbornly widespread and that national economic growth had delivered little benefit to most Mozambicans, his time on the diplomatic circuit and his flying visits to the cherry-picked poor communities that had benefitted most from donor aid left him with the opposite opinion. He argued that there had been meaningful positive change. It was easy to understand how he had formed that could-be-true view from his vantage point.

Mozambique's free-market transition had energised the leisure sector in Maputo. The cosmopolitan capital city had a small affluent elite and plenty of opportunity for fun if you had some cash in your pocket. But this boom was largely jobless growth and little money trickled down to the majority of Mozambicans, who remain resolutely poor. When Frelimo dismantled the state's socialist machinery, this brought deindustrialisation, job losses and great social hardships as well as ushering in investors hungry to capitalise on Mozambique's natural resources.[152] Intended beneficiaries of economic liberalism were local entrepreneurs. I carried out extensive fieldwork with small business people in Maputo and some of the poorest market and street traders during the heights of Mozambique's 'success'. Despite the growing economy they faced stagnation in their standards of living and were trapped in persistence poverty.[153] They went without meals, they struggled to provide for their families, they scratched a living on a few dollars a day. The poor were being left behind, while a handful of Mozambicans became super rich. Beyond Maputo when I travelled around the country, I saw endless poverty. In many rural provinces people were as poor as anywhere on earth.

Economic growth alone is not enough to combat poverty. New money must reach the poor. Although poverty levels declined across Mozambique in the years immediately after the civil war, they remained stubbornly stable in the 2000s and 2010s. In 2020, the UN reported 72.5 per cent of people still lived in poverty.[154] Across sub-Saharan Africa the percentage in poverty was 55 per cent. Throughout the period in the 2000s and early 2010s, when the United Nations was led by Annan and Ki-moon who championed Mozambique's reputation, it was at the bottom of the UN's own Human Development Index (HDI). By 2020 it was still below all neighbouring southern African states. Remember that Mozambique was long held up as a beacon of development success in comparison to other African countries by the UN leaders! This is a bullshit comparison and one that is so tragic and matters because the liberal economic approach and investor-friendly policies were being praised as delivering success for political reasons. Rather what they were achieving was worse than the policies in comparable countries. Neoliberal ideology resulted in the persistence of poverty for most Mozambicans.

Shattering the Myth

By 2020 the false narrative of Mozambique as a nation on the rise had becoming increasingly difficult to sustain. Reality was biting back. The UN leadership no longer talked about it as a comparative success story. The nation faced mounting challenges: a political scandal over corrupt bank loans, unmet development needs, organised crime, an economic slump, political conflict and devastating cyclones.[155] Most concerning was a rise in violent attacks involving both Renamo supporters and Islamic militias in the north of the country that would later erupt into full-blown conflict. Both capitalised on the weakness of the police and security services. Tellingly, whereas his predecessors heaped praise on Mozambique, the Portuguese UN Secretary-General António Guterres highlighted the state's failures to control violence. He was 'shocked' by reports of massacres including the 'beheading and kidnapping of women and children'. As a UN statement continued, 'He strongly condemns this wanton brutality. The Secretary-General urges the country's authorities to conduct an investigation into these incidents and to hold those responsible to account.' Guterres further called for all parties in the conflict to follow human rights law.[156] In early 2020 as many as fifty people died in attacks by fighters linked to Islamic State.

These atrocities were part of a wider conflict centred on Cabo Delgado, a northern province that was the site of a multi-billion-dollar natural gas project, but among the poorest parts of Mozambique. With limited government services, rural people lost access to the land they relied on for agriculture due to the expansion of mining and gas extraction. Locals were unqualified for new jobs in the natural resource sector. Without land or opportunity some youths were prone to the messages of radical preachers and joined the insurgency. The republic's police force, that should be providing national security, mainly kept close to the government in the capital, helping Frelimo tighten their grip on power, and helping themselves to bribes on the streets. Cabo Delgado is more than 1,600 kilometres from Maputo. With Mozambique's crumbling infrastructure it would take days to drive there, but for most ex-pats and visiting international politicians and diplomats who never stray far from the delights of the city, it might as well be another country. That is not to say that the collapse of security in Mozambique isn't having an impact in Maputo. In the last five years there has been a rise in high-profile kidnappings for ransom in the capital, which the failing police service have been unable to curb. In 2022, there were twelve recorded nationally and at least $35 million was paid in ransoms.[157]

Mozambique is sliding back towards civil war and the poor in the far north of the country are facing the worst consequences.[158] Four thousand people have been killed and nearly a million have fled their homes because of the violence, in a conflict that has received little global coverage.[139] Since 2021 the Southern African Development Community has sent forces, which includes troops from the South African National Defence Force, to fight armed rebel groups alongside Mozambique's army. Amnesty International has named this a 'forgotten war' and has obtained video of Mozambican and South African forces burning corpses, which they report is part of a wider tragedy of 'violence against civilians, extrajudicial executions and other human rights violations and violations of international humanitarian law'.[160] The legacy of Mozambique's decades of so-called development success is a tragically failed state.

Two decades of misleading international comparisons hid this unfolding catastrophe. Successive leaders of the United

Nations and the wider donor community promoted a vision of Mozambique, which distorted the reality. At the global level, authoritative voices like Kofi Annan and Ban Ki-moon argued it was doing better than similar African states as they wanted other nations to follow the same policies that Maputo had adopted. On the ground, foreign aid workers' overall perception of Mozambique's so-called development success was distorted by their favourable impression of life in and around the capital, where the expat lifestyle was more pleasurable than in other highly impoverished developing societies.[161] Collectively, the international community drew upon the distorted, selective and ideological use of economic metrics and the lazy half-truths of personal experiences to formulate comparisons that concealed the true persistence of poverty and the failures of the Frelimo government. The next chapter takes a wider perspective on the ways in which international development has failed to close the gap between rich and poor countries.

CHAPTER 8

Why are Certain Countries Poor?

Dismantling comparative models of development

A Ladder of Development

The discussion of the failure of development in Mozambique in the previous chapter drew on different evidence, experiences of a corrupt police force, reflections on expat life, field research of livelihoods, data on the poverty ratio, and reporting on conflict. Perhaps most persuasive in debunking the positive comparison was the nation's rank in the UN's Human Development Index. The HDI combines different statistics on life expectancy, education and per capita income. This is a better measure than just using a financial indicator like GDP (gross domestic product) which reduces development to economic growth. As the evidence from Mozambique illustrated, when an economy is growing, the cake can be getting bigger and bigger, but if the slice the poor receives does not grow, they will remain impoverished and hungry.

As a means of comparison, the HDI is far from perfect, and it still draws heavily on national economic performance. The distorting impact of this is well evidenced by the position of

Ireland, which was second in the world for development in 2020 only behind Norway. It came ahead of other affluent nations including Switzerland, Sweden and 13th-placed Britain. Ireland's performance in health and education was average for nations in the 'Very High' development group, but what boosted its rank was a gross national income (GNI) per capita of $68,371, which was nearly 50 per cent higher than for the UK. Anyone who knew the two countries will be able to tell you that Irish people were not one and a half times as wealthy as Brits, and that there was poverty in both countries. Instead, the metric was heavily distorted. Ireland's income was greatly exaggerated by the inflow of profits to multinational corporations based in Dublin that took advantage of its controversial tax haven status.[162] This predominantly foreign wealth did not lift the development of most Irish people. In 2020 the HDI provided a really bad means to comparing living standards in the UK and Ireland.

Ireland's silver medal position was short-lived and by 2023 it had slid to eighth, a position that still over-represented Ireland's level of development as it was distorted by a GNI which had risen to $76,169, nearly ten thousand dollars greater than Switzerland, the country which by then had the highest HDI rank.[163] The bottom-placed country was South Sudan, and as conflict raged in the north of Mozambique, it remained only six places higher at 185th of 191 countries.

Rigorous technical analysis has elsewhere deconstructed the HDI metric and questioned the quality of the data and the assumptions that go into the formula.[164] This is not the place to further interrogate the index in fine detail, but suffice to say that it is contested, yet is still probably the best readily available global measure of poverty and prosperity. As with any numerical comparison, the underlying data and methodology must be considered critically as they can produce distorted comparisons, but figures on life expectancy and education are usually accurate and reliable indicators, which moderate variation in income like the Irish instances. Sticking with the index, here I want to look at the way in which the HDI is used to divide countries into four human development groups – Low, Medium, High and

Very High – as a route into thinking about how international development is compared across time as well as space, as this chapter bridges between the discussion of place-based and historical comparisons. Policymakers at the UN and elsewhere conceptualise development as a series of stages, like a ladder with each country on a step, and all of them on the way up to the top 'Very High' rung. Given enough time, everyone will get to the top deck, but how helpful is this concept?

Geographical and historical comparisons are often combined to locate different nations at higher and lower rungs on the development ladder. So, we could think of contemporary Mozambique down in the Low development group as being fifty or a hundred years *behind* Switzerland at the top of the index. The most influential thinker to theorise development in this way was the American economist, Walt Rostow. Writing in 1960, he used the experiences of rich nations, principally Britain, as a basis for comparison. Rather than the UN's four groups of development, Rostow divided countries into five historical stages: the traditional society, the preconditions for take-off, the take-off, the drive to maturity and the age of high mass consumption. Since the Industrial Revolution in the later eighteenth century, Britain progressed from being a *traditional* to a *high mass-consumption* society in the mid-twentieth century, later to be surpassed as the developed country par excellence: the United States of America, which, in its post-Second World War boom, was an iconic model of a modern, affluent consumer society. Every other nation could also be located in one of these five stages with, for example, the poorest countries in Africa in the 1960s being in the *traditional* society stage.

Rostow's model seems intuitive at first. It makes sense to compare contemporary poor nations with basic incomes, short life expectancy and limited school provision to the earlier history of a European nation that had comparative low levels of wealth, health and education nearly two hundred years earlier. The problem with this model was that it failed to capture what drove the creation of wealth and development in the rich nations. High mass consumption in Europe and America was interlinked with the export of natural resources, first from colonies and later from independent yet impoverished nations of the Global South. Mozambique's cotton was woven into Portuguese textiles, Indian tea quenched the thirst around English breakfast tables, and Liberian rubber shod the wheels of American cars. The industrial development of the mature, *high mass-consumption* societies of the 1960s was dependent on the continued export of cheap minerals and agricultural goods from the colonies and ex-colonies of the Global South. The progress of Britain and the US was not due to purely national processes but depended on global trade. Their *take-offs* had been triggered by colonialism and the import of cheap resources. For the Mozambiques, Indias and Liberias of the world, there was no one left for them to colonise and help push them up the ladder of development.

The wealth of some nations is connected to the impoverishment of others. African countries in the 1960s were not fifty, a hundred or more, years behind in comparison to Britain and other Western nations. They were part of the same shared global history that had produced uneven development. Africa remained poor because of centuries of colonialism and economic inequalities. The comparative model that posits that some nations are stuck waiting on the ground floor of history and once they have leapt on to the development ladder, they will reach the same heights as developed nations is a fantasy. Africa was poor, not because it hadn't yet been incorporated into the modern global economy, but because it played a subordinate role supporting the prosperity of the rich nations.

Stuck in the Waiting Room

A further issue with a comparative model of global history is that it promotes the vision of one type of Western society as the aspirational goal for the rest of the world. Implicit in Rostow's five stages of economic growth (subtitled *'A non-communist manifesto'*) was the idea that a Western nation, and especially 1960s America and the suburban world of motor cars, refrigerators and white nuclear families, which was a progression from the earlier British template of a Victorian consumer society, was *the* model nation. No matter what Rostow believed at the time, we can now look back and see clearly that the US was no model society in the early 1960s. America had myriad issues to resolve at home. Martin Luther King Jr was leading the civil rights movement in its non-violent fight for racial equality. Second-wave feminists campaigned for women's rights. The gay liberation movement was in its infancy. Then, as now, even the richest nations on earth had fundamental inequalities that needed to be addressed, as well as failures in health, education and the environment. There has never been a utopian country at the top of the development ladder to compare the others against. In 2023, the Swiss did not look down from their alpine summit completely free of impoverishment but faced their own development challenges. Switzerland's poverty rate was low, but still 8.7 per cent and one in twenty people suffered material and social deprivation, as well as problems of gender and racial inequality.[165]

This issue has not prevented Rostow's theory from shaping development policy for over half a century. He himself argued persuasively that the United States should help poor nations develop and rapidly transition through his five stages. As an advisor to President Kennedy, Rostow's influence can be seen in JFK's 1961 inaugural address: 'To those people in the huts and villages of half the globe struggling to break the bonds of mass misery, we pledge our best efforts to help them help themselves.' The language of geo-historical comparisons remains commonplace in the aid sector. The world's most prominent development economist Jeffrey Sachs wrote that 'sweatshops are the first rung on the ladder out of extreme poverty', there are scholarly books with titles like *Catch Up*, and UN development policy documents captioned 'Leaving no one behind'.[166] The overarching message is that the poor countries of the world are stuck in the past and if they want a better future, they have to follow the upwards path of the West.

Under these models, developing regions are deemed to be doing poorly in comparison to developed places due to internal conditions, which present obstacles to modernisation and social change that include factors such as the natural environment. Prominent environmental determinists, like the best-selling author of *Prisoners of Geography*, Tim Marshall, popularised the falsehood that physical geography overwhelmingly constrains development: 'Geography has always been a prison of sorts – one that defines what a nation is or can be, and one from which our world leaders have often struggled to break free.'[167] It is an intuitive could-be-true line of argument – that nature shapes the fate of nations – but one that is widely discredited by academic geographers as naïve. Environmental determinism elides the fact that many seemingly inhospitable locations around the world have produced prosperous societies: Florida, Hong Kong and the Netherlands are all locations with major environmental challenges; a humid and hurricane-prone climate, poor geology and drinking water supply, and low-lying flood-vulnerable land, respectively, that would seemingly make them unlikely places for some of the richest societies on earth, but they have escaped these 'prisons' because of their broader economic and political geography.

As well as unhelpful notions of environmental determinism, cultural comparison which rates some groups as less sophisticated or more savage than others, has also served as a powerful tool of subjugation and helped reproduce what the influential geographer James Blaut called the 'colonizer's model of the world'.[168] Colonial theories of modernisation, like Rostow's sequence of transitions from traditional to post-industrial societies, characterised the early societies as culturally inferior. For instance, their 'particularistic' values with strong kinship and family ties were viewed as an obstacle to development as opposed to the 'universalistic' values which characterise modern European societies with wider social circles.[169] These hierarchies are replicated in mainstream culture. They will be familiar to anyone who has played a computer strategy game like *Civilization*, where you guide a chosen culture to advance from the Stone Age to the near future. In the real world, people with histories of colonisation have been forced to live comparatively in ways that consistently hierarchised societies and reproduced patterns of inequality and racism. In the 1960s, Mozambican cotton farmers would be considered 'backward' in comparison to Portuguese industrial workers even though both were working in the same economic system. This is a bullshit comparison because it was only the inputs of Mozambican cotton which enabled the factories of Lisbon to become modern. Indeed, many Portuguese people lived in poverty in the twentieth century. Some who arrived as colonial settlers in Mozambique were so poor and 'backward' they didn't have shoes.[170]

This comparison is further shown to be a distorted record of reality when a temporal dimension is used to rationalise the differences. Some development models conceptualise developing countries as ten, fifty or even a hundred years behind developed ones. There was a 'development gap' to be narrowed.[171] Africa, Asia and Latin America needed to 'catch up' with Europe and North America, as if non-Western societies sat in the waiting room of history.[172] But colonised people do not exist on another timeline, no more than they are meek, powerless avatars in some grand computer game. They were people who had been subjugated. What were the Mozambican cotton growers of the 1960s supposed to do to advance their society? Find another nation to colonise and exploit so they could progress to being factory workers rather than peasant farmers? Even after they triumphed in their independence struggle, Mozambicans' social progress was stymied by the wider relations, including tensions with neighbouring apartheid South Africa and the geopolitics of the Cold War.

The problem with either environmental explanations or notions of cultural inferiority is that they ignore the wider historical and contemporary political and economic relationships that make countries rich and poor. Here I argue that comparisons need to be *relational* and consider connections between countries, rather than focusing on what happens within a nation's borders. What is absent from comparative analysis like Marshall's, Rostow's and Sachs's is an awareness of the deeper relations between the developing and developed countries and the historical processes that have produced uneven development.[173] Capitalist relations that bind the affluent nations and the marginalised places of the world economy have generated a continual 'development of underdevelopment'.[174] Rather than developing countries, such as Mozambique, being on the early steps on a teleological ladder of progress, their underdevelopment is a permanent condition. Colonialism developed crucial comparative advantages that protect the rich economies – for instance, control of global banking networks, high-quality education sectors, legal systems, huge reserves of capital, the dominance of political structures like the UN and WTO, and tariff and trade barriers. In tandem, the underdeveloped 'peripheral' regions of the world are locked in an inferior status and committed to the service of core economies, providing natural resources, agricultural products, tourism destinations and a supply of low-cost migrant labour that can fill gaps in the job market. These patterns of relationship are further sustained through indebtedness and weak terms of trade, which undervalued the goods and services produced in the developing world, as well as the transplanting of bullshit ideologies, like the neoliberal policies that had such a devastating impact on the development of Mozambique in the 2000s and 2010s.

When countries like South Korea, which was poorer than many countries in sub-Saharan Africa in the 1950s, have escaped poverty, a crucial ingredient has been a realignment in their relations to the wider geopolitical world. Seoul benefitted from preferential relationships with Washington, was able to control its own imports and exports, avoided indebtedness, and nurtured and protected domestic industries, rather than its economy being exploited by a neo-colonial power. South Korea lacks natural resources and has an indigenous culture that is very different to the Euro-American model, but these internal factors did not hold the nation back. It was able to steadily and strategically insert itself into the global economy over the last seventy years.[175]

Bad Hospitals and Good Doctors

The discussion of the persistence of geo-historical comparison and the need for alternative relational comparisons has been relatively conceptual and deserves a case study. Drawing on my own fieldwork on healthcare in Sierra Leone, the remainder of this chapter introduces the *could-be-true, but isn't* comparative perspective, and secondly provides the alternative relational comparison analysis to explain differences in healthcare outcomes between Sierra Leone and the UK.

Hospitals are worse in Africa than in any other region in the world. In Sierra Leone they are worse than in most of Africa. When I published my research in 2020, Sierra Leone had the fifth-lowest life expectancy and the second-highest infant mortality rates in the world.[176] For further comparison, the differences between the United Kingdom and Sierra Leone could not be starker: four child deaths per 1,000 live births in the UK versus seventy-nine in Sierra Leone; life expectancy is eighty-one and fifty-four years respectively; and income is $46,071 against $1,668.[177] There is evidently a chasm in the basic conditions of life between these nations. So, is it not helpful to think about the two places as being at different historical steps on the same development ladder? Taking life expectancy as a historical comparison, Britons could expect to live to the age of fifty-four more than a century ago, way back in 1912. It therefore seems to make sense. But there are real problems with this type of historical comparison, especially as there is a connection between good healthcare in the UK and weak healthcare in Sierra Leone.

The international doctors and nurses I interviewed readily made unfavourable comparisons between their experiences of Western hospitals and facilities in Sierra Leone. One interviewee termed Connaught Hospital, the principal referral hospital in the capital Freetown, a 'hellhole'. People were 'dying all the time of stuff they shouldn't die of'. An example, among many, was of an anaemic thirteen-year-old girl who died because she did not get a blood transfusion, 'something that is the bread and butter of what happens in the UK and we would never allow to happen'. Resources at Connaught Hospital were even 'behind Haiti'. Historical comparisons were often made as the healthcare workers tried to make sense of the conditions they faced. For instance, a physician recalled observing a whole chest cavity full of fluid: 'It almost took me back, because I trained twenty-five years ago . . . But you never really see them in Western countries now . . . it's a little bit like going back in time as well.' One published surgical report even analysed how government hospitals in Sierra Leone were worse in 2010 than the facilities of the Union Army during the US Civil War more than 150 years earlier.[178] The judgements of these health professionals about the level of care available are shocking and undoubtedly accurate, but what is not so helpful is when these comparisons are framed historically. Just because the healthcare available may be similar to that in other places at different times does not mean the underlying circumstances of the two periods and locations compare.

Moving around the hospital interviewing local and international staff, I saw the suffering of patients and the tough working conditions, but I was not stepping into the past, rather walking through a painful present. Wards with poor hygiene and a lack of drugs were part of a globalised world of smartphones and the internet where patients were as keen to talk to me about last night's Manchester United game as their medical care. Most of the foreign doctors and nurses I talked with had not been trained in the history of international development, they were experts in medicine not sociology. Prior to travelling to Sierra Leone, they drew from a well of general knowledge that tries to explain the differences between rich and poor nations as being the result of local factors such as corruption, warfare, weak governments, disasters, a lack of natural resources or some other domestic issues, rather than understanding impoverishment as a condition that is related to a global history of colonialism and is sustained by unequal world trade.

The clearest way to pull apart the historical comparison is to think about the employment of Sierra Leonean doctors and nurses at home and internationally. Connaught Hospital was vastly understaffed, but the quality of local healthcare workers was not the problem. As a Western doctor explained, the Sierra Leonean clinicians' 'anatomy knowledge and technical skills were fantastic; it's just all the other supporting elements that need work'. As another described: 'One of the surgical doctors is trained to an incredibly high standard, he knows what's good. Professor X exactly the same.' So, these doctors were not stuck in the past practising the medicine of a hundred years ago. The same went for the nurses, who are in demand overseas. An estimated 60 per cent of Sierra Leonean-trained nurses emigrate. They seek a better life in the UK, Canada, the US and nearby, but more affluent, Ghana. Emigration shows that we need to understand that the problems of healthcare in Sierra Leone were linked to the better health and employment conditions in more affluent nations. There are 520 Sierra Leonean health workers in the NHS and many more employed in other support jobs and private care homes, as well as thousands across other developed countries. The number in the NHS may seem small but is equivalent to 16 per cent of the entire public health workforce of Sierra Leone.

Relational Comparison

Sierra Leone desperately needs more health workers to improve patient care, but the majority of those that are trained locally want to emigrate and make a better life for themselves in other more affluent countries. The nurses I talked with always asked about opportunities to come to London. This is logical. You can't blame anyone for wanting to emigrate. Work at Connaught Hospital was hard, and salaries were too low to support even a basic standard of living. Nurses survived by selling medicines to patients and doctors subsidised their meagre government salaries by working in private clinics. The pull to emigrate is a problem of twenty-first-century globalisation, not something that Western nations had to face earlier when they transitioned through different developmental stages. Doctors and nurses in Edwardian Britain enjoyed relatively good salaries and weren't compelled to seek new opportunities overseas. We can't think of Connaught as being a museum-like hospital of the past. It exists now in today's interconnected world. The Sierra Leonean Ministry of Health must try to improve the health of the nation while dealing with new and evolving challenges, not the world of a hundred years ago.

Not only was the immigration of health workers a challenge that the West did not need to overcome as it progressed up a development ladder, the ongoing, continued improvements in healthcare of Britain and other Very High development countries are boosted by the same movement of healthcare workers out of low development countries. This further bolsters their HDI. There are 5,819 African nationals working as doctors in the NHS. In total around 27 per cent of doctors in the UK were trained in developing countries. If fewer doctors and nurses left the world's poorest countries for the richest, what is sometimes called the 'medical brain drain', then there would not be such a gap in healthcare. And yet there is a very really need for more healthcare workers in Britain's NHS, a problem shared by nearly every country in the world. Coronavirus illustrated the fragile capacity and understaffing of British hospitals, but the scale of the shortfall in Africa is truly staggering. There are 280 physicians per 100,000 people in the UK. On average across sub-Saharan Africa there are twenty per 100,000, but in Sierra Leone just two per 100,000.[179]

How do development programmes, like the one at Connaught Hospital that brought Western healthcare workers to work in impoverished settings, fit into this picture? Can aid work help push nations up the development ladder as Rostow and JFK anticipated in the 1960s? Some inspiring people make tremendous sacrifices like those that I talked with who selflessly risked death as they worked through Sierra Leone's 2014–16 Ebola outbreak. Although such individuals do amazing, lifesaving work every day in difficult circumstances, the overall scale is tiny. It is a cliché, but they are a sticking plaster on a gaping wound. There are systemic problems that global development programmes cannot answer. Worldwide there are far too few health workers, and they are in demand across a globalised job marketplace. Like any employment market, those with much-needed skills tend to move to where wages are highest. Few people head in the other direction for an overseas adventure. African healthcare workers migrate to work in British hospitals in numbers that dwarf the countermovement of UK aid and volunteers.

National comparisons hide the globalisation of the health sector. The high standards of hospitals in rich countries and the long life expectancies are the apex of healthcare the rest of the world is measured against. These high-ranking national health outcomes are not just a result of the histories and conditions internal to these societies, but rather are relational and depend on global flows of migration and draw upon resources, medicines and scientific discoveries produced around the world. Equally, rather than being stuck in the past, Sierra Leone's poor healthcare is a prisoner of the present, trapped not only by the outflows of skilled people, but by wider structural challenges. Even if all the Sierra Leonean health workers trained locally were retained, there would still be a huge shortfall in the ratio of doctors to patients and multiple other elements of the national healthcare system that needed desperate attention. All of which would require money that Sierra Leone does not have. Ultimately, poverty resulting from uneven international trading relationships and an absence of industrial development block improvements in medical provision.

Oftentimes, comparative models project visions of how people want the world to be rather than how it is. In international development, comparisons frequently support contested ideas, like those of neoliberal economists at the WTO, as to why there are differences between rich and poor countries. Here the examples of Sierra Leone, as well as Mozambique from the previous chapter, have illustrated that ideological and simplistic historical models distort our understanding of global inequality. These subjective worldviews shape vital policies and thus bullshit comparisons can have dangerous consequences for the world's poorest inhabitants. Yet even progressive, critical development research and policymaking depends upon the use of comparative statistics. To cast light on global inequalities, metrics and models need to be deployed with integrity to provide as objective a vision of international development as possible, while acknowledging that every study will contain subjectivities. I have drawn heavily on published data to bolster my arguments, with the caveat that some data like the HDI can be misleading.[180] Despite the myriad, and sometimes interconnected, global challenges facing society – climate change, war, migration – poverty remains a gargantuan problem. To lift the poorest out of impoverishment we need to continue to make comparisons, but to think about the wider relationships, those real-world political, economic and historical connections between rich and poor. The last aspect, history, is especially important to comprehend as analogies from the past are critical devices for understanding the contested politics of the present, but many such comparisons are riddled with half-truths.

PART 3

History

CHAPTER 9

Is China a New Colonial Power?

Misunderstanding the past clouds judgement of the present

Rising China

Built on a bedrock of granite, concrete engineering has remade the mouth of the Pearl River Delta. Rising towers of steel surround Hong Kong Harbour visually joining sky and shorelines. The reflected glare of water on glass sustains the illusion. As darkness falls, the spectacular straight-line profiles of skyscrapers are lit in fluorescent pinstripes. Nightly light shows criss-cross Kowloon Bay. Chinese financial might and engineering prowess built the new Hong Kong–Zhuhai–Macau Bridge, the longest sea crossing on earth, and the sheer scale of the span looks impossible. Out of sight, Hong Kong's world-class mass transit system is a marvel of metropolitan transportation. Tunnels criss-cross the bay. Underground stations deliver passengers into the subterranean roots of high-rise towers and multi-storey shopping malls, feeding in office workers and consumers like water up the xylem of a Dawn Redwood. One tower, the HSBC Main Building, was the world's most expensive in 1985, but now looks like a junior partner among the financial titans.

Hong Kong went from a British colonial backwater to the most dynamic city in the East. Recently it has been surpassed by Beijing's rapid rise. The Communist Party of China's self-confidence has led it to all but rip up the 1984 Sino-British agreement that granted it special status and preceded the restoration of Chinese control of the semi-autonomous territory in 1997. China's utter dominance has led to the suppression of Hong Kong voices that call for democracy and the imposition of new security laws that remove most of the freedoms that this special administrative region enjoyed.

Further from home, Chinese political influence and financial muscle is having tremendous purchase in new territories. Huge investment is building roads across Africa, developing ports in the Indian Ocean, and even delivering new nuclear reactors to Britain. Beijing is regularly accused of acting like a colonial power. There is a mini-publishing industry turning out titles such as *When China Rules the World*, *Bully of Asia*, *Belt and Road: A Chinese World Order* and *China's Second Continent*, with the last of these books analysing empire building in Africa, which alongside Southeast Asia is characterised as a region of Sino neo-colonialism. Discussing China's growing influence, Hillary Clinton said, 'We don't want to see a new colonialism in Africa,'[181] and Malaysian Prime Minister Mahathir Mohamad, after returning from a visit to Beijing, warned fellow Asian leaders to be wary of 'a new version of colonialism'.[182] Many commentators, from the *South China Morning Post* to *Al Jazeera* and *The New York Times* have further questioned if China is now a colonial power, but does the historical comparison between the colonialism of Portugal in Mozambique or Britain in Sierra Leone and China's new global reach make sense? Is China following the colonial model or is this just the clumsy use of a metaphor? To properly understand why this could-be-true comparison is unhelpful, we need to first understand the full horrors of European colonial history. A record of racism, slavery, famine and war was the legacy of five centuries of empire, but in Britain in particular, there is a collective amnesia around the painful truths of the colonial era.

European Colonialism

In 1492, Europeans began the so-called 'Age of Discovery'. Rather than 'discover' barren lands, these voyages brought Spanish and Portuguese mariners into contact with other sophisticated societies, and in the process changed the world forever. Conquistadors received a final blessing in Belém before setting out across the Atlantic in their modest thirty-metre wooden caravel ships. They carried with them a powerful and unknown weapon: diseases that would nearly annihilate the Aztecs, Incas and other peoples of Central and South America. An estimated 80 to 95 per cent of the indigenous population would die from smallpox, influenza, measles and other pathogens that had co-evolved in the Old World and to which the first Americans had no immunity. The population of Mexico went from 15 million to 1.5 million.[183] In exchange, the Iberians returned to Lisbon and Seville with their caravels straining under the load of hordes of treasure, alongside valuable new crops: potatoes, tobacco and cacao beans for chocolate. An unimaginable financial windfall of gold and silver, a depopulated and easily controlled new continental territory, and a range of exotic plants provided the inputs of capital, land and resources required to kick-start the growth of Europe's colonial capitalism.

Wealth circulated between European societies and the British, Dutch and French would follow the Iberians westward. They established colonies across the Atlantic, developed shareholding and new banking practices, and became the world's first global capitalists. This new economic system spread in lockstep with colonialism and delivered economic growth. But this was a pattern of development based on spatial inequality. As Europe grew rich on Aztec gold, Brazilian chocolate and Caribbean sugar, Central American societies were decimated by disease, Amazonians were coerced into plantation labour, and West Africans were kidnapped, transported in torturous conditions, beaten, raped and forced into generations of slavery. Twelve million souls were taken across the Atlantic in 45,000 voyages over 400 years. Two million died in transit.

This transatlantic Columbian Exchange was the catalyst for worldwide colonial domination. Rather than innate European superiority or ingenuity it was a cocktail of· luck, pathogens and politics that spurred Europe's rise. Once colonial models of exploitation centred on the Atlantic Ocean were established, Europeans turned to new territories in the Old World and beyond. In time, Africa, Asia and later Australasia would fall under the control of the British, French and other European powers. Prior to this moment, levels of development were similar across late Medieval Europe and Eastern civilisations. When the Portuguese navigator Vasco da Gama arrived by sea in India in 1498, he marvelled at the riches of the ruling Zamorin of Calicut. At first, the Portuguese and other Westerners came as equals. European merchants were hungry for Indian spices and soon began to pay for these luxuries with gold recycled from the Americas, however with wealth came authority and the balance of power would shift decisively. Later under British rule, India would become the most important colony in the world.

The British began trading through the Indian port of Surat in 1608. Colonial authority expanded gradually, and it was not until the eighteenth century that the British East India Company seized control of large swathes of land from the declining Mughal Empire. In the 1750s, the defeat of the Nawabs of Bengal left the company in control of a vast state. It was then able to tax the population and extract a huge revenue. This was the launch pad for the steady accumulation of territory, wealth and power that would draw the whole subcontinent under British influence. Rebellions against the East India Company's rule led to the formalisation of the British Crown's colonial control in 1858.

Far from introducing civilisation to India, Britain captured and repurposed sophisticated societies. Colonial bureaucrats took over the roles of the Mughal Empire, assumed command of the economy, exploited the poor and stifled local culture. Impoverishment in India was hard-wired to economic development in Britain, as illustrated by the textile trade. Cheap raw cotton was exported from India to northern England providing the raw material for the world's first Industrial Revolution. Costly manufactured clothing returned to India and was paid for by the export of other materials that further fuelled British growth. A relationship of structural dependency was cemented. This was reinforced through laws banning the import of India textiles to Britain. The Bengali city of Dhaka, once a hub of weaving industries, experienced wholescale economic collapse. After a century of British rule, tigers and leopards roamed once-prosperous streets.[184]

Britain's Indian Empire has long been fondly recalled, especially so in the decades following independence. Teatime period dramas where the love interests of pale young colonialists played out against a romanticised vision of a technicolour India, were a mainstay of British TV schedules. At moments there were tensions between Europeans and Asians, but the subtext was often that these were the unavoidable growing pains of development. The good outweighed the bad, with Indians thankful for the arrival of Manchester-built railway locomotives, cricket from the playing fields of the Home Counties, and the gift of the Queen's English. This type of comfortable myth has been resilient and for British audiences at least, the true impacts of Indian colonialism are still little known. Colonialists like Churchill, Queen Victoria and Rudyard Kipling are all celebrated.

At the outset, the East India Company was grossly irresponsible, draining resources from what had been the rich Kingdom of Bengal. Administrators grew wealthy, as did a quarter of the members of the British Parliament who were company shareholders. This plunder created huge stresses on the local population and a famine in 1769–70 left as many as ten million people dead. A drought was the trigger, but the circumstances were man-made. This region had not experienced a famine in the previous century. Relentless colonial revenue collection depleted farmers' savings and exhausted village food stores and left them with no resilience to failing rains. Despite the mounting death toll, British tax policy continued unabated, and more revenue was collected in 1770 than the previous year.

Colonial famines would continue to strike Indian communities. Crop and water shortages resulting from monsoon failures and droughts at the end of the nineteenth century were on a biblical scale. Fields were parched. The earth cracked. Plant stalks stood as dry as tinder. Between 1876 and 1902, estimates suggest that between 31.7 and 61.3 million people died of famine (to render the scale of this loss of life, globally 48 million civilians and soldiers died in the Second World War).[185] By being drawn into the British Empire, Indians faced indebtedness, land seizures, increased taxation and obligations to grow non-food crops, such as cotton, opium and tea, all of which depleted food security and left them newly vulnerable to climatic events. Make no mistake, these were man-made disasters. Millions were unable to survive because of British imperial greed and not fluctuations in weather. These were victims of colonialism not prisoners of geography.

Famines continued into the twentieth century, most notably in Bengal in 1943, where Churchill refused to provide relief. The Nobel Prize-winning economist Amartya Sen argued that despite challenges such as crop disease and the fall of Britain's Burmese colony to Japan, there were sufficient food supplies in the region. Mass deaths resulted from wartime inflation, speculation and hoarding that forced a spike in prices and made food unaffordable. Market forces could have been corrected, but the colonial government continued to export India's rice elsewhere in the empire, removing food in the most famine-affected regions, to deny them falling to the Japanese in case the British forces could not hold eastern India. The Viceroy lobbied for relief which Churchill aggressively rebutted. This demonstrates the cruelty and fragility of British rule. Unable to feed the colonised population, unwilling to control the market, and too fearful of defeat to act to save lives. Three million died. A final colonial atrocity.

Since independence in 1947, the Indian population has increased dramatically and despite repeated droughts, famine has been eliminated through investment in agriculture, improved food distribution and effective emergency response.

The New Silk Road

Further east, Southeast Asia was another region dominated by European colonial powers. First it was the Dutch, later the

British and French, and then in recent history, the Americans through their disastrous neo-imperial Vietnam War. With post-colonialism and peace, the region became synonymous with backpacking. College-age kids and dropouts treated it as a giant adventure playground for enjoying surfing, stir-fries and smoking pot. In parallel, Southeast Asian economies were exerting their independence, building industry, rapidly growing, and moving from low- to middle-income status. The tourist trade is still a mainstay, but rather than Westerners on gap years predominating, there are new vacationers with more cash in their pockets. Chinese tourists pack Thai beaches, Malaysian fish markets and Singaporean shopping malls. The yuan is now the primary source of tourist spending. In tandem with the shifting identities of holidaymakers, there is a growing Chinese influence across the region. China is becoming a major economic and political player, so much so that many Southeast Asians fear neo-colonialism.

Away from the tourist sites, Chinese actions spread throughout the region, starting with the Mekong, the mighty river that rises in the Tibetan plateau and passes through five countries before meeting the sea in southern Vietnam. Geopolitical power flows from powerful China at the head to smaller, weaker nations below. China is reshaping the hydrology of the region. Upstream, the narrow and deep river passes through sparsely populated lands ideal for dams. Chinese companies have built eleven along the high river. Further south, below the plateau and towards the sea, the Mekong runs wider and slower, fanning out at the Delta. This fertile landscape teems with plant and animal life. With each new concrete barrage, the flow is altered, and the sediment loads and fish stocks that support millions of farmers and fishermen are reduced. Hydroelectric dams help electrify Chinese growth, but the environmental costs are borne downstream. Communities throughout Southeast Asia's biggest river basin face livelihood challenges because of China's water policy.

Dam construction is just one facet of China's building ambitions. Southeast Asia is the first notch on the 'Belt and Road Initiative' a huge chain of infrastructure projects that are having a major impact on economies stretching from the shores of the

South China Sea to the heart of the Mediterranean. Rather than a single belt, this is a multi-stranded approach linking the economies of Eurasia, in what is popularly known as the 'New Silk Road'. There have been headline-grabbing stories of a train that travels all the way from Yiwu to Madrid on a 21-day, 13,000-kilometre odyssey. Though rather than a continuous marathon from China's industrial heartland to the Spanish capital, this is more of a multi-stage relay. Locomotives, rail cars, crew and maybe even much of the cargo is swapped out along the eight-nation journey, as the train traverses at least three different gauges of wider and narrower tracks.

Back in Southeast Asia, high-speed rail, port facilities and thousands of factories are remaking the region's economic geography. The latter includes garment and textile firms that have relocated from China in search of lower wages and reduced costs. Thousands of young female factory workers are exploited in the newly industrialised towns of Cambodia and Vietnam. They are angry and resentful at the harsh working conditions. These are approaches that Chinese managers learned back home where they enforced strict discipline in the 1990s and 2000s. Local elites argue that Chinese money is helping to develop their nations in the same way that the cities around the Pearl River Delta have grown in recent decades. So, some welcome Chinese investment, but others fear it. Elsewhere, Chinese business interests in the Philippines and Laos have taken advantage of weak regulation to set up offshore gambling, which is illegal in China. With betting has come . corruption, organised crime and undocumented migration. The Chinese state has also played fast and loose with international law. Throughout the South China Sea, the People's Liberation Army has remade uninhabited islets into military installations and reefs into runways for fighter bombers. Beijing is bolstering its internationally unrecognised claim to nearly all of this marine region.

In some respects, Southeast Asia is treated as Beijing's backyard. But although it may be a bully at times, this is not the colonialism of old, with its formal political control, taxation, plantation agriculture, racialised legislation and atrocities. To take tourism, is this truly emblematic of a relationship of dominance? Despite huge leisure spending by planeloads of Chinese holidaymakers, Southeast Asia is not dependent on servicing these clients. There are still millions of Western visitors and beyond tourism, great economic diversity. Japan remains the region's major source of foreign direct investment. It is easy to overstate the economic importance of China. Next to return to dam building on the Mekong, this is not colonialism. International water politics is a problem common around the world in shared water basins including those of the Danube, Nile and Zambezi. What is particular on the Mekong is there is one strong upstream state and multiple weaker nations down water.[186] China is throwing its weight around, yet on this issue and others, Southeast Asian nations have considerable agency and could do more if they were less competitive with one another and more co-operative in their negotiations with their powerful neighbour. In other political arenas, Southeast Asian nations have demonstrated their political bite and forged bilateral relations that counterbalance Beijing's influence. Malaysia has courted more Japanese capital, and Thailand and Vietnam in particular have looked towards Washington as well as Tokyo. There are strategic and dynamic relationships shaped by decision makers in Bangkok, Hanoi and Kuala Lumpur, unrecognisable from the domanial status they endured under colonial rule.

Moreover, Southeast Asian economic powerbrokers often view Chinese partners favourably as they are predictable commercial stakeholders. The leaders of Myanmar (present-day Burma) appreciated their *business as usual* approach at a time when the regime faced international condemnation for the military crackdown on the Rohingya, the scene of many human rights abuses. The generals that call the shots in Naypyidaw are neither naïve nor Chinese vassals. Southeast Asian politicians have far more agency in these relationships than their colonised forebears, who had only minor voices in imperial administrations. Sticking with Myanmar, this flexibility was demonstrated when local leaders sought to scale back a Chinese deep-water port when they became concerned they would be saddled with too much debt and give their Chinese lenders too much leverage over their affairs.

China's role in Southeast Asia is not new; there have been millennia of interactions. There are different types of Chinese interest rather than one monolithic China. In Malaysia, Thailand, Singapore and elsewhere, Chinese people are important parts of the national population and have interests that do not mirror the Chinese state. Overseas, Chinese have lived throughout Southeast Asia for countless generations. President Xi Jinping likes to cast them as 'members of the Chinese family'.[187] A statement that has stoked tensions between ethnic Chinese business people and nationalists in Indonesia and Malaysia, but no one can seriously draw parallels between powerful ethnic Chinese interests and the racialised European elites of the colonial period. Many Southeast Asians are winners as well as losers from the growing ties with Beijing, but what about in other weaker and poorer regions of the world where billions of yuan buy more influence and control, and the relationship may be closer to colonialism?

China in Africa

Kabwe is right in the middle of Zambia, on the main road that links the capital, Lusaka, and the Copperbelt, a rich sequence of geological formations that spans Central Africa. It is a dusty town in need of renewal. Economic life is tenuous. Social life is fragile. Along the road are kiosks selling scratch cards for cell phone credit, plastic sachets of high-strength alcohol and not much else. For a dollar or so you can connect to the outside world or escape from reality. Kabwe is famous for two things. The first is that it is the world's most polluted town.[188] A century of lead mining, much of which was under British colonialism, has poisoned generations of children. The state-owned smelter closed in 1994. The jobs have long gone, but lives will be affected by the deposits of toxic dust and the poisons that have seeped deep into the soils for generations. The second is that it was home to Zambia China Mulungushi Textiles (ZCMT).

The Mulungushi textile factory was completed in 1981 with aid from China. This was during an early era of cooperation between China and Africa. China also helped build the TAZARA Railway that passes through the city. This 1,860-kilometre line links the port of Dar es Salaam in eastern Tanzania to the Zambian mines, connecting the Copperbelt to the Indian Ocean. TAZARA provided a lifeline for exporting valuable metal at a time when the South African apartheid regime was strangling the economies of neighbouring independent black states. That Chinese-African partnership is fondly remembered and is a legacy that advocates of increasing ties are keen to celebrate. ZCMT has had a less happy history. After being set up by the Chinese, it operated under Zambian management until 1996 when it was forced to close. The African factory was uncompetitive in the globalised clothing and textile sector. The next year it reopened with new investment from Qingdao Textiles as part of a new wave of Chinese engagement in Africa.

At first, the people of Kabwe welcomed the return, but as one weaving machine operator I interviewed characterised it: 'The way we are seeing there'd be a future, but what happened is a hell.'[189] Chinese managers brought with them their experiences of industrialisation that worked in China as well as in Southeast Asia, but would fail in Africa. The Mulungushi factory was uncompetitive: high costs, weak energy supply, competition from imported new and used clothes and poor access to overseas markets damaged business. To reduce costs, salaries were suppressed to the absolute minimum. Pay was so low that employees could not support their families. Work conditions were barbaric. As another factory worker I interviewed discussed, 'the salaries, that was too low for us to sustain our working . . . It was like slavery. It was just survival of the fittest.' The Chinese overseers disciplined the workforce and introduced unpopular night shifts. Many workers simply just up and quit their jobs. As the factory's spinning and weaving looms were worked harder and harder, the remaining workforce was exposed to greater and greater risks. Horrendous industrial accidents were commonplace.

Sitting in a small, bare-walled concrete house across the road from the now derelict ZCMT factory, a young ex-worker calmly, yet heartbreakingly, talked me through how his forearm had been ripped from his body at the elbow by one of the machines. He received minimal composition and was left with broken promises, medical bills and a hopeless future. As well as a devastating record of disabilities, the period was marked by worker protests and confrontations. In 2006 the factory closed, the machines fell silent, and the site went to ruin. Qingdao did not leave though. Next door was the cotton gin that had supplied raw materials to ZCMT. This continues to operate, processing raw cotton from farms throughout central Zambia. The ginned fibres are now exported to China, feeding their profitable clothing factories.

Cotton, copper and that most precious of resources, oil, have attracted new Chinese engagement in Africa. From Angolan gas to Zimbabwean diamonds, the vast natural wealth of the world's poorest continent has fuelled Chinese growth in the last two decades, but also triggered an economic boom in some African nation. China's investments have grown exponentially, sparking new enterprises and reigniting depressed economic sectors. A quarter of a million Chinese have settled in Angola setting up import businesses, working in construction and finding new opportunities in agriculture and forestry. China National Offshore Oil Corporation is drilling in the Gulf of Guinea and the Indian Ocean, and new roads, railways and ports are being built across the continent bringing much-needed investment to a fragile and fragmented transport infrastructure. As the example of Mozambique illustrated, economic growth is not the same as development, and the local impacts of new economic activity need careful analysis. What is clear is that these uneven partnerships are nothing like the coercive patterns of trade of the colonial era such as the brutal Portuguese cotton-growing sector in Mozambique.

Chinese President Xi Jinping casts these new relationships as a meeting of equals: 'China and African countries are destined to be good friends, good brothers and good partners, and

China-Africa cooperation stands as a fine example of South-South cooperation.' Beijing certainly enjoys close ties with most governing parties in sub-Saharan Africa. In contrast, many African opposition politicians have compared the increasing Chinese influence to the colonial activities of the Belgians, British, French and Portuguese. In 2007, Zambian opposition leader Michael Sata went further still: 'We want the Chinese to leave and the old colonial rulers to return . . . at least Western capitalism has a human face; the Chinese are only out to exploit us.'[190] He accused the Chinese of paying slave wages, flouting safety standards, damaging the environment and corrupting leaders across the continent. In a remarkable U-turn, after Sata won the 2011 presidential election, he soon mended fences and dropped the neo-colonial rhetoric. In 2013 he made a high-profile visit to China, met with Xi Jinping and talked about close Africa-Asia relations. When Sata died in 2014, the only two non-African government dignitaries at his funeral were a minor British royal and a powerful Chinese Minister. Sata was first a popularist and then a realist who changed his tune when he realised how China's financial power could benefit his agenda, but does his original argument that China is a neo-colonial power comparable to the old European imperialists really stack up?

In terms of scale, impact and influence, China is not close to matching the old colonial powers. European colonialism dominated the whole of Africa. In 1884, the Berlin conference brought the British, French, Portuguese and other powers together, and round the table they carved up the continent into different European territories. The map of Africa was literally redrawn. Straight lines cut through communities. Politicians traded the lives of people they would never meet, like chess grand masters swapping pawns. The scale symbolises the utter contempt and sheer power the Europeans held over Africans. Secondly, the impacts of colonialism extended across everyday life: forced work in plantations, mines and agriculture, imposed languages and religions, but more than anything governed through violence: military campaigns, brutal policing and the imprisonment of freedom fighters, these terrors were all part of the arsenal of empire. Mulungushi Textiles is one of the worst examples of contemporary employment practices, but the impact of Chinese managers there was nothing like the coercive labour practices and state violence of the colonial era. Thirdly, to take influence, China may be the largest foreign player in many African nations, but it does not dominate every aspect of economic life. Drawing on the most recent figures on foreign direct investment stock, China was only the fifth largest investor with 46 billion dollars, behind the Netherlands, France, United Kingdom and United States.[191] In other metrics, such as lending, China does top the charts, but there is a plurality of other influential foreign interests. Like their counterparts in Southeast Asia, today's African leaders are wise to their power and can choose to work with different global investors.

Making Sense of Beijing's Influence

China is shaping Africa's trajectory, but it is one of many forces impacting the destiny of the world's poorest continent. Across the globe, a rising China is changing the geography of the world economy, but not through formal imperialism. Decisions made in Beijing can influence governments in Addis Ababa, shape the flows of rivers in Southeast Asia, and build new railroads across Eurasia, but none of these impacts are on the same scale as the global transformations wrought by European colonialism. The effects of China's new overseas projects are in no way comparable to the impacts of the Columbian Exchange, the slave trade, or British control of India. The future China is helping to make will not resemble the world of the colonial past.

A lack of understanding of the true horrors of European empires helps explain why China's global ambitions are often compared to colonialism. I know first-hand that knowledge of the wide-ranging and long-lasting effects of British colonial rule is weak, even among well-educated school leavers. We need to decolonise school curriculums. For the past decade I have taught a first-year university module that covers the historical geography of colonialism and its exploitative role in the making of the modern world. The majority of my students, who have diverse ethnic and cultural backgrounds and strong academic records, enter university with little critical understanding of the ways in which Britain abused overseas territories. If we don't understand what colonialism was, or have a rose-tinted view of empire, then it is unsurprising that the colonial label is mistakenly reused to cast shade on China.

Britain's imperial policies showed a callous disregard for non-European life. Decisions made in Whitehall led to untold deaths and blocked progress in colonial territories. The Palestinian writer, Edward Said, characterised the European projects as exercises in orientalism: the people of Africa, Asia and the Middle East were held in contempt as inferior 'others'. An attitude that enabled inhumane treatment. Colonialism depends on maintaining 'us' and 'the other' hierarchies informed by race, religion or culture. European regimes continually faced challenges – protest, rebellion and insurgency – from oppressed others. Political control was backed up by the ever-present threat of violence. The ways in which stronger nations wield power in weaker territories today does not compare. There is not the political control, explicit racism or the unconcealed threat of force. There are no slave ships. No uninvited gunboats in foreign harbours. No colonial administrators blocking famine relief. The arguments here are not an excuse for Beijing's international ambitions. China can be self-serving, exploitative and do damage to local people and environments, but these are not the violent and racialised colonial models of old.

Rather than reflecting the colonialism of the past, the ascent of China and its great influence represents a huge shift in the core of the world economy. Two hundred years ago, London was the epicentre of financial power. Once the sun began to set on the British Empire, Washington rose to be the global hegemon and shaped economic life throughout the twentieth century. The centre of gravity has now moved east. China first became the workshop of the world, but with its vast accumulation of cash through the early years of the twenty-first century, it is now the banker as well. In late 2020, the IMF determined that China overtook the USA to be the world's largest economy: a momentous historical moment that received little attention in the midst of the global Covid-19 pandemic and the chaotic aftermath of the 2020 US election.[192]

Identifying Beijing as the new global powerhouse should be the start rather than the end point of geopolitical analysis. The world is becoming increasingly multi-polar. China may be the great new power, but there are others on the rise as well including Brazil, India and Indonesia. The sovereign wealth funds of nations rich in natural resources – Norway, Saudi Arabia, the United Arab Emirates – provide other powerful sources of investment and lending. And the influence of the older economic centres – Britain, the United States and others – have not gone away. All of these nations seek to shape the world beyond their borders.

Having sat in the shadow of a derelict factory and seen the broken dreams and damaged bodies of impoverished Zambians is to see the human costs of Chinese-led globalisation. Across Africa there have been tragic mining accidents, evictions and protests as a result of China's business ventures. In Southeast Asia, there have been labour abuses, environmental damage and criminality, but similar injustices accompany the actions of other foreign investors in both regions. Beijing may now be the single most powerful foreign influence on the world's stage, yet none of the Chinese actions are unique nor approaching the high crimes of colonialism. As a model the comparison does not work. China doesn't literally enslave people, allow famines to ravage rural populations, or suppress rebellions with violence. For Western, Asian and African political leaders, including Hillary Clinton, Mahathir Mohamad and Michael Sata, to draw such direct parallels between European imperialism and China's ascendancy is duplicitous. They should know better than to fan the flames of popular anti-Chinese sentiment by casting Beijing as a dangerous expansionist colonial power. However, if we think of it more metaphorically, as a figure of speech, some of the words and phrases that surround colonialism can be applied to cast light on the actions of China in Africa – and other exploitative foreign powers – even if they are not literally applicable. While in the measured language of academic writing and government reports this type of metaphorical communication is misleading and should be avoided, and politicians and journalists should steer away from misapplying inflammatory phrases, it is understandable, indeed justifiable, for people living through injustice, who otherwise struggle to communicate their deprivation, to resort to a lexicon of slavery, empire and colonialism. This might sound like a double standard, and it is. There is a different acceptable register for the deployment of comparative metaphors in formal communication and the use of analogies by people living under harsh conditions of exploitation. The next chapter continues to explore the challenging and divisive use of historical analogy through a discussion of segregation in Israel-Palestine and apartheid-era South Africa.

CHAPTER 10

Is There Apartheid in Israel?

An analogy that does not fit the injustice

The Handmaid's Protest

Margaret Atwood's feminist dystopian masterpiece, *The Handmaid's Tale,* has a colossal cultural imprint. After publication in 1985, the novel soon amassed praise and literary prizes, and ever since has been a mainstay of bookstores and libraries around the world. This is despite, in a case of life imitating art, the novel featuring in the America Library Association's top 100 most banned and challenged book list for the past three decades.[193] Reading is central to our intellectual and political freedom, but this is outlawed in the world of *The Handmaid's Tale.* Gilead, the vivid and terrifying setting Atwood imagined, is a vision of a near future that is so scary because it is believable and could almost conceivably happen. The US has been superseded by a theocratic regime that reinterprets the Old Testament and creates a new militarised and strictly hierarchised society which is at its harshest in its complete degradation of women. The few females who remain fertile after catastrophic environmental pollution must forcibly reproduce children and are assigned to a ruling class of male Commanders. In 2017, the alternate reality became a TV

167

hit and Elisabeth Moss's intense and captivating performances in the lead role of Offred brought the nightmare to life for millions of viewers.

The Handmaid's Tale has not yet proved prophetic, but is so iconic that motifs from Atwood's world have become a metaphor for suppression widely used in social protest. In 2020 following the death of Supreme Court Justice Ruth Bader Ginsburg, a vigil of women dressed as handmaids mourned the loss of the liberal judge and feared how Donald Trump would replace her. As one berobed protester lamented outside a federal courthouse in Santa Ana, California, 'He doesn't have a lot of respect for women. We might as well be handmaids.'[194] This symbolic, affecting comparison was repeatedly made through the Trump presidency by women across the nation. Many feared America was becoming like Gilead. Maybe not in a literal sense but this could-be-true comparative vision of a fascist state was arresting.

Atwood's provocative symbolism has carried far beyond its origins in a fictitious New England. In March 2023, Britain's prime minister, Rishi Sunak, welcomed his Israeli counterpart, Benjamin Netanyahu, for talks at Downing Street. His visit was met by hundreds of protesters, including flanks of women in the long scarlet-red dresses and distinctive starched white bonnets. They silently marched to draw attention to the plight of women and rising totalitarianism in Israel. The costume had become a sign of resistance. Hundreds of women in dozens of protests around Israel have taken a stand in red with their heads bowed and hands clasped to communicate their fear that the overhaul of the judiciary will leave women and minorities silenced and unprotected.[195]

Handmaids were not the only protesters that met Netanyahu in London. Many others chanted, shouting 'Shame!' in Hebrew as they demonstrated against the leader's right-wing policies. One slogan read: 'We are Israelis and Jews living in the UK demonstrating against Prime Minister Netanyahu, who is leading a judicial coup turning Israel into a dictatorship.'[196] Another protester wore a Netanyahu mask and clutched a banner that read 'I ♡ Apartheid'. A simple but powerful provocation.

This visit occurred six months before the terrifying attacks on Israeli Jews by Hamas on 7 October, which left some 1,200 dead, mostly civilians, many of whom were killed in brutal circumstances, sexual violence and 240 people taken hostage, and triggered a bombardment and invasion of Gaza that by the end of 2023 had led to over 20,000 Palestinian civilian deaths, according to the Hamas-run Gaza Health Ministry.[197] The losses of life and the atrocities committed on the brutal Saturday in early October and in the weeks of conflict that followed, must all be mourned and condemned. There is no monopoly on suffering or excuse for barbarism. The death of a single innocent soul is enough to make the case to immediately stop violence, but at the time of writing, there is no end in sight to this tragedy.[198] The scope and scale of the initial Israeli response was widely condemned. After the Israeli Defence Force (IDF) launched their assault on Gaza, the apartheid analogy featured prominently in the global denunciations of Netanyahu's regime's actions. Pro-Palestinian demonstrations in London, in support of the population of Gaza, carried 'End Israeli Apartheid' placards produced by the Palestine Solidarity Campaign. Spain's second deputy Prime Minister, Yolanda Díaz, condemned 'Israeli apartheid' against the Palestinian people.[199] And a petition started by US-based reporters, which attracted signatures from over 1,500 journalists, called upon reporting of the conflict to use words including 'apartheid', as well as 'ethnic cleansing' and 'genocide'.[200] The apartheid comparison was part of the lexicon of opposition to Israel's military assault on Gaza.

Apartheid: Model, Metaphor or Legal Definition?

There can be few examples of pairs of territories which are distant in time and space, that have been compared as often as apartheid-era South Africa and contemporary Israel and Palestine. Across the media, political discourse and advocacy campaigns, the comparison has long been mobilised to raise awareness of the plight of the Palestinian people and direct condemnation towards the government of Israel. In 1997, Nelson

Mandela drew a direct link between emancipation in South Africa and Israel when he proclaimed, 'We know too well that our freedom is incomplete without the freedom of the Palestinians.'[201] The use of the parallel spread to the extent that Boycott, Divestment and Sanctions (BDS), a Palestinian-led movement for freedom, justice and equality has, since 2005, organised an annual global Israeli Apartheid Week 'to raise awareness about Israeli apartheid'.[202] The BDS movement grew and gained support from a diverse range of organisations and individuals including the American Anthropological Association, the Mayor of Barcelona and the Disciples of Christ Church.[203] Before the Hamas-Israel war, leading international voices had made the comparison including Jimmy Carter, Noam Chomsky, Naomi Klein and Archbishop Desmond Tutu. The United Nations, via its agency the Economic and Social Commission for Western Asia (ESCWA), once used the language of an 'apartheid state' in a report on Israel.[204] Even Tamir Pardo, a former head of Israel's Mossad intelligence agency, speaking in September 2023, added his voice to the small number of Israelis who describe the political situation as apartheid: 'There is an apartheid state here . . . In a territory where two people are judged under two legal systems, that is an apartheid state.'[205]

Beyond the original South African context, the 1998 Rome Statute that established the International Criminal Court (ICC), defines apartheid as a general term for an 'institutionalised regime of systematic oppression and domination by one racial group over any other'.[206] So as Pardo's analysis suggests, there is a legal basis for assessing if states are practising 'apartheid', but how appropriate is it to assign this label, which is so evocative and inherently associated with the historical segregation of South Africa, to other societies? Scholars have sought to interrogate the similarities of Israel-Palestine[207] and have provoked a heated reaction and counter-claims that the apartheid comparison is an attempt to delegitimize Israel.[208] Amnesty International has argued Israel's actions meet the ICC definition.[209] Israeli Foreign Minister, Yair Lapid, was angered by Amnesty's position, saying such 'extremist language . . . will pour fuel on to the fire of anti-Semitism'.[210] Carter's views have likewise been deemed by Jewish figures in the United States to be on the border of anti-Semitism.[211]

In general terms, metaphorical comparison can effectively draw attention to injustice as the examples of *The Handmaid's Tale* highlighted, and they can enable the relatively powerless to assertively voice their message. Trump's America or Netanyahu's Israel was not literally like Gilead, but that fictitious parallel drew attention to gender inequalities and legal injustices. Metaphors can be powerful tools for protest. In contrast, as the previous case study of China's global ambition and European colonialism demonstrated, comparisons for comparisons' sake that shoehorn one geo-historical process into the model of another flattens complex differences and reifies similarities, providing more of a catalogue of commonalities rather than an explanation of what is driving injustice.[212] The apartheid analogy is not like the handmaid comparison. It is not simply metaphorical, but invokes memories of South Africa, even if the proponents of the 'apartheid Israel' label base their discussion on the Rome Statute and detach apartheid from the South African context.[213] Despite this legal disassociation, when the term 'apartheid' is applied to Israel, by BDS, international politicians and journalists, it conjures up mental images of Mandela imprisoned on Robben Island and township uprisings and suggests a literal equivalence between the two societies: that the South African model of segregation can be applied to Israel.

My intention here is not to further inflame the debate and interrogate if the ICC definition fits the current *legal* situation, but rather to explore if the social experience of life in apartheid-era South Africa and Israel-Palestine before the Hamas-Israel War were directly analogous. Here I discuss how vulnerable groups of women and men in both South Africa and Israel-Palestine were economically marginalised. Using case studies of cross-border work, I explore the similarities and differences, analyse what lessons from the former can tell us about the latter, and ask if drawing the two societies together offers any solace for those desperate to resolve the never-ending tragedy in the Middle East.

Understanding Apartheid

From before apartheid's instigation in 1948 until its fall in 1994, South Africa was controlled by two co-dependent white groups. The nation was politically dominated by Afrikaners that descended from Dutch settlers who first arrived in the southern part of Africa in the seventeenth century. Economically the nation was led by the culturally distinct English speakers who controlled the mining, manufacturing and commercial agricultural sectors. Most traced their heritage back to British colonialism in the nineteenth century and they retained international links with businesses in the UK and cultivated connections with the US. *Apartheid* is an Afrikaans word that means 'separate development' and is related to the racial division of communities. The apartheid-era South African state used geography to carve up the country into big expansive white spaces and fragmented, impoverished black spaces, with the goal of furthering the political and economic projects of the white minority rulers. The advancement of the white community depended on racial exclusivity and forced segregation produced a landscape of social and economic dislocation.

The black majority (which in the language of apartheid encompassed African, Indian and Coloured people [*sic*]) were segregated into townships on the fringes of white cities and isolated rural labour reserves, which included semi-independent homelands. They intersected with white space only through subordination and oppression. The 1970 Bantu Homelands and Citizenship Act assigned a restricted citizenship to all black Africans who lived in one of ten tribal homelands, and these became pseudo-national states for the black African (also classified by the government as Bantu) population and were known as Bantustans. The act created impoverished labour reserves and relocated 3.5 million black Africans to the impoverished Bantustans – or South Africa's 'dumping grounds'.[214] These small impoverished rural spaces were ruled by newly created Chiefs, as these were invented 'traditional' territories that were the product of modern racism. Movement into South Africa proper was strictly limited, and Africans were excluded from any rights to land or political participation in white space. Signs on beaches, buses, toilet doors, services counters and nearly all public spaces hailed '*blankes alleen* / whites only' or '*nie-blankes* / non-whites'. Life was reorganised along racial lines. Separateness was not confined to economic and political spheres; socially, races were completely divided. Interracial sexual relations were outlawed. The spatial, gendered and hierarchical divisions of the apartheid era served as an inspiration for *The Handmaid's Tale* alongside the oppressive societies of Czechoslovakia and Iran. In the original novel, African Americans are called the Children of Ham and were expelled from Gilead, as Atwood has said: 'They put them into closed "homelands". Like apartheid South Africa.'[215]

The production of Bantu societies created a reserve army of labourers to work in the white-owned economy. The apartheid state established a huge bureaucratic infrastructure to manage the segregation and to control the flow of millions of workers through internal surveillance. Movement of blacks was regulated through a passbook (*dompas*) that had to be carried by all Africans and only permitted unemployed migrants to stay in urban areas for three days to look for work. Adherence was strictly enforced by police who further used pass laws to intimidate workers, including dawn raids to check the papers of women and men asleep in dormitories. Police made use of the Boerboels, Rhodesian Ridgebacks and German Shepherds that were the literal attack dogs of apartheid, trained to secure white spaces against black bodies.

Apartheid protected the powerful racial minority from wage competition and suppressed the overall cost of labour. This enabled the white population to sustain political control and provided a low-cost labour force to support the mining, agriculture and manufacturing sectors. The black majority lived in communities marked by 'acute poverty and malnutrition, grotesque overcrowding, haphazard but intensive political repression, [and] extreme dependence on wage earning in "white" South Africa'.[216] The hierarchy was not just racialised it was also gendered. Under apartheid, male black labourers worked in the white-owned economy, from Cape fruit farms to

Gauteng gold mines and from stevedoring in Durban's dockyards to domestic service in the suburbs of Johannesburg, this last sector being one of the narrow ranges of roles that also employed black women.[217] There was an oversupply of workers in the late 1970s and 1980s, leading to high levels of unemployment (around 25 per cent) and suppressed wages. African wages were so low that they were a quarter of white pay in manufacturing and – a frankly astonishing – *twenty* times lower than white wages in the mining sector.[218]

One of the reasons apartheid was so attractive to white business owners, including the major anglophone mining companies, was the low labour cost. Black pay was kept low because the cost of reproducing and maintaining the African male labour force was borne by the workers' families.[219] Women's work, including substance farming in the homelands, subsidised the low wages of migrant male workers. There was a co-existence of a black, primarily male, labour force employed in the white economy and separate black female-led households in the African labour reserves. These two separated modes of production *articulated* with one another to suppress the overall cost of labour. Articulation meant that both the male wage labouring in the white economy and the separated female work of social reproduction – raising the family, growing food crops, providing a place for rest and retirement – in the segregated Bantustans were co-dependent on one another. The male worker needed a Bantu home to return to and support him, and the female partner needed income from the male wages in the white economy. Apartheid guaranteed a cheap and controllable workforce, predicated on the Bantu homelands providing a labour force that was subsidised by the work of women – and older (often female) children too – who faced ever greater impoverishment.[220] Male wage earners could be absent for many months, even years at a time, creating a tremendous burden on women. This included the mental well-being of women faced with the uncertainty of prolonged marital separation, relationship breakdowns, and estrangements and the detrimental impacts on physical health when husbands returned home with sexually transmitted diseases, including HIV.[221]

Apartheid Geography

The discussion above has sketched out some of the basic structures of apartheid society. In simple terms it was a vast, repressive economic system for managing the selective employment and systematic exploitation of millions of black workers, but a short summary cannot do justice to the full complexity and dynamics of people and place. South Africa is a huge, diverse and expansive country. Today it is one where the legacies of generations of division still mark society, as the discussion of the role of South African dogs and their owners in Chapter 4 illustrated. Although formal segregation ended nearly three decades ago, urban spaces remain starkly divided between the affluent and very white suburbs, and the deprived black townships.

My overarching image of the nation is one of big landscapes and wide-open spaces, huge farms and wild countryside. I've driven from north to south, through the Highveld, across the Drakensberg mountains that inspired Tolkien's *Lord of the Rings*, to the wild southern coast where the Atlantic and Indian Oceans crash together. I regularly visited Kruger National Park when I lived in Maputo. This world-class safari destination draws in millions of visitors a year. You can drive for hours spotting elephants, giraffes and springboks and not see another car. This nature reserve is almost the same size as Israel, larger if you include the adjacent Limpopo National Park across the border in Mozambique.

There is then already an apparent scalar difference between the 1.22 million square kilometres of South Africa and the 22,145 square kilometres of Israel. To contextualise these numbers, South Africa is almost twice the size of Texas, Israel is just larger than New Jersey. In their most basic geography, they are incomparable. The gap is not so big in population but still of a different magnitude: South Africa was around 35 million people in the mid-1980s at the height of apartheid, and the combined population of Israel and Palestine today is just under 15 million. More significantly is population density. In contrast to sparsely populated South Africa, Israel-Palestine is among the world's most crowded areas. There is also a key demographic difference, and here the numbers are contested, but the broad picture is clear. In South Africa the White population was under 20 per cent, whereas across Israel-Palestine, Jewish citizens and Palestinians are of roughly equal population size.

As well as these basic geographical differences, the political schisms across the two societies are very different. In Israel-Palestine, despite the complexities of identity, the conflict is consistently reduced to a binary one. Whereas in South Africa, outside of the exclusive category of 'white', which itself was a composite of people with different cultural and linguistic heritages, under apartheid there was differentiation between racial groups, which had some different rights, and African identity was fragmented by the creation of Bantustans. This heterogeneity was reflected in post-apartheid South Africa which was self-styled as the inclusive 'Rainbow Nation' which proclaims 'unity in diversity'.[222] This includes, in alphabetical order: Afrikaner, Bapedi, Batswana, European, South Asian, Sotho, Xhosa, Zulu and many other ethnic groups. During the apartheid era, the opposition African National Congress's (ANC) position was that a post-racial South Africa would belong to everyone, non-White and White alike, and this included dismantling the fictitious, invented traditions of the Bantustan territories. In contrast, the exclusive claims of Israel and Palestine, and the 1990s Clinton-backed Oslo Accords that anticipated a two-state solution, are built around ethnic-national identity and separate religious practices within defined borders, although there are also advocates of secular, one-state or other multi-state solutions. Following the Hamas attacks on Israel, any peaceful outcome seems remote and the idea of a single Rainbow Nation-esque solution is inconceivable as a near-term resolution.

These geographical and political realities are important to appreciate before we consider if the apartheid label is an appropriate term for explaining the contemporary situation in Israel. There are many more axes against which their similarities and differences could be compared: forced evictions and displacements, social exclusion, legal rights and cultural dislocation. Here, employment is serving as a signal case for disrupting the application of the apartheid model to Israel, and specifically the impacts of low-wage cross-border male work on the women left behind.

Cross-border labour played a small but important economic role in both Israel and Palestine before the horrific Hamas attacks. As in apartheid South Africa, the marginalised group temporarily entered the restricted space occupied by the dominant community and undertook low wage work that supplemented the economy of the powerful group. Palestinians typically worked in the construction sector in East Jerusalem and Israel at low rates of pay and often without health provision, vacation allowance or payslips.[223] Additionally, their labour was back-breaking, and health and safety regulations were lax.[224] Their wives remained in Palestine and supported their husbands through their domestic labour.

In the Palestinian lands, as in the Bantustans, there was widespread unemployment and Israeli businesses could capitalise on a captive low-wage workforce. While there are structural commonalities, the realities of the two systems are very different in terms of scale of employment, bordering, distance and work patterns. Firstly, the South African system was huge, and was *the* general system of employing mass labour. It led to millions of black people entering white space to work, whereas in contrast, only a small proportion of Palestinians commuted into Israel for work.[225] Secondly, the borders are incomparable. White South Africa space was too big to fully secure and demark by walls or fences, so movement was regulated by the passbook system with regular checks and enforcement by police in urban areas. There was also a punitive permit system in Israel,[226] but the segregation was primarily by the hard borders between the West Bank and Gaza Strip and Israel. An armoured separation wall and hi-tech checkpoints physically divided the communities and tightly regulated movement. Thirdly, the spatial relationships were different. Male Palestinian workers commuted short distances to work in Israeli space, whereas long distances, often hundreds of miles, physically separated the black homelands from employment in the white economy in South Africa. Fourthly, Palestinians daily commuted and were unable to stay overnight in Israel, whereas long absence and dormitory living characterised the black experience of work under apartheid. African men lived in simple hostels in white South Africa for months, even years at a time, separated from their families. There are then fundamental empirical differences in the scope and scale of the cross-border labour systems of these two uneven societies.

Despite the lack of fit between the massive apartheid labour model and the situation in Israel-Palestine, historical study of the experiences of women in the Bantustans can still provide analytical tools that can be applied to understand the contemporary inequalities endured by their counterparts in Palestine. In both systems there is an articulation between male employment in the dominant economy and female-gendered domestic work that supports the male labour force. To animate the livelihoods of women left behind, here I will share some findings from a research project I undertook with my colleague Mark Griffiths who has worked extensively in Israel-Palestine. Our collaborative paper brought together our respective expertise, his from the Middle East and mine from southern Africa.[227] Mark's data came from fieldwork with Palestinian communities, and mine from archives on South Africa, but it was apparent from the outset of our analysis that these were two very different societies and cultures, yet we could use similar tools to investigate them in concert.

Cross-Border Lives

To start with an oral history from South Africa, Florence Mongake of Mogopa, North West Province,[228] recounted that before apartheid, men of her community 'would be at home with the cows' but after they 'joined the mine . . . they would leave you for three years and you would be pregnant and the men is gone and you must make sure your children are eating'. Similarly, Elsie Motsusi[229] talked about life in her North West community of Braklaagte: '[the men] would live by the hostels; they would leave the wives and kids to starve.' Impoverishment was tied to the cross-border labour as the testament of an unnamed woman from Transkei Bantustan illustrates:

> We feel lonely in this desolate place where so many of our husbands must leave to find work, and stay away all year, sometimes many years. We have pity for our husbands. We know why they must take town girls [commercial sex workers/second wives] – men are men – and we also know why they want us to stay home, to keep a home for him and to make a place for his children because we have no rights for a place in the cities.[230]

The woman's husband worked more than 800 kilometres away in Cape Town, and his absence led to a disintegration of family life. For this woman, and Florence and Elsie, and millions of other family members, cross-border labour brought a heavy psychological load as well as impoverishment:

> This woman had an irresponsible [sic] husband who worked in the white suburbs and came home only when he desired. One late afternoon when returning from work I see this old woman sitting on a small stool, her shoulders bent inwards and her face clasped in her hands. She was sitting beside a brazier fire and on the fire was a boiling pot . . . they hadn't had a meal for three days, and the pot on the brazier was just filled with water.[231]

The image here of a suffering woman is stark. Her condition is a product of the apartheid labour regime. This degradation of African households became a pre-condition for the supply of cheap labour to the White economy as poverty compelled the next generation to seek work in White space.

Moving forward in time and across to Palestine, interviews with women in Al-Walaja cast light on how they suffered under a very different cross-border labour system. To work in Israel, Palestinian men had to pass through checkpoints in the border. At Checkpoint 300, a securitised space of turnstiles, metal detectors and sensors, between Bethlehem and Jerusalem, each morning 4,000–7,000 male labourers would enter an overcrowded facility to cross using a so-called 'eight-hour' permit that enabled West Bank Palestinians to work in Israel.[232] Permits were denied for reasons including: 'dismissal from an Israeli company; union activity; imprisonment; political activism; or being too old (over fifty), young (under thirty), unmarried and/or childless.' The 'married with children' condition meant that a man had to leave a wife and at least one child behind, with profound effects on their families.

Husbands were typically away from the home for up to sixteen hours, as they would leave for work at 3:00am to pass through the checkpoint. When they were at home, men were 'exhausted from the long hours he's been away' and even 'tired, angry . . . and [already] stressed about the next day' and this diminished their capacities to contribute to domestic labour. Saud's husband would leave early and return late, so she had to carry out domestic work that was intensified by his absence, such as preparing breakfast and dinner twice. Aside from him sitting with the family for half an hour a day, he was an absent presence in the family home. Hayam felt this increased burden: '[because he's absent] I have to deal with family duties alone, we can't share responsibilities [so] I have to organize all family issues, house requirements, deal with the children . . .' Labour conditions and the checkpoint in this way foreclosed an even division of housework and childcare. Randa made this point explicitly: 'because he's away a lot and so tired at home . . . the responsibilities that my husband should do but can't are fulfilled by me. I cover for the husband and the wife at the same time!'

For the women and men living with cross-border work, the system created physical and emotional stress. The Checkpoints were chock points, overcrowded and stressful environments. Tala explained how this tension returned to the family home with her husband:

. . . before [working] he has to pass the checkpoint. It's always overcrowded and it affects him physically; once he came home with a broken rib because of the pushing and squeezing . . . he gets angry, it is not easy for him, he wakes up early and goes into the overcrowded place with gates and inspections; this affects him at work and affects him when he comes home, because he is angry at home too . . .

Her daily life was also made 'emotionally difficult': 'he is tired emotionally, and for us we remain *uncertain* about his day, don't know if he passed, how his day went, so it's *emotionally difficult* for us too . . . at home with the responsibilities'. Karima reflected on the ways that the stressful commute affected her daily life and responsibilities: 'I feel pressure, I'm always under stress. I should not get angry, but internally, I'm angry and stressed out . . . it's too much pressure for any mother to have to deal with on her own.'

These stories show how women's lives were intimately bound to Palestinian men's low-wage, cross-border labour in East Jerusalem and Israel. While the women did not participate formally in the Israeli labour market, their days were filled with the domestic work that sustained the men who worked in the Israeli economy.[233] In this way, as in the Bantustans of South Africa, there was a bond – an *articulation* – between Israel's low-wage sectors and female domestic work.[234] There are strong parallels in the economic structures which degrade women's lives in each geo-historical moment. Both groups suffered material deprivation and severe psychological damage, but they are not directly comparable.

The South African apartheid model of society does not describe the general economic situation in Israel-Palestine nor the gendered experience of the minority of households engaged in cross-border work. Millions of South African women and children were left behind in the Bantustans and experienced years of absence, spatial distancing and infidelity. That was normal life under apartheid. Apartheid was culturally abhorrent but was primarily a huge South African economic system for managing and exploiting millions of black workers.[235] There has never been a comparable systematic approach to using Palestinian labour to support the Israeli state. Segregation in Israel-Palestine is primarily underlined by ethnic-national tension, and the recent exploitation of commuter workers was a collateral effect of separation. The social experience of Palestinian women married to cross-border workers was also qualitatively different, and thus was not life under apartheid.

The distinctive injustices Palestinians suffer deserve not to be mislabelled as a facsimile of another time and place. This is not to imply that life for Palestinians is easier – or indeed worse – than the struggles that black South Africans experienced. It is different. As the tragic scenes from Gaza in late 2023 demonstrated, the threat to life was acute, the bombings and military interventions by the IDF that led to thousands of female and child civilian casualties in a matter of weeks were of a greater order of magnitude than actions by South African apartheid forces.

Despite the fundamental differences, lessons from one society can be used to help analyse the injustices in another time and place. The work I have done on both societies in tandem has enabled me to carry the idea of articulation from the South African context in which it was developed and apply this theory to Israel-Palestine. Understanding South African apartheid-era articulation and its effect on female well-being furnished me with the intellectual tools to better explain the social experiences of Palestinian women whose husbands worked in Israel. Thus lessons from the African women's past can help us understand the injustices suffered by Palestinian families in the early 2020s. Next, the argument will zoom out to the international scale to see if there are lessons from the wider geopolitical context of apartheid South Africa that can be applied to understand Israel.

The Geopolitics of Segregation

One of the statues in London's Parliament Square is of Jan Smuts, the South African military leader and statesman. Although not an architect of the 1948 apartheid policy, Smuts shaped the wider landscape of segregation and was an avowed white supremacist as well as a friend and colleague of Churchill. Early in his career he had served the British Empire and played a role in the 1917

Balfour Declaration, in which Britain announced its support for a Jewish homeland, as Smuts saw the geopolitical advantages of a state friendly to the West close to the Suez Canal.[236] Throughout the modern history of Israel, from its very inception in 1948 it has faced aggression from neighbouring Arab states and garnered sustained support from Western allies. As Netanyahu's visit in early 2023 illustrated, the British government remained a firm friend of his regime, despite the discontent surrounding some of his policies. Critically, following the vicious terror attacks by Hamas in October 2023, the staunchest support for Israel came from the United States and continued as the IDF mounted its far-reaching response. Israel is the largest cumulative recipient of US foreign assistance since the Second World War and has received $158 billion, more aid than any of the world's impoverished countries, nearly all of which has been military assistance.[237] The funding reflects robust domestic support for Israel in the US, a mutual commitment to democratic values, and shared strategic goals in the Middle East.

Smuts' geo-strategising also foreshadowed a close relationship between South Africa's apartheid regime and Israel and there is a long history of cooperation – often covert – that has shaped policymaking in Israel, at least until the fall of apartheid.[238] Both Israel and South Africa have a geopolitical significance that has raised their global status. Through the 1970s and 1980s, the South African economy, and especially its gold and platinum mines where hundreds of thousands of African men laboured, produced vast profits for domestic and international firms including Anglo American and Oppenheimer. The apartheid system provided the economic and political foundation that sustained the pro-Western white government that was a vehemently anti-communist ally of Washington. In 1973, the United Nations passed the Apartheid Convention, which declared the crime of apartheid and racial segregation. It passed by ninety-one votes to four against. The opponents were South Africa, its allies the United Kingdom and the United States, and Portugal which still clung on to colonial power in Mozambique. After the independence of Angola and Mozambique, Pretoria sought to dominate southern Africa.

From the mid-1970s, US-backed interventions by South Africa in Angola led to sustained conflicts with the communist-aligned People's Movement for the Liberation of Angola (MPLA) and its Cuban allies.[239] There was also support for Renamo in Mozambique to destabilise the neighbouring, black-ruled country. The apartheid security apparatus served a global as well as a national agenda by stemming the development of socialist states throughout the Cold War era.[240]

Israel likewise has a strategic geopolitical significance that belies its relatively small population and size. It is a major player in the international arms and surveillance industries. These technologies are first developed in places like Checkpoint 300 and then sold to the West. Since 9/11, Israel emerged as a 'showroom' for state-of-the-art security equipment.[241] The separation wall and its checkpoints have become 'a selling point for businesses involved in its construction'[242] that received a further boost after President Trump was elected and promised to build a wall along the US-Mexico border. Shares in Israeli companies such as Mahal, Elbit and Elta received huge injections of capital in 2016.[243] Prior to Hamas's ferocious raid in 2023, Palestinian territory served as a grim test case for how Israeli hardware could be used to impose segregation, surveillance and controlled movement. Since the Israel-Hamas war, the fallibility of Israeli border security was exposed. Firstly with tragic results for Jewish civilians living aside the border, and secondly, a collateral effect of the IDF's offensive in Gaza has been a bolstering of Israel's defence and security sectors and a surge in the stock prices of major US arms manufacturers including Lockheed Martin Corporation and Northrop Grumman Corporation.[244]

In both South Africa and Israel, segregation was not solely a domestic policy but a dynamic of international economic and political relations. It is no coincidence that when the Cold War ended in 1991, the apartheid regime soon fell, although there is more to this important chapter in South African history explored elsewhere.[245] Two decades later, the American 'War on Terror' shaped the politics on the ground in Israel-Palestine. The two episodes of segregation can be brought together for discussion, but that does not mean there is apartheid in Israel. Lessons from South Africa's recent history have helped me understand the Israel of today. Firstly, the idea of articulation that explained how women suffered in the Bantustans is a concept that can be used to make sense of domestic life in Palestine. Secondly, when we pan back to examine both geo-historical moments from a global perspective, we can understand how the West supported South Africa in the Cold War and why Israel is an important security ally of the US today. Both divided societies are legitimised by geopolitical support, rather than solely being functions of national politics.

Apartheid is an Afrikaner denomination for an explicit and very particular state policy. Despite the ICC legal statute, I don't think the word travels beyond its original context as a general label to be applied in other times and places. For four years I was an editor of the *Journal of Southern African Studies* and read countless pieces of historical scholarship that examined the cruel particularity and dynamics of apartheid, a racialised system of development riddled with injustices but also occasional contradictions. Apartheid was South African in the way that Jim Crow referred to racial exclusion in the United States, or the Aboriginal Protection Acts did in Australia. Beyond my criticism of the appropriateness of the comparison, there is a sobering reason to stop applying the apartheid label to Israel-Palestine, which concerns what initiated the comparison and what came after political segregation in South Africa.

Despite their close alliance between 1948 and 1994, the apartheid Israel comparison only took off after Mandela was released and a post-apartheid South Africa began to emerge. The analogy gained currency as implicit within the labelling is the idea that there is a similar trajectory towards a post-segregation future for Palestinians and Israelis. This is problematic, because the post-racial future black and white South Africans anticipated in the mid-1990s was not the society they have today. Although the legal structures of apartheid have all been dismantled, as the government's own Statistics South Africa Department notes in 2023: 'South Africa is known as one of the most unequal countries in the world' and the 'labour market is heavily racialised and gender-biased'.[246] It is a country where guard dogs and private security protect the rich. Where murder rates and violent crime are among the highest in the world. Poverty is widespread, life expectancy is low, and power and water shortages are a crippling reality of daily life. South Africa is a better place than it was three decades ago, but it is not a model society for others to emulate. No matter how unimaginable it may seem for victims of violence across the Palestinian and Israeli communities, how painful it is to look forward, and how hard the process of reconciliation will be, Israel-Palestine needs to find a peaceful future of its own making and one that improves livelihoods for everyone rather than just dismantling the formal structures of segregation.

CHAPTER 11

Can the Fight against Climate Change Be Won Like the Space Race?

Why we need more than technology to tackle environmental crisis

From Petrol to Electric

It is early in 1964, a cold January. Snow is draped over the French Alps north of Monaco. Crowds are gathered by the roadside in anticipation. The metallic buzz of a small four-cylinder engine sounds down the mountain. Hurtling on the edge of control, half driving, half skidding downhill comes a tiny rally car. Driver and co-driver are wedged inside, like a pair of grown-ups in a child's pedal car. Shoulder to shoulder leaning into the camber, shifting their body weight more like Tour de France cyclists on an alpine descent than motorists, guiding it round a tight hairpin bend at breakneck speed. There is a flash of light as the car crosses the apex of the curve and the six headlights meet the camera lens. The Pathé news reels are black and white, but your mind's eye pictures it bright in signal red. The Mini maintains momentum at all costs, speeds out of shot and attacks the next section of the stage.

This pocket rocket burst into the public consciousness after claiming an unexpected victory in the glamorous Monte Carlo Rally, beating every larger and more powerful car in the process. To say it was headline news would be an understatement. Driver Paddy Hopkirk was flown back to Britain for primetime television interviews, and he received a telegraph from Prime Minister Sir Alec Douglas-Home and a signed photograph from the Beatles. The Mini became an icon of the swinging sixties, as at home on London's hip Carnaby Street as on continental rally stages.

As well as John, Paul, George and Ringo, famous owners included the American film star Steve McQueen and Enzo Ferrari. Celebrity endorsements and motor sport victories helped to embellish its cool status, but Alec Issigonis's design classic's success was underpinned by functionality. The front-wheel-drive car was small, economical and affordable as well as being great fun to drive. Minis helped bring motoring to the masses. Alongside the Volkswagen Beetle, Citroën 2CV and Fiat 500, it was one of the people's cars that flooded Europe's roads. Car ownership became a reality for households around the world.[247] Affordable motoring revolutionised society, but millions of new fossil-fuelled engines pumped carbon emissions into the atmosphere and transformed the global climate.

Fast-forward six decades and the biggest innovation in the history of the car is changing the way we drive. Sold alongside petrol-powered versions, a new MINI[2] is available that ditches the four cylinders and replaces internal combustion with electric power. Alongside other electric cars, MINI Electric offers a simpler driving experience and promises a bright-green new future for the car industry. Out of curiosity I took a brand-new MINI Electric for a test drive. Much was familiar. The indescribable, yet alluring, new car smell, a stubby automatic gear stick, a dashboard that mimics the 1960s original, and an overall design that mirrors the petrol-powered MINIs parked across

---

[2] When Mini was relaunched by BMW in 2001 it was rebranded as MINI.

the dealership. Tentatively I took the borrowed car out with soft hands on the wheel and light feet on the pedals.

From a standing start, the MINI would accelerate instantly. Power arrived like the flick of a light switch, but when taking my foot off the pedal there was a disconcerting grab of deceleration as the car harvested energy as it yielded velocity. A characteristic of electric vehicles is their regeneration of energy to maximise battery life. Despite its impressive performance, after not much more than a quarter of an hour, the novelty of electric power was beginning to fade. Another fifteen minutes passed, and my eye was increasingly drawn to the battery gauge. Like the power bar on my ageing iPhone, the level of charge was plummeting at an alarming rate. After a short drive around town, I was already well below 80 per cent. The car's multicoloured display had only promised a 105-mile range at the outset. Far less than the advertised 145 miles. When I was back at the dealers, I queried this with the salesman. He attributed it to the MINI only having a few hundred miles on the clock and not yet being run in. Maybe that was right, or maybe it was bullshit. Tests have found ninety miles to be a realistic maximum.[248]

Cherry-Picking Data

Nissan markets their electric Leaf model as having 'zero tailpipe emissions' for 'more sustainable driving'. This is correct as though electric cars may not directly emit gases, the driving is only more sustainable and not pollution-free. Energy for electric cars comes from a power plant somewhere which in many cases still burn fossil fuels. How then can we compare the true cost of carbon emission of petrol and electric cars? As one prominent motoring YouTuber demonstrated, in the most extreme cases, when electric cars are drawing from the dirtiest fossil fuel-generated electricity and compared to the most efficient petrol cars, then equivalent electric journeys can actually contribute more CO_2 emissions per mile.[249] While this could be true, it was an extreme example using carefully selected data. In reality, electric cars in the UK nearly always generate fewer emissions per mile travelled as the supplies of electricity are rapidly becoming greener. Another comparison made by the analysts Transport & Environment argued that an average electric car will consume just 30 kilograms of irrecoverable metals, about the size of a football, in its batteries over a lifetime, whereas a petrol car burns 17,000 litres of fuel, equivalent to a 90 metre or 25 story high tower of oil barrels.[250] The problem with this blunt comparison is that it fails to cite the environmental costs associated with charging the battery.[251] Both comparisons show that different narratives around the efficiency of electric cars can be generated to serve selected audiences.

The ultimate bullshit comparison is one that came from a PR company called Clarendon Communications and was reported in *The Times*, *Daily Mail* and *Daily Telegraph*. A 'groundbreaking' study 'which has been drawn from independent, referenced data' claimed that electric cars need to travel 50,000 miles before matching the carbon footprint of petrol vehicles, suggesting there was little difference in the sustainability. The report was commissioned by companies including Aston Martin, Honda and McLaren. The *Guardian* later revealed that the car makers had written the report themselves and that Clarendon Communications was a company registered under the name of Rebecca Stephens, a part-time nurse whose husband James Stephens was a director of Aston Martin. The report was subsequently debunked.[252] Michael Liebreich, the founder of Bloomberg's clean energy research arm BNEF, raised concerns in a Twitter thread: 'What we can't have is the auto industry and fossil fuel incumbents twisting the discussion to their own advantage using sock-puppet PR companies and underhand tactics. The time for that is over.'

Having read widely and considered the science, I am not in doubt that electric cars are more sustainable, but equally I know I could cherry-pick data, and use particular journey patterns and time frames to make a convincing argument that they are no greener than their petrol-powered equivalents. Comparisons are easily manipulated if you play with the metrics. Comparing two cars, such as a petrol and electric MINI, in isolation is not helpful. There is too much complexity in car manufacturing and energy production and too many variables in patterns of use to forensically audit the full environmental impacts. The relative performance of electric versus petrol ultimately hinges on how green the electricity is that charges the battery packs and how long the car is used for to offset the material and energy consumption associated with manufacturing. This equation can be changed by government actions: more support for renewable electricity and incentives to extend vehicle life will increase electric car sustainability.

The positive environmental impacts of a transition to electric automotive power need to be examined at a global rather than an individual scale. However, most often the comparisons that appear across the motoring sector and journalism discuss particular vehicles and individual consumers. More worryingly, interest groups use data to author comparative narratives to leverage different arguments but present their findings as robust facts. We need to step back from these unhelpful comparisons and think about the bigger picture and consider the system changes needed for a wholesale transition to electric power – including expanded charging networks, novel ownership patterns, greener energy production, optimum battery and vehicle size. Carbon emissions are a global problem. There is only one shared atmosphere, so we need joined-up thinking rather than comparative approaches about individual problems fixed by changes to consumer behaviours.

Cheating Tests

Picture that moment in the doctor's surgery at the start of an appointment. You're sitting patiently at their side looking at some posters promoting healthy eating or maybe worse lying prone on a bed staring at the ceiling waiting as they read through their notes. Then the questions start: How often do you exercise? Do you eat healthily? Do you smoke? How many units of alcohol do you consume in an average week? You hesitate for a second before you answer almost honestly, maybe adding in an extra gym session, forgetting a few biscuits, and doing a tally of one of your quieter drinking periods. Or maybe this is just me who feels they must represent a better version of themselves when they go for a check-up? Really the only person I'm cheating is myself, as if the doctor has a full and honest picture, they can better assess my well-being. But what happens when a car lies during the automotive version of a 'health' check? How and why would that happen? The story of how cars cheated during testing is one of the dirtiest environmental scandals of the twenty-first century and at its heart is a comparison between the emissions of diesel and petrol engines.

The difference between diesel and petrol engines is how they burn their fuel. Petrol provides explosive power when a spark plug ignites the fuel, whereas diesel ignites under compression. Initially, diesel engines were designed to run on cruder fuel than high-grade petrol, giving it a reputation as being dirtier. Diesel fuel was only standardised in the 1950s when it increasingly became used in motor vehicles, most often buses, lorries and vans, yet was still considered the dirtier option. In 1990 only 12.9 billion litres of diesel were sold in the UK versus 32.8 billion litres of petrol, yet by 2006 equal amounts of each fuel were being sold, and by 2019 30.0 billion litres of diesel were sold against just 16.9 billion litres of petrol,[253] due to a huge rise in the number of diesel cars sold.

Volkswagen was one of the major proponents of diesel fuel in the late 1990s and 2000s. Their best-selling Golf had a new TDI (Turbocharged Direct Injection) fitted in 1993. These engines had injectors that sprayed fuel into a combustion chamber, enabling it to burn more completely, reducing exhaust emissions and producing more power, which was further boosted by the turbo. The engines were smoother and more powerful than older diesel technology. Direct injection engines were used across VW cars and the other brands owned by the group including Audi, Seat, Skoda, Porsche and even Bentley. These cars won many press awards, including the 2009 Green Car Award and an Audi TDI even claimed victory at the Le Mans 24 Hour race in 2006. What most impressed consumers was their superior fuel economy compared to petrol equivalents. A 1997 1.6 litre petrol Golf and a 1.9 TDI both produced around 100 horsepower and had near identical performance figures. But the petrol version did thirty-nine miles per gallon versus fifty-three miles in the diesel.

Volkswagen ran adverts celebrating the TDI's fuel efficiency in comparison to petrol power. A memorable TV spot from 1996 was 'Gas Station'. In this ad, two rural folk from New Mexico discuss the strange UFO-like apparition that passed by their remote gas station without needing petrol. It was identifiable only by the strange sign on it that looked 'Kinda like a Vee and a Dublyer'. The ad simply finishes with the tag line 'Golf TDi. Up to 891 miles between fill-ups'. It was not just the car makers pushing buyers towards the black pump. In the early 2000s the UK government provided incentives to purchase diesel cars including lower road tax, because the greater fuel efficiency was believed to make these cars more environmentally friendly than petrol. However, the environmental comparison was deeply flawed as it considered fuel consumption rather than having robust data on emissions that affect local air quality. Volkswagen promoted the technological miracle of fast, cheap and green diesel vehicles. In reality, the TDI system was dirty and failed to combine good fuel economy with compliant emissions.

As recently as 2015, VW was continuing to brag about their diesels' green credentials: 'This ain't your daddy's diesel. Stinky, smoky and sluggish. These old diesel realities no longer apply. Enter TDI Clean Diesel,' but this bravado was built on a lie. Governments test vehicles before approving them for the road. Exams compare what comes out of their exhaust pipes with what is permitted by law. VW had built software that recognised when their cars were in the testing labs and being put through standardised procedures. Like the patient lying to their doctor, this computer code triggered the engine to behave in a different way and changed diesel injection to fool the smog testers by giving readings that falsely showed that the emissions were a lot cleaner. Those diesel engines produced far more emissions under real-world conditions versus during their health checks and much more than their petrol equivalents. In the US, the Environment Protection Agency eventually found that nitrogen dioxide was being emitted up to forty times the government standard.[254]

Nitrogen dioxide is harmful for human health, irritating lungs and causing breathing difficulties, especially when it is found in high concentrations in urban areas.[255]

The cars were designed to present a false, greener, better version of themselves under testing. The cars were peddling bullshit. In 2015, the EPA began to notice discrepancies between tests and the full scale of the scandal was soon uncovered. Volkswagen admitted that about 11 million cars worldwide, including eight million in Europe, had been fitted with so-called 'defeat devices' that cheated tests between 2009 and 2015.[256] Less than two years later, a US federal judge ordered VW to pay a $2.8 billion criminal fine for 'rigging diesel-powered vehicles to cheat on government emissions tests'.[257] Volkswagen Group CEO Martin Winterkorn resigned and was charged in the United States with fraud and conspiracy. Worldwide the scandal cost VW $33.3 billion in fines, penalties, financial settlements and buyback costs. Other manufacturers including Volvo, Renault, Jeep, Hyundai, Citroën and Fiat were also found to be cheating emissions tests, further illustrating how ill thought out the procedures were. Frustratingly, decades earlier, concerns had been raised about the validity of the testing regimes, which were 'unrealistic' with a 'predictable' pattern of cycles that did not strain engines. As a report from 1998 by Per Kågeson argued, the test 'allows car manufacturers to design their cars to pass tests and results in cars producing higher levels of pollution when driven on the road'.[258]

A Moonshot

We choose to go to the moon. We choose to go to the moon in this decade and do the other things, not because they are easy, but because they are hard, because that goal will serve to organize and measure the best of our energies and skills, because that challenge is one that we are willing to accept, one we are unwilling to postpone, and one which we intend to win, and the others, too.[259]

Famous words, stirring words, powerful words from President Kennedy in 1961. These words helped change the world. They brought together a nation, corralled resources, stimulated scientific endeavour and directed energy towards achieving a single goal that many thought impossible. More than half a century later, this moonshot is often referenced when an even greater global challenge is discussed: climate change. Could the achievements of NASA in the 1960s be an inspiration for solving the impending environmental crises? Does it make sense to compare the space race and efforts to tackle climate change?

Making an environmental problem into a space mission is a good way to grab attention.[260] US Energy Secretary Jennifer Granholm has said that fighting climate change is 'our generation's moonshot'.[261] Microsoft has launched a 'moonshot' to go carbon neutral by 2030, meaning they would be removing more carbon from the atmosphere than they produced.[262] Kyushu University in Japan has launched a 'moonshot' to produce machines to filter carbon dioxide from the atmosphere.[263] And newspapers from the *Financial Times* to the *New Statesman* have called for a 'moonshot' to address the climate crises. It is certainly a word that beckons boldness and experimentation.[264]

There are two characteristics of the 'moonshot' that are invoked when it is used as a comparative model for the climate crisis. Firstly, the Apollo missions of the 1960s and 1970s had commitment and unity of purpose. Getting to the moon required unprecedented expenditure $26 billion between 1960 and 1973, equivalent to more than $200 billion today. A huge workforce with a wide range of technical and scientific skills was put to the task. Coordination between different areas of government and the private sector was essential. It was also risky and controversial, with many Americans questioning if it was an appropriate use of resources at a time when the nation faced many injustices. Political support from the very top was essential to maintain the project, as were flexibility and ingenuity at every level of the mission.[265] Secondly, it had a clearly defined goal. Success and failure were very easy to measure. Once Neil Armstrong stepped out of the lander (and made it back home safe with his crew), it was mission accomplished.

Starting with the first characteristics, it is right to say that addressing climate change also requires massive change and action across science, business and government. Yet there is a fundamental difference of scale. The lunar missions leveraged the resource of one single – albeit very powerful – nation with a then population of 185 million, of which 400,000 were directly involved in the project. The climate crisis is a global issue which touches the lives of all eight billion people. The space race happened against the backdrop of the Cold War. Nationalism was a powerful force in unifying America's efforts – you can't picture the rockets of NASA and the spacesuits of the astronauts without the stars and stripes. There is no such equivalent cultural glue to hold the population of the world together. We are not all invested in the challenge. On the one hand, Extinction Rebellion protesters are willing to face prison when they call for action, while at the same time climate sceptics are still an influential voice in the global media, and thirdly there are millions if not billions around the world who are poor and lack formal education required to understand the emerging crisis or the political influence to demand a response. Visiting the moon involved many complicated parts operating together including rockets, guidance systems, life support, lunar landings and more. Tackling climate change is an infinitely more complex set of problems. As the example of the challenges faced with the transition to electric cars showcased, it is not easy to rework key aspects of society, even when the problem is relatively discreet such as swapping from one car power source to another.

Secondly, the type of outcome that will resolve each challenge is utterly incomparable. The Apollo missions had a simple goal: get to the moon. Yes, there were some further mission criteria, but the big prize was obvious to everyone, and ever since it was achieved, NASA's manned space programmes have dwindled in scale. In contrast, what is the goal of the climate science community? Halting global temperature rises at 2° Celsius, 1.5° or 1° or less? Reducing carbon dioxide concentrations in the atmosphere to 300 parts per million (PPM) or allowing 400 or 500 (PPM) or going back to the levels from the pre-Industrial

Revolution? Stopping the melting of ice caps and disappearance of glaciers? Capping carbon emissions at a certain level per person? What is the time frame for achieving whatever goal is selected? There are many different targets that could be set, and the scale of societal change required to deliver some of the more ambitious versus less progressive aims is totally different. Politicians, business leaders and scientists have repeatedly failed to reach consensus. So the lack of a single agreeable target versus the simple: 'We choose to go to the moon' illustrates how it simply doesn't work as a comparison.

More fundamentally, the mission-goal model of a moonshot is completely at odds with the actions needed to reconcile the relationships between humans and the natural environment. Living sustainably is something that will forever need attention. There can't be an end point. It needs a permanent reorganisation, not a fixed-term solution like the Apollo programmes. Into the future, humans will always need to restrict net carbon emissions alongside the release of other harmful gases. Yet global environmental change is not just about releasing less CO_2 into the atmosphere but a much broader suite of wider, often interconnected, environmental issues. 'Fixing' climate change will not alone repair the damage done to the planet as there are a much more expansive suite of problems – including ocean acidification, species extinction, deforestation and water pollution – that are also life-threatening. We must re-evaluate what type of natural environment we want to sustain.

When searching for an analogy maybe the Industrial Revolution, the period that spurred the beginning of the climate crises, is a better comparison. The Industrial Revolution changed the world forever. In the same way that resolving global environmental change will never have a definitive 'end', the Industrial Revolution doesn't really have an agreed 'start'. From around the 1780s, there were innovations in the use of automated machinery, like the textile-weaving power looms in northern England that transformed not only the production of goods, but also society. These new machines built upon earlier technological leaps forward from elsewhere. At the heart of the Industrial Revolution, though, was a social change – the factory – rather than a new technology. Modern factories reorganised work not just in textiles but across a wide range of new goods including bicycles, biscuits, bricks, pins, rifles, soap and washboards and these new cheap products changed everyone's lives.[266] The Industrial Revolution was not just about scientific discoveries, but also new ways of organising the economy and society. Maybe a comparable environmental revolution is what is required today with new tech and also new political ideas and economic systems? But there does not appear to be the leadership to will this into action. While the G7 and other political institutions bring leaders together and presidents and prime ministers call for action on climate, their speeches fail to catalyse change. When Kennedy launched the moonshot his words were famous, stirring and powerful. Sadly, when Joe Biden and others speak on the environment, their contributions are forgettable, insipid and empty.

Environmental Revolution

How then can we bring about an environmental revolution? I'm not a climate scientist, but I work alongside some excellent ones. On a weekly basis I go to talks in my geography department and hear the latest cutting-edge research. Two lessons I've repeatedly learned are a) the problems facing the planet are probably worse than you think and b) the rate of change is rapid – between the time I write this, and you read it, any figures that I have cited on global environmental change will already be out of date. Sometimes these departmental seminars leave me feeling bewildered and hopeless. Oftentimes I'm impressed by the incredible geographical research, but despair that this work is not reaching the right audience and shaping policy. The problems, be they technological, political, social or economic, are stacked high and look insurmountable. How can we feel anything but anxious and scared of the future? How will I talk to my children about the global environmental crises that will shape their lives? I don't have all the answers, but I have begun to understand the nature of the problem.

One building block for an environmental revolution is understanding that we need to reorientate society from high-density energy to low-density energy. What does that mean? Well, fossil fuels are the input for the current high-density systems – burning petrol, diesel or coal can release a lot of energy relative to their size. In contrast, renewable power sources are lower density, they cover more area and are immobile: hydroelectric dams, solar farms and windmills can only be built in certain places and batteries are heavy and charging them is a slower process than filling up petrol tanks. Therefore, we need to be innovative in finding local solutions to energy generation rather than taking a one-size-fits-all approach and look for a wholesale like-for-like replacement of the old fossil fuel energy systems. Electric cars are improving, and the range of newer and more expensive models are a vast improvement on the MINI I test-drove, but maybe part of the solution to transport is to have smaller cars with shorter ranges for local journeys. Many different answers are needed to resolve the multitude of problems we face with climate change and stretch well beyond energy use.

This multi-pronged approach was well encapsulated by my colleague, Tamsin Edwards's research for the BBC Radio 4 series *39 Ways to Save the Planet*. This series sliced global environment problems into different sectors and examined innovations – including in the diverse fields of bamboo-growing, steelmaking, rewilding, legal reforms and tax policy – that could begin to steer us towards a sustainable future.[267] Importantly, none of these are a panacea in isolation, but the cumulative effect of changes like these and many more behavioural and technological shifts could have revolutionary potential.

To briefly reconsider the auto sector, we can see what sorts of shifts may be required there. We should not fixate on comparisons with the status quo when searching for answers to the environmental crisis, but think about the bigger picture and sector-wide revolutionary approaches that are fundamentally more sustainable. For cars this means not just swapping energy systems but thinking about the huge volume of new cars sold. In the UK, the consumer credit-based car market is dependent on a relentless cycle of new purchases. Far too many cars are manufactured, but government is always supporting the development of new vehicle factories and car sales as they bring tax revenue and economic growth. Overproduction is part of the problem, but the flipside is overconsumption. Herein lies a fundamental issue with the way new electric vehicles are sold, which as with their petrol counterparts are being purchased on finance for short-term use and sold on after a few years. The transition to electric vehicles is not resolving this problem. Rather than being part of a revolutionary new transport system, electric Teslas and MINI Electrics are a green-ish substitute for dirty old technology. Cars, be they electric or combustion, are purchased at an utterly unsustainable tempo. We do not just need to switch to greener fuel sources but think about greener models of vehicle use and ownership.

Humankind's desire to circumvent problems like climate change with shiny new products means that rather than dealing with the underlying issue, we invent something to cancel it out. Buying a new electric MINI instead of a petrol one is not the answer. We know that cars are environmentally toxic, but giving up the freedom is, it seems, too much to ask. Here I would be the first to stick my hand up and take my part of the blame. But I'm a subject of a wider system. There needs to be more progressive taxation and regulation for me to give up a petrol-powered car. The comparison needed in the transport sector is not between individual green and dirty cars, but between an environmentally sustainable society and one that promotes overconsumption of energy and resources.

CHAPTER 12

Why Is Britain Obsessed With the Second World War?

How historical comparison builds an exclusive national identity

War Movies

After the famous MGM roaring lion, a rattling drum march echoes through the speakers, building softly, softly, quietly, quietly, then loud and hard. The screen shows the peaks and valleys of Bavarian mountains in the dark of the night. The names of the stars appear in a Teutonic script as red as the flag of Nazi Germany – Richard Burton, Clint Eastwood, Mary Ure – then the title: *Where Eagles Dare*. A warplane soars overhead, camouflaged, flying low against the alpine background. Inside are elite allied paratroopers disguised as Wehrmacht soldiers on a top-secret mission: free an American general who knows the plans for D-Day before he yields the secrets under torture. The prisoner is held captive in an impregnable German castle: the *Schloss Adler*, the Castle of the Eagles.

This was my favourite film as a boy and is still my number one. *Where Eagles Dare* is an action-packed thriller that never fails to draw me into its world of adventure where British and American heroes overcome impossible odds. *Eagles* is like a heist movie set against the background of the Second World War. At first it is a race against time to free General Carnaby, but the mission evolves as the plot unravels and becomes fiendishly complicated. The initial tension between the experienced British commander, Burton, and the younger American hardman, Eastwood, develops as they become brothers in arms. Ure's spy helps them access the inner sanctum of the mountain-top citadel. Burton leads his team forward, while Eastwood dispatches tens of Nazi soldiers: seventy-three by one count. Ure makes tens of kills as well, in an early action role for a female lead.[268] This is a simple battle between good guys and bad guys.

What attracted me in my formative years was the daring bravado, action and stunts; the vertigo-inducing set-piece fight with ice axes on the roof of a cable car is pure movie gold. When I watched my VHS home recording as a child I was captured by the simple context of the plot: this film was a triumph over evil, as the Brits beat the Nazis. It made me proud. Now when I occasionally sit down to watch it out of nostalgia, I view *Eagles* for the thrills. This is something of a guilty pleasure. I am mindful of the more complicated geopolitics of the Second World War when watching movies that glamorise the exploits of the Allies. While there is no doubting the cataclysmic horrors of the Nazi regime, the Allied war effort was more complex than simply good overcoming evil. The war involved an alliance with Stalin's oppressive dictatorship, the RAF firebombing Dresden, the US atomic bombings of Hiroshima and Nagasaki, the abuses of colonial subjects in support of the British Empire, and famines in Bengal that cost millions of lives. The complex morality of the war rarely makes it into Hollywood productions.

Where Eagles Dare was part of a whole generation of 1950s and 1960s war movies that were endlessly repeated on British screens in my early 1990s childhood. Others included *The Great Escape, The Heroes of Telemark* and *The Dam Busters*. Their common tropes were heroic male figures that took on the Nazi regime in a battle of plucky Allies defeating the German war machine.

This movement of films was made in the aftermath of the war and became the foremost cultural legacy of the global conflict in the UK. British film-makers are continually drawn back to the Second World War. Recent blockbuster war movies include *Dunkirk* (2018), *The Imitation Game* (2014) and *The Darkest Hour* (2017). In the last named, Gary Oldman won an Oscar for his portrayal of Winston Churchill. This sympathetic biographical treatment was praised by Conservative critic Charles Moore as 'superb Brexit propaganda'. Sometimes it seems every moment in modern British history is compared to the Second World War.

Moore's comments might have chimed with the narrow majority of the British population that voted for Brexit in 2016 and wanted to take back control of their country rather than pursue further European integration, but are far from a universal view. An opposing newspaper critic, Afua Hirsch, agreed that Oldman's Oscar-winning portrayal was propaganda, but was disparaging of Moore's glowing commentary and argued the film was 'a great example of the kind of myth we like to promote in modern Britain. Churchill has been rebranded as a Tube-travelling, minority-adoring genius, in line with a general understanding of him as 'the greatest Briton of all time'.[269] The myth of Britain standing alone and succeeding in its darkest wartime hour against near-impossible odds is one that sustains the notion of a small island nation defeating a more powerful foe, but this conceals the dependency of the British war effort on support from its empire.[270]

The current generation of war films are more nuanced than those of the *Where Eagles Dare* era. Contemporary features are careful in their treatment of characters that are more complex than the macho heroes played by Burton and Eastwood. *The Imitation Game* centred on a sensitive portrayal of the code-breaker Alan Turing's closeted homosexuality. In this cryptography drama, for instance, most of the fighting takes place elsewhere. Despite this, the genre still reinforces Britain's wartime mythology. *Dunkirk* showed the fears and terror of British troops and was epically dramatic, but less bombastic when combat filled the screen. The most memorable set piece featured an iconic Spitfire piloted by a stoic hero, in a scene that could have come from a 1960s director. As critic Geoff Dyer writes, the movie had the power to have a particular effect on Britons of a certain age:

> . . . it was like witnessing a dramatized, massively enhanced projection of some of the components of the national culture that had formed me and my contemporaries. The film was designed to be immersive; what it immersed me in − symbolically expressed by the Spitfire gliding silently on to the beach where the stuff of consciousness yields to and is cushioned by the claims of the unconscious − was the experience of seeing what was already there, waiting for the film as it landed in my head.[271]

Film-making plays a key role in sustaining 1939–45 at the forefront of the nation's psyche, to the extent that everything from football, to Brexit and Covid-19 is viewed through the lens of the Second World War. Let's all 'keep calm and carry on' and overcome the odds. Any challenge the nation faces can be encapsulated by the metaphor of Britain standing alone against the existential threat of Nazi Germany.

'Two World Wars and One World Cup'

England hosted the 1996 European Football Championship. The home team started the tournament better than expected. After a draw against Switzerland, they waltzed past Scotland, and beat a star-studded but splintered Dutch team. In the knockout stages they overcame Spain in the quarter-finals after a penalty shootout. As the team progressed, the catchy anthem 'Three Lions (Football's Coming Home)' echoed from the terraces and enthusiasm surged through the nation. The next opponents in the semi-finals were Germany. As anticipation built, the British tabloid press resorted to bullshit comparisons. The front page of the *Daily Mirror* featured two of England's most celebrated players, the combative Stuart Pearce and the mercurial Paul Gascoigne mocked up in Second World War helmets, with the title 'ACHTUNG! SURRENDER: For you Fritz, ze Euro 96 Championship is over'. A line paraphrasing a fictitious German officer accepting the surrender of British soldiers in a 1960s war movie. The wartime metaphor is repugnant on many levels, but I think it is at its worst in implying a moral equivalence between German soldiers fighting under an oppressive regime of the distant past, and a young generation of professional footballers that represented a modern, democratic and progressive society. England went on to lose on penalties and Germany proceeded to win the final. Following their victory over the Czech Republic at Wembley, the champions sang England's own anthem, 'Football's Coming Home', when they arrived back in Frankfurt Airport.

Fourteen years later, England hadn't made it any further in tournament football, but there was a sense of anticipation around a golden generation of footballers led by the Italian manager Fabio Capello. I was in South Africa for the 2010 World Cup with two friends that had travelled out to Africa. After making the long drive from Maputo to Johannesburg to collect them, we drove through the night to Port Elizabeth. Our first England match was the last group stage game, a one-nil victory over Slovenia at Nelson Mandela Bay Stadium. Next, England faced Germany in the knockout stages in Bloemfontein. We hadn't anticipated travelling to Bloemfontein as we'd optimistically believed England would qualify first in their group rather than as runners-up and would avoid the Germans. Bloemfontein, the 250,000-person city that is culturally more Afrikaner than anglophone, didn't seem ready for the influx of tens of thousands of English fans either. After finding some overpriced accommodation, we headed out into town to soak up the atmosphere ahead of the big match. This atmosphere turned out to be toxic.

English football fans have a reputation for hooliganism and violence that traced back to notorious rioting in the 1980s, and the worst instances involved clashes with German supporters. After defeat by West Germany in the Italia '90 World Cup, there were riots back home and attacks on German fans and cars, and the seaside town of Brighton looked like a 'battlefield'.[272] There was violence at the Euro 2000 tournament that brought shame on the nation. Bare-chested supporters hurled cafe furniture across the usually genteel square of Charleroi. Belgian police resorted to water cannons to break up clashes between English and German fans. The violence in Belgium was widely condemned. A spokesman for Tony Blair said the prime minister was disgusted: 'He is determined that anybody who seems hell-bent on going abroad and causing destruction should be condemned by everyone. The Belgian police have our full support for cracking down on hooligans as hard as they need to.'[273] However, some thought the riotous English were justified in their attacks. The day after the game, a columnist for the *Daily Mirror*, Tony Parsons, could not resist calling the Germans 'Huns' and making a comparison to the World Wars: 'yes, do mention the war . . . they had it coming' as Parsons reminds his readers in a column that 'boys in their teens died at Anzio'.[274] A battle that was fifty-six years earlier. This is a very English disease. As the German culture minister, Michael Naumann, said during the 2010 World Cup: 'There is only one nation that has decided to make the Second World War a sort of spiritual core of its self-understanding and pride.'[275]

I'd witnessed mild tensions at Premier League matches back home, but I hadn't been to an England game before the Slovenia match, which was uneventful both on and off the pitch. Thus, I wasn't prepared for the xenophobia of that June day. By the time we reached the strip of bars in Bloemfontein colonised by England supporters, the atmosphere was already intense, but still jovial. Fans filled the road and the whole street rocked with anticipation. There was shouting and singing, and 'Three Lions' echoed down the street. At first, there were small pockets of German supporters, but they disappeared as the day wore on and more huge pint-and-a-half bottles of Castle lager were drunk. Then the chanting started to turn dark as a vocal minority pitched in with the macabre: including 'Two World Wars and One World Cup' and 'Ten German Bombers'.

The lyrics to these chants all show a lack of care about whom they offend. I doubt any England fans stopped to think about what their Italian head coach felt about the songs. Should

Capello have remained seated when idiotic supporters chanted 'Stand up if you won the war'? It all felt completely mindless. The intensity of the repetitive 'Ten German Bombers', which has an accumulative song format like the kids' song 'Ten Green Bottles', whipped the crowd into an ultra-nationalistic frenzy.

In 2017, England manager Gareth Southgate described 'Ten German Bombers' as 'completely unacceptable' and the English Football Association agreed to ban the chant in 2021. While the worst lyrics have been outlawed, the FA is not blameless. An officially sanctioned – and it must be said, widely decried – England supporter band has long played the theme tunes to Second World War movies such as *The Dam Busters* and *The Great Escape* at home and away games. This drumbeat contributes to the comparisons between the ambitions of the English football team and the war.

When the Second World War chanting started on the streets of Bloemfontein, we left to find the ground. Arriving early in the Free State Stadium, the atmosphere inside was less toxic, although media reports showed pictures of English fans dressed in RAF uniforms waving inflatable fighter planes. From an English perspective, this was not a game for the ages. The golden generation of the late 2000s of David Beckham, Steven Gerrard and Wayne Rooney suffered a humiliating 4–1 defeat. With our dreams of watching England progress to the final in Johannesburg dashed, I took my friends back to Mozambique for the rest of their holiday to escape the football.

Blitz Spirit

The interventions by Tony Blair, Michael Naumann and Gareth Southgate demonstrate that leaders are sensitive to the ways in which the history of the Second World War can be misused. Far beyond the world of football it remains a national obsession and often becomes *the* frame of reference for the most pressing issues of the day. In the 2010s this was the Brexit debates, at the turn of the next decade it became the way in which the nation comprehended the global pandemic.

As coronavirus hit in 2020, British politicians and journalists were quick to make Second World War comparisons. Opinion writers called for 'Churchillian language' as the newly elected Boris Johnson and other senior figures scrabbled to invoke the stirring rhetoric of a conflict that finished decades before they were born. The wartime analogy captured the public imagination and there was a national call for a 'Blitz spirit'. In factories, the repurposing of high-tech production lines to rapidly manufacture ventilators was akin to the rush to build wartime Spitfires. At home, Captain Tom, a centenarian veteran, who had served in India and the Burma Campaign at the time of the Bengal famines, raised £33 million for health charities by walking a hundred lengths of his garden. In the skies, a Spitfire painted with 'THANK U NHS' and the names of 80,000 health workers and volunteers made a tour of hospitals. These nostalgia-tinged interventions captured media attention and widespread praise, but what message did they convey to the more than 2,000 German doctors working in the NHS? As well as the European neighbours researching vaccines with which the British government needed to cooperate to resolve the pandemic. Moreover, despite hundreds of media stories, the Spitfire-inspired ventilator manufacturing delivered few machines, charitable giving was a drop in the ocean compared to the huge increase in public health spending, and moral boosting air displays affected only a tiny percentage of healthcare workers who were alert and sensitive to the underwhelming spectacle of a lone aircraft. Collectively, the Second World War inspired nothing more than a symbolic contribution to the colossal Covid-19 response that was completely disproportionate to its cultural effect. So, the comparison was a distraction in terms of a metaphor catalysing a response, but does invoking Churchill and the Second World War make sense as a model to capture the impacts of Covid-19?

In 2020 as in 1939, there was a strengthening of state authority and spending, but few other meaningful similarities. Staying at home, shutting down the economy and social distancing could not be more different from wartime mass mobilisation, increases in industrial output and conscription into military life. During the pandemic, Britain was depicted as standing square alone against the virus foe which Johnson confusingly termed an 'invisible mugger'. The prime minister pledged to build a 'world-beating' track and trace system, as if this was a competitive arena where the most important metric was Britain's comparative performance. As the disaster unfolded, the government began to shun national comparisons and Britain's performance was evidently worse than most counterparts. A surge in infections in the winter months were the result of a new mutant virus believed to originate in southern England, but government mismanagement of the pandemic had meant that many more people became infected in the first place, creating the conditions for the mutation to occur.[276]

Towards the end of 2020, Britain became the first country to start a national programme of vaccinations. Government Minister Gavin Williamson claimed the UK got the coronavirus vaccine first because it was 'better' than other countries: 'We have obviously got the best medical regulators, much better than the French have, much better than the Belgians have, much better than the Americans have,' he told LBC Radio, and continued with this line: 'That does not surprise me at all because we are a much better country than every single one of them.' The response from the European Commission spokesman, Eric Mamer, was scathing: 'We are definitely not in the game of comparing regulators across countries, nor on commenting on claims as to who is better . . . This is not a football competition; we are talking about the life and health of people.'[277] On the eve of the vaccine rollout, Health Secretary Matt Hancock christened the moment 'V-Day' invoking the VE and VJ Days that marked the end of Second World War hostilities in Europe and Asia-Pacific. Following the first jabs, Hancock cried on television and said, 'It makes you so proud to be British.' The Pfizer/BioNTech inoculation being used was not a British vaccine, but a multinational effort, developed in Germany by a company led by two doctors of Turkish origin and manufactured in Belgium. The British Second World War analogy could not have been less appropriate. This was a breakthrough to benefit everyone on the planet. A moment to celebrate unity, not an opportunity for petty nationalism.

Britain was relatively successful with the vaccine roll-out in the first half of 2021 and was ahead of its European neighbours in reaching key milestones of the proportion inoculated, which led to a reprisal of the national comparison by the government and their outriders in the mainstream press. This, though, was a selective rendering of Britain's so-called 'success' in tackling the pandemic, as the more important metric of deaths and disease prevalence evidenced a disastrous mishandling of the health crisis that was much worse than in many other European nations. Consistently throughout the pandemic, the overall messaging from the country's leaders was isolationist, mirroring the myth that frames wartime Britain as a lone outpost against Nazism. That was another misremembered history. Rather than self-sufficiency, the wartime island nation was dependent on the rest of the world. The British Empire was an expansive military-industrial machine. Churchill did not lead the UK as a lone power but made common cause with the United States, the Soviet Union and other nations, and forcibly drew upon vast resources from overseas colonies to contribute food, fuel and weapons to an eventual Allied victory. The resolution to Covid-19 would also depend upon global cooperation, the sharing of expertise on transmission and treatments, imports of personal protective equipment and the pooling of scientific knowledge to build novel vaccines. The Second World War and Churchillian comparisons were a lazy and dangerous distraction.

War Returns to Europe

My daughter was born on Valentine's Day 2022. I loved her completely from the moment I first saw her peaceful perfection. Although she is my third child, the early weeks were disorientating. Day and night were pulled together. Our curtains were half closed against the late winter days and dim lamps half lit the night. We all stumbled towards a new routine of family life, but it was a disquieting time for her to enter the world. Covid was lingering over Britain. The last of the legal restrictions on life were being dismantled, though there were still many cases. Things were better, but far from back to normal. There was at least a collective sense of relief that the worst of the pandemic was behind us. I spent a lot of time on the sofa cradling my newborn girl with 24-hour TV news on in the background. The pandemic was no longer the headline and reports of an impending war filled the airwaves with a new terror.

On 24 February, Russia mounted its invasion of Ukraine. This was the biggest land attack in Europe since the Second World War, the type of conflict that I never imagined in my lifetime. Maybe it was because my emotions were heightened as I watched the televised tragedy unfold with a ten-day old on my lap, but this was a world-shifting moment. More affecting than 9/11, or the close-to-home London bombings of 7/7, or the distant wars in Afghanistan and Iraq. This was truly terrifying; I couldn't sleep or concentrate on anything. The scale of the conflict, its relative proximity, and the existential fear of nuclear escalation rocked me to my core.

President Vladimir Putin's justification for the assault on Kyiv was to de-Nazify the Ukrainian leadership. It was an absurd notion to suggest the government of President Volodymyr Zelensky, who was born to a Ukrainian Jewish family, was comparable to Hitler's Third Reich, but this is what was implied. Russian Foreign Minister Sergei Lavrov called Zelensky 'a Nazi and a neo Nazi'.[278] Ukraine had suffered the full horrors of the Second World War when occupied by Nazi Germany. The Holocaust involved the mass murder of Ukrainian Jews, and one and a half million lost their lives.[279] There was violence on a huge industrial scale: imprisonments, mass shootings, concentration camps, ghettos, forced labour, starvation, torture and mass kidnappings. Before the 2022 invasion, modern Ukraine was an emerging nation becoming increasingly prosperous, Kyiv was liberal and open, there with an imperfect democracy and a slow-burning border conflict with Russia, but nothing about it was comparable to Germany in 1939.

David Fishman, a professor of Jewish history, explains why Putin calls Zelensky a Nazi: 'This propaganda is an attempt to delegitimize Ukraine in the eyes of the Russian public, which considers its war against Nazi Germany its greatest moment, and in the eyes of the Western public who may not know much about Ukraine except that it's next to Russia.'[280] A tiny proportion of Ukrainians are ultra-nationalists and have used Nazi insignia, but the same minority fascist views can be found in the US, Britain and indeed Russia. In the Second World War, a small number of Ukrainians collaborated with the Nazis, as did the French, Danes and other occupied peoples, but ten million Ukrainians fought in Stalin's Red Army alongside the Russians. Comparing Ukraine and Nazi Germany is bullshit.

As the fighting has ground on, Putin continues to draw historical parallels between Soviet participation in the 1940s' 'Great Patriotic War' against Germany and the present-day 'special military operation' in Ukraine. In September 2023, Putin gave a speech that invoked the memory of Soviet military victories during the Second World War, including turning points in the battles of Stalingrad and the recapturing of the Caucasus and Donbas, and he attended a concert in honour of the Battle of Kursk's eightieth anniversary. Putin has criticised the attitude of the West towards Germany in the 1930s before the outbreak of the War, while ignoring the Molotov-Ribbentrop Pact that allied the Soviet Union with Nazi Germany. This agreement between Hitler and Stalin permitted the Soviet invasion of the Baltic states, and partitioned Poland between Germany and Russia in 1939. This analogy was used as a frame of reference as he argued the same pre-conditions in Ukraine needed intervention today. The passive West let Hitler launch the Second World War. In Putin's bullshit worldview, Russia is rising to head off the development of another Nazi state. By making persistent references to the Second World War, Putin is also signalling to the Russian people that this is a big and prolonged conflict and a fundamental struggle for their nation.[281]

Misremembering the Second World War

One of my childhood friends had an oversized rifle-green shirt that he would wear when we played in the woods. It was West

German army surplus. On the shoulders there were badges the size of postage stamps with the black, red and gold bars of the modern German flag. Once, after a day of tree climbing and den building, he went back to his grandmother's house for tea. She kept the shirt to launder. When he got the uniform back, it was neatly pressed and folded like the dress shirt of a new military recruit, and the German flags had been carefully unpicked and thrown away. This old lady wouldn't let her grandson run around in German army fatigues. That English grandmother had a limited grasp of contemporary geopolitics. It was the early 1990s, Germany had just gone through a peaceful reunification and Western Europe's largest and richest nation was an important NATO ally. At that moment in history, we stood together facing the diminished threat of a fracturing Soviet Union, rather than there being any political animosity between Bonn and London. Despite this reality, the grandmother was stuck in the past, living in the shadow of the Second World War. That was how she understood the world.

Half a century after the Second World War, even as a child, I thought her perspective was silly. I would now say it was archaistic, but as we move further forward in time, the shadow of the Second World War stretches ever longer and remains salient. Only around 2.5 per cent of British people alive today were born when the global conflict ended, but it is still a national obsession. When Prime Minister Rishi Sunak hosted an Artificial Intelligence Safety Summit in November 2023, with attendees including Elon Musk, the venue was Bletchley Park, chosen because it was a significant location in the history of computer science and the home of British Enigma code-breaking in the Second World War.[282] Even with this most forward-looking of topics, Sunak attempted to remind the world that AI had origins in the UK and the wartime work of Alan Turing: 'I want to make the UK not just the intellectual home but the geographical home of global AI safety regulation.'[283] The conference itself was criticised as a mess, and lacking purpose as big US companies had already signed up to an American government pledge on safety. Critics argued the real audience for the summit was domestic and the venue was intended to conjure up associations with Britain's leading role in the global conflict and cracking the Nazis' code. One tech executive speaking on condition of anonymity suggested the hosting of the summit was 'government by photo op'.[284]

It isn't just the Second, but even the First World War – which nobody alive can remember – that is a persistent frame of reference for British identity. Driving round the Shires it is not unusual to see the dark outline of a First World War English Tommy, with tin helmet and bayoneted rifle standing in silent vigil as you enter a village. Around him may be a flourish of poppies, once a dignified reminder of the war dead, and increasingly these red flowers are a potent symbol of British identity. This now ubiquitous motif adorns cars and vans, newspapers and football shirts in the run-up to Armistice Day and is increasingly associated with nationalism and largely divorced from its original meaning as a symbol of peace.[285] In what must be the nadir of tasteless acts of remembrance, a human-sized poppy with oversized clown shoes waddled on to the pitch holding hands with an RAF airman at a Tranmere Rovers football match in 2019. The love for poppies knows no bounds among some Britons. I once overheard two old ladies in a charity shop bickering over a pair of poppy-printed curtains. The argument was not over who would buy them – neither had any need for the drapes – but over who adored poppies the most.

The British tendency to reflect on contemporary events like the Covid pandemic and the emergence of AI through the lens of the global conflicts of the twentieth century illustrates how historical comparisons are both resilient but often lazy and unhelpful. The Second World War was not a positive national experience. It had crushing effects. Britain was far poorer and diminished on the world's stage by 1945 and endured a devastating toll of deaths, debt, social anxiety and poverty. A painful legacy partially mirrored in the fallout of coronavirus, but this echo is not the comparison that the Conservative government and their media cheerleaders wanted when it invoked Churchill and Spitfires at the outset of the pandemic response. Britain's wartime battles and twenty-first-century struggles to overcome the coronavirus crisis are viewed as national endeavours, rather than understood as global challenges dependent on cooperation and unity, not isolation and exceptionalism.

Britain is not alone in misremembering the Second World War, but it would be absurd to suggest singing 'Ten German Bombers' outside a football match was tantamount to firing cruise missiles at Kyiv. By drawing the UK and Russian examples together for discussion in the same chapter, my intention is not to imply any moral equivalence between both countries' Second World War comparisons, but rather to suggest that it is not a distinctly British characteristic to use a bullshit reading of the past to narrate the present. The terrifying ways in which Putin's regime has used fabricated memorialising of the Second World War to justify his own acts of terror serves as a vital lesson of the dangers of distorting the past and the need to think critically about how history can corrupt the present.

CONCLUSION

A Woman Needs a Man Like a Fish Needs a Bicycle

Unveiling bullshit comparisons

Challenging Authority

The battered hardback cover of my favourite childhood book was the colour of double cream and held together by yellowed stripes of Sellotape. *Winnie-the-Pooh* by A. A. Milne rested on a small wooden night stand at my bedside, like a divine text. In my edition, the hand-drawn illustrations of E. H. Shepard brought the magical tales to life. The Winnie-the-Pooh stories had been sold to Disney in the late 1960s, and in many subsequent versions the characters were reimagined. Shepard's beautiful hand-drawn sketches became uniform, soft, bulbous figures lacking subtlety. Pooh Bear morphed into a modern teddy bear shape with a toddler-friendly smile. His friends from the Hundred Acre Wood – Christopher Robin, Piglet, Tigger and Eeyore – were all redrawn, with exaggerated features. They became simple, easily reproduced cartoons, not the rich characters alive in ink lines I first encountered on the pages of my treasured storybook.

In 2013, the G20 group of powerful nations met in Saint Petersburg, Russia. Xi Jinping had recently risen to the presidency of the People's Republic of China and was attending his first summit of world leaders. During the conference he was pictured outside in shirtsleeves walking alongside US President Barack Obama. The youthful American leader looked tall, lean and energetic, and in contrast Xi was stout, laden and cumbersome. A meme soon began circulating that juxtaposed a photo of the world's two most powerful men with a cartoon of Disney's Winnie-the-Pooh and Tigger, one a plodding-looking bear and the other an effervescent tiger. Later when Xi Jinping and Japanese Prime Minister, Shinzo Abe, met and endured an achingly awkward handshake, wags on social media responded with an image that compared Abe to the depressed donkey Eeyore with Xi reprising his role as a gloomy Pooh Bear.[286] When Xi attended the opening ceremony for the Hong Kong–Zhuhai–Macau Bridge in 2018 alongside the Hong Kong Chief Executive, Carrie Lam, the pair were likened to Winnie-the-Pooh and his best friend Piglet. Lam wore blush pink and walked half a stride behind Xi. Piglet, always bright in pink, is known for being timid and naïve, although unflinchingly loyal to Pooh. For the many Hong-Kongers that saw Lam as a puppet of China, these characteristics were reflected in her leadership.

Winnie-the-Pooh has been banned in mainland China since mid-2017 because of the jibes made at Xi's expense. The Disney images became a coda for dissidents and have been censored from social media. The 2018 film *Christopher Robin* was even denied a Chinese release. There is no place for Pooh Bear behind the great Chinese firewall. So does that make Winnie-the-Pooh and Xi Jinping a bullshit comparison? While it is not nice to ridicule anyone for their appearance, Xi and those around him look thin-skinned and vain, and they clearly saw the parallels as an affront to his status. This is a *good* comparison – Xi and the other politicians targeted were primarily being satirised for their public actions rather than their personal images. Here is another progressive example of the double standard in the use of disparaging metaphors. A catchy, not-really-true metaphorical device can be used by those who otherwise lack a voice to highlight injustice, and this is the type of accessible message that can disperse through social media. A confident and truly popular leader would be able to laugh off such a silly comparison. That wasn't the case for Xi who stamped out the memes. The absurd censorship of a series of children's stories is a sign of weakness rather than strength. Moreover, it speaks to an inability of China's leadership to comprehend criticism. There is zero ability to metabolise dissent.

The example of Pooh and Xi illustrates how metaphorical comparison can be used as a focal point to draw people to form new opinions. This can have positive or negative effects as the use of such metaphors is subjective. Stamping out the comparison in China may have suppressed an opportunity for internal dissension, but at the same time, the ban on Winnie-the-Pooh drew global attention to the comparison. The light-hearted media stories that followed were only a news sidebar but will have contributed to introducing a new international audience to the autocracy of the Chinese leadership.[287]

'In the end, an iceberg lettuce won.' So begins an article in *Time* magazine on the fall of the short-lived Prime Minister Liz Truss. To American readers, British politics in the 2020s must seem utterly bizarre. As well as being satirised as leader of 'Britaly' by *The Economist*, the durability of Truss's premiership was compared to a vegetable. The British tabloid, the *Daily Star*, started the joke with a live video stream asking, 'Which wet lettuce will last longer?' The stunt captured the imagination as millions logged in to check on the survival of the sixty-pence lettuce, as *Time* observed it 'gripped the nation and underscored the chaos at the heart of Britain's government'.[288] The wilting lettuce outlasted Liz Truss and she announced her resignation after just forty-four days in office. This was another personal comparison that served a wider political objective.

Both the Truss and Xi metaphors were examples of powerful political figures being challenged by either traditional or social media. Their proponents were punching upwards, but many comparative memes are not on the side of the angles. There are countless dehumanising and upsetting bullshit comparisons that target public figures – racist images of black people and monkeys, body-shaming comparisons of celebrities at different life stages, and mockery of LGBTQ+ communities – horrific opinions that do not bear further discussion. There is no simple answer as to when and how bullshit metaphors are justified as critiques of public figures, but I would say rarely. I even think it is worth stepping back and questioning the Truss example. Would the wet lettuce comparison have been made of a male leader? I fundamentally disagreed with her politics, believed she was ill-equipped for the job of prime minister, and remain glad that she swiftly resigned, but in hindsight there is something about this highly personal and arguably gendered attack which does make me feel that perhaps the widely reported joke went too far.

Dismantling Bullshit Comparisons

A woman needs a man like a fish needs a bicycle is a feminist slogan attributed to the Australian social activist, Irina Dunn in 1970[289] and popularised by Gloria Steinem, a leader of second-wave feminism in the United States. It is a humorous comparison that follows the familiar template that 'you need *something* like you need a hole in the head', but softens the analogy with whimsy. It served the feminist movement well fifty years ago, but now feels outdated. It can be true that women may get along just fine without men, but setting two genders up in opposition to one another is not now a progressive way to conceptualise social relations. For example, when I was recently taking my two youngest children to a playgroup, I was struggling to manoeuvre the bulky double buggy through a narrow doorway. As I jostled our way in, the pram just scraped the door jamb and a watching old lady quipped, 'Typical male driver.' I brushed the comment aside as I focused on unbuckling an infant and a toddler and setting them to play with building blocks. With the children settled, I stopped to think about what she had just said and for comparison's sake flipped the gendering in my mind. If my wife had been trying to coax the buggy through that same space and an old man had heckled her with 'typical female driver', would that have been acceptable? No. And it isn't acceptable that she said the inverse to a man. The subtext of her comment was that the playgroup was a woman's space. To be fair it wasn't a 'you're not welcome here' but it was a 'you don't know what you're doing here' jibe. Dads often face these types of social exclusions. In 2018, Daniel Craig suffered very public mockery over his parenting. TV presenter Piers Morgan compared Craig with his on-screen persona, James Bond, and questioned his masculinity for wearing a baby carrier in an infamous tweet: 'Oh 007 . . . not you as well?!!! #papoose #emasculatedBond'.[290]

I bring these vignettes aside the 'a woman needs a man like a fish needs a bicycle' comparison to illustrate how the feminism of the 1970s which spawned the slogan is now out of date. If we want to create a society where men and women are treated equally as parents and guardians of young children, we need to shed the gendering of activities like pushing a pram or wearing a papoose. We need to bring the roles of genders together, rather than think how women can manage without men or vice versa. Inclusion rather than parallel tracks should be the common goal. There is a long way to travel to meet this aspiration.

Countering Bullshit Comparisons

We need to rip away the magicians' cloaks that shroud comparisons to reveal what they conceal. The first examples in *People* illustrated how bullshit comparisons prioritise the individual in society and reify certain identities: male, white, aggressive and competitive, as being more meaningful and valuable. Comparison pits people against one another rather than promoting cooperation. It atomises society compelling us to be individual and assertively entrepreneurial, rather than privileging collaboration, recognising the teams that make great people, and acknowledging the social advantages that enable some to succeed while others fail. Excessive and inaccurate comparison can be a socially corrosive process that entrenches inequalities across families, workplaces and wider society.

Comparisons of people can be brutalising. To return to the arch-bullshitter, Donald Trump makes provocative use of *Metaphors.* He compares his political opponents to 'vermin': 'We pledge to you that we will root out the communists, Marxists, fascists, and the radical left thugs that live like vermin within the confines of our country,' he proclaimed to a crowd in New Hampshire.[291] This dangerous metaphorical language has been called out for the invidious comparison that it is. Historian and cultural critic, Ruth Ben-Ghiat, raises deep concerns about the impact of the 'othering' of groups such as political opponents, or as Trump has widely done so elsewhere, immigrants, as signs of his authoritarianism: 'You need to get people to feel they have an existential threat facing them,' argues Ben-Ghiat. 'And the more they feel uncertain and fearful, the more the strongmen can appear and say, "I alone can fix it."'.[292] Trumpian bullshit is widely critiqued, but the broader misuse of metaphors for personal attacks by Trump's supporters, other politicians, journalists, and authors from across the political spectrum need to be robustly critiqued. It is the job of a free press, academia and a wider engaged civil society to continually castigate such abuses of language as they matter, not because they are deplorable turns of phrase, but because they can have real-world consequences and be a harbinger of totalitarianism. Trump's dehumanising language clearly echoes Fascist speech.[293] My hope is that *'that's a bullshit comparison'* becomes a ready response that eviscerates toxic metaphors.

After *People*, the evidence from the *Place* section expanded in scale and illustrated how the fundamental relationships between places are absent from popular comparisons. Here I argued that geographical comparisons need to be relational. At its most basic, relational comparison is an argument that there is an interconnection between places that produces winners and losers. For some schools to be outstanding, others must be inadequate, and for some nations to be developed, others must be developing. To correctly compare places that are prosperous and impoverished we should not just consider the circumstances of place X or Y in isolation and list their similarities and differences.

Rather the relationships between conditions of poverty in one place and affluence elsewhere need to be analysed together. This enables us to identify connections between their levels of progress or their relations to wider networks, be that the English university system, international tourist markets, the globalised healthcare sector or the world economy. Mapping these contours of inequality can enable policymaking that reshapes the relations between successful and failing places.

To return to another touchstone example, England's Ofsted school inspections exemplify how *metrics* produce bullshit comparisons of *places*. These simplistic single-word evaluations are increasingly deplored. The Beyond Ofsted Inquiry, chaired by former schools minister Lord Jim Knight and funded by the Teachers' National Education Union, has said the system is 'toxic' and 'not fit for purpose'. While the Department for Education maintained Ofsted has a 'crucial role' in reassuring parents, Knight countered, arguing: 'It's created a culture of fear in our schools, and if anybody thinks that fear is the basis for sustained improvement, rather than support, then I think they've got it completely wrong.' The former Schools Minister's robust language all but says the school inspection metrics are bullshit.[294] Perhaps the next time these or other rotten metrics are skewed in an inquiry, they'll be called out as *bullshit comparisons*.

Thirdly, the last section, *History*, argues that a selective reading of the past provides material to develop analogies that serve present-day agendas. The Second World War is an immovable anchor for a certain brand of British values, the space race offers false hope of a readily achievable solution to climate change that pretty much allows us to live our lives, business as usual, and casting China as a neo-colonial power conceals the ways in which Western nations have exploited the Global South for centuries. Historical comparisons are some of the most egregious, but also persuasive, ideological tools. A well-presented historical analogy may at first appear objective and authoritative, but when distorted by the bias of an author, comparison can be manipulated to champion ideas that stand as obstacles to social, political and environmental progress.

The apartheid analogy flattens the complexity of the Israel-Palestine conflict, but it is not the only egregious comparison that has been applied to the situation. As this ongoing tragedy continues to unfold, other historical comparisons are loudly invoked to try and understand the disquieting present. In the aftermath of Hamas's terror attacks of October 2023, Israel's former prime minister, Naftali Bennett, repeatedly referred to his enemy as 'Nazi Hamas'.[295] Suggesting Nazi Germany was a *model* for Hamas's raids on Israel is a deeply misleading parallel to draw. The Nazi analogy would be understandable from a widow in the raw intensity of grief, a victim of rape, or someone facing the nightmare reality of not knowing if they will ever see a kidnapped loved one again, but not from an experienced statesman. At such moments, politicians should be in command of their rhetoric and use words deliberately to set the tone for the nation. Drawing a direct comparison between Hamas and the Nazi regime was disproportionate. The threat posed by Hamas was of a different order of magnitude, and although Hamas's 1988 covenant called for the destruction of Israel, as a combat force it is inherently weak and was unable even to mount a defence of Gaza from the IDF's invasion. Hamas's barbaric surprise terror attacks against civilian and military targets was a tragedy for Israel unparalleled in the twenty-first century, but Hamas does not pose an existential threat akin to the Third Reich, as Israelis are protected by the overwhelming military superiority of the IDF and are the region's dominant power.

Bennett's comparison was a brazen instrumentalisation of the Holocaust and a collective vilification of Palestinians.[296] This misuse of the memory of genocide is a conceit that has been repeatedly deployed by Israeli leaders on the political right. Among the first to critique the comparisons of a conflict between Israel and its neighbours and the Holocaust was Isaac Deutscher, a Polish historian of Jewish heritage. Writing in 1967 following Israel's crushing victory in the Six Day War, he argued that for Israel's government, 'Nothing was easier for their own propagandists, aided by Arab verbal threats than to play up the fear of another "final solution" threatening the Jews.'[297]

Prophetically, Deutscher believed that the IDF's far-reaching military success in 1967 would be a disaster for Israel itself as it spawned a '"doctrine" that holds that Israel's security lies in periodic warfare which every few years must reduce the Arab states to impotence.' The same may well be true in the aftermath of Israel's inevitable military accomplishments in Gaza. Lessons from the past can help formulate answers to the problems of the present, but false comparisons cannot.

Like dirty windowpanes, bullshit comparisons give murky, distorted perspectives to the world. The arguments in this book should give you the means to break them. The examples in the conclusion from Ben-Ghiat on Trump, Knight on Ofsted, and Deutscher on Nazification, have cast daylight on toxic metaphors for people, misleading metrics of places, and false models from history. This book is a call to do more to illuminate bullshit comparisons. It is not meant to be read as a tirade against comparison, but rather is positioned as a helpful and hopeful guide.

Comparisons can spotlight injustices and provide the stimulus for progressive action. Use comparisons carefully and selectively. When you read a comparison from any source: in politics, the media or your own social circle, stop and think about it critically: What agenda might the comparison be trying to advance? How could it be misrepresenting gender? Might it be promoting a colonial mentality? Could it be pushing market forces further into everyday life? And do remember you can always call bullshit on a comparison floundering in the dark waters between fact and fiction.

Acknowledgements

I am very grateful to Renata Kasprzak for her persistent confidence in the book, and support in getting a wild idea to a wide audience. The Contested Development Research Group, in the geography department at King's College London, gave valuable feedback and encouragement on several draft chapters. All my colleagues at King's are a constant source of inspiration, the department buzzes with excitement, and I can't imagine ever working elsewhere. Phil Hubbard led me into the world of animal geographies which gave me the confidence to write about dogs. Lisbon has been a constant source of inspiration and the fieldwork I did there with Archie Davies helped me think differently about urban change. I'm thankful for Clare Herrick bringing me into the Sierra Leone research as I would have never otherwise ventured to study hospitals. Writing on Israel-Palestine has been the hardest topic I have ever worked on, and Mark Griffiths' bravery and care in approaching that field has been an inspiration. Over many years of research in Mozambique, including trips across to South Africa, and projects in Zambia, there were many friends that encouraged and assisted me, oftentimes on prickly, controversial topics. I wholeheartedly acknowledge their help, but it is better to leave them unnamed. Finally, the most important acknowledgement is the constant love and support of Emma Rigby.

References

1   The White House, 'William J. Clinton: The 42ⁿᵈ President of The United States', *The White House*, https://www.whitehouse.gov/about-the-white-house/presidents/william-j-clinton/, 2023.

2   D J Trump, *Great Again: How to Fix our Crippled America*, (New York: Simon and Schuster, 2016), p.11.

3   H G Frankfurt, *On Bullshit*, (Princeton and Oxford, Princeton University Press, 2005).

4   H Ramer and J Colvin, 'Trump compares himself to Nelson Mandela after filing for New Hampshire primary', *PBS News Hour*, https://www.pbs.org/newshour/politics/trump-compares-himself-to-nelson-mandela-after-filing-for-new-hampshire-primary, 23 October 2023.

5   G Lakoff and M Johnson, *Metaphors We Live By*, (Chicago: The University of Chicago Press, 1981).

6   D Shariatmadari, 'Swarms, floods and marauders: the toxic metaphors of the migration debate', *The Guardian*, https://www.theguardian.com/commentisfree/2015/aug/10/migration-debate-metaphors-swarms-floods-marauders-migrants, 10 August 2015.

7   The Economist, 'Welcome to Britaly', *The Economist*, https://www.economist.com/leaders/2022/10/19/welcome-to-britaly, 19 October 2022.

8   I Lambertini, 'A remark from Ambassador Ingio Lambertini', *Italian Embassy in the UK*, https://twitter.com/ItalyinUK/status/1583083342320525313/photo/1, 20 October 2022.

9   C Goodhart 'Problems of Monetary Management: The U.K. Experience', *Papers in Monetary Economics*, 1, 1, (1975) p.1–20.

10 P Adab, A M Rouse, M A Mohammed, T Marshall, 'Performance league tables: the NHS deserves better', *British Medical Journal*, 324, 7329, (2002), p.95–98.

11 Indy100 Staff, 'Michael Gove might be prime minister, so people are resharing this ridiculous exchange', *Indy 100*, https://www.indy100.

com/celebrities/michael-gove-might-be-prime-minister-so-people-are-resharing-this-ridiculous-exchange-7301081, 1 July 2016.

12 S Weale, 'Former inspector says Ofsted statement that most England state schools are good is 'nonsense'', *The Guardian*, https://www.theguardian.com/education/2023/oct/24/former-inspector-says-ofsted-statement-that-most-england-state-schools-are-good-is-nonsense, 24 October 2023.

13 B Forgács and C Pléh, 'The Fluffy Metaphors of Climate Science', in Shyam Wuppuluri and A. C. Grayling (eds) *Metaphors and Analogies in Sciences and Humanities*, (New York: Springer, 2022), 447–477.

14 H Davidson, 'China bans celebrity rankings in bid to 'rectify chaos in the fan community'', *The Guardian*, https://www.theguardian.com/world/2021/aug/27/china-bans-celebrity-rankings-in-bid-to-rectify-chaos-in-the-fan-community, 27 August 2021.

15 A Brooks, *The End of Development*, (London: Zed Books, 2017).

16 A Brooks, 'Controversial, corrupt and illegal: ethical implications of investigating difficult topics: Reflections on fieldwork in southern Africa.' In J Lunn (ed) *Fieldwork in the Global South: Ethical Challenges and Dilemmas*, (Abingdon: Routledge, 2014) p.34–48.

17 S Marche, *The Next Civil War: Dispatches from the American Future*, (New York, Simon and Schuster, 2022).

18 G Roberts, 'Whose 'Stalingrad' will Bakhmut be?', *Responsible Statecraft*, https://responsiblestatecraft.org/2023/03/14/whose-stalingrad-will-bakhmut-be/, 14 May 2023.

19 D Hannan, 'Emmanuel Macron, the new Napoleon? No, he's a Poundland Putin' *The Daily Mail*, https://www.dailymail.co.uk/debate/article-9547241/DANIEL-HANNAN-Emmanuel-Macron-new-Napoleon-No-hes-Poundland-Putin.html, 5 May 2021.

20 N Kampouris, 'UK PM Boris Johnson Compares Brexit to Tortures of Greek Hero Prometheus', *Greek Reporter*, https://greekreporter.com/2019/09/25/uk-pm-boris-johnson-compares-brexit-to-tortures-of-greek-hero-prometheus, 25 September 2019.

21 ITV News, 'Who was Cincinnatus, and why did Boris Johnson mention him in his speech?' *ITV X*, https://www.itv.com/news/2022-09-06/boris-johnson-likens-himself-to-roman-who-returned-as-dictator-in-final-speech, 6 September 2022.

22 Frankfurt, *On Bullshit*.

23 K Davies, 'Siblings, Stories and the Self: The Sociological Significance of Young People's Sibling Relationships', *Sociology*, 49, 4, (2014), 679–695.

24 W O Eaton and L R Enns, 'Sex differences in human motor activity level', *Psychological Bulletin*, 100, 1, (1986), 19–28.

25 R Shelton, 'Bottom Shuffling Babies' *University Hospitals Dorset: NHS Foundation Trust*, https://www.uhd.nhs.uk/uploads/about/docs/our_publications/patient_information_leaflets/Childrens_therapy/Bottom_shuffling_Babies.pdf, 1 February 2021.

[26] S Özçalskan and S Goldin-Meadow, 'Sex differences in language first appear in gesture', *Developmental Science*, 13, 5, (2011), 752–760.

[27] UC Davis Health, 'When to start potty training: what age should kids start (and do boys really take longer)?' *UC Davis Health: News*, https://health.ucdavis.edu/news/headlines/when-to-start-potty-training-what-age-should-kids-start-and-do-boys-really-take-longer/2021/03#:~:text=Girls%20learn%20faster%2C%20usually%20completing,cues%20from%20the%20older%20kids, 3 March 2021.

[28] J K Geddes, 'Developmental Differences Between Boys and Girls', *What to Except*, https://www.whattoexpect.com/first-year/development-and-milestones/differences-boys-girls#:~:text=Yet%20both%20are%20wrong%3A%20Studies,parents%20believe%20boys%20start%20sooner, 15 December 2021.

[29] F Keegan, 'Take It From A Late Bloomer: Stop Comparing Yourself To Other People Your Age', *British Vogue*, https://www.vogue.co.uk/article/being-a-late-bloomer, 9 July 2023.

[30] J Jerrim, P Parker, N Shure, 'Bullshitters. Who Are They and What Do We Know about Their Lives?' *IZA Institute of labour Economic: Discussion Paper Series*, 12282, (2019).

[31] NBC News, 'UK Immigration Minister Resigns Over Illegal Cleaning Lady' *NBC News*, https://www.nbcnews.com/news/world/uk-immigration-minister-resigns-over-illegal-cleaning-lady-n25611, 9 February 2014.

[32] A Mahdawi, '"Who's the man?" Why the gender divide in same-sex relationships is a farce', *The Guardian*, https://www.theguardian.com/lifeandstyle/2016/aug/23/same-sex-relationship-gender-roles-chores, 23 August 2016.

[33] NPR, 'Same-Sex Couples May Have More Egalitarian Relationships', *NPR: All Things Considered*, https://www.npr.org/2014/12/29/373835114/same-sex-couples-may-have-more-egalitarian-relationships, 29 December 2014.

[34] M Macasero, 'Who is the GOAT of basketball? Taking a closer look at the five greatest players ever', *Sportsskeeda*, https://www.sportskeeda.com/basketball/news-who-goat-basketball-taking-closer-look-five-greatest-players-ever, 27 June 2023.

[35] K Jain, '"Patrick Mahomes Has a Chance to be the 1st Michael Jordan of Football," Opined NFL Analyst Max Kellerman After Super Bowl LVII', *The Sports Rush*, https://thesportsrush.com/nfl-news-patrick-mahomes-has-a-chance-to-be-the-first-michael-jordan-of-football-opined-nfl-analyst-max-kellerman-after-super-bowl-lvii/, 13 August 2023.

[36] J Livesey and A Milne, 'Diego Maradona: Legend or cheat? From Hand of God to cocaine battles, everything you need to know', *The Mirror*, https://www.mirror.co.uk/sport/football/news/diego-maradona-legend-cheat-hand-21731786, 21 March 2020.

37 T Beattie, 'Lionel Messi arrival at Inter Miami causes "unprecedented" issue at sponsors Adidas', *The Mirror,* https://www.mirror.co.uk/sport/football/news/lionel-messi-inter-miami-shirt-30525769, 22 July 2023.

38 S Lowe, 'Bojan Krkic: 'I had anxiety attacks but no one wants to talk about that. Football's not interested' *The Guardian,* https://www.theguardian.com/football/2018/may/18/bojan-krkic-interview-anxiety-attacks-football, 18 May 2018.

39 E Corbella, 'Who is Marc Guiu? Barcelona's 17-year-old goal-scorer: origins, comparisons and . . . how Xavi sees him', *Marca,* https://www.marca.com/en/football/barcelona/2023/10/23/6536653c268e3ea5028b456f.html, 23 October 2023.

40 S Lowe, 'Bojan, the anxious wonderkid, is back at Barcelona guiding next generation', *The Guardian,* https://www.theguardian.com/football/2023/nov/03/bojan-the-anxious-wonderkid-is-back-at-barcelona-guiding-next-generation, 3 November 2023.

41 V Gouttebarge, H Aoki, and G M Kekhoffs. 'Prevalence and determinants of symptoms related to mental disorders in retired male professional footballers', *Journal of Sports Medicine and Physical Fitness,* 56, 5, (2016), 648–54.

42 DW, 'Martin Bengtsson and the Dark Side of Football', *DW Kick off!,* https://www.youtube.com/watch?v=KyEz8xh3og0, 21 April 2016.

43 Kuper, 'Ronaldo vs Messi: who won?' *Financial Times,* 4 June 2023.

44 The Blizzard, 'A Game for Individuals', *The Blizzard,* https://www.theblizzard.co.uk/article/game-individuals, 1 December 2014.

45 W Downes 'BOOT-IFUL Neymar to bank £750,000 from Nike for finally beating Cristiano Ronaldo and Lionel Messi to Ballon d'Or', *The Sun,* https://www.thesun.co.uk/sport/football/5719998/neymar-nike-ballon-dor-money/, 4 March 2018.

46 A Wonke, 'Ronaldo', *Universal Pictures* (2015).

47 L Donegan, 'Wie genius pitted against big boys', *The Guardian,* https://www.theguardian.com/sport/2004/jan/15/golf.lawrencedonegan, 15 January 2004.

48 J Strege, 'Wie has chance to become 'second only to Danica Patrick' in endorsement earnings among U.S. women athletes', *The Loop,* https://www.golfdigest.com/story/michelle-wie-has-opportunity-t, 26 June 2014.

49 D Dethier, 'Michelle Wie dishes on her playing future, funny conversations with Tiger Woods', *Golf,* https://golf.com/news/michelle-wie-tiger-woods-playing-future/, 9 October 2019.

50 PGA Tour, 'Interview with Michelle Wie', *PGA Tour: Archive* https://www.pgatour.com/news/2008/07/25/wietranscript072508.html, 25 July 2008.

51 A Licata, ''We won't accept anything less than equal pay': US Women's Soccer team speaks out after mediation talks quickly break down', *Business Insider,* https://www.businessinsider.com/megan-rapinoe-us-soccer-equal-pay-negotiations-2019-8?r=US&IR=T, 15 August 2019.

[52] C Kelly, 'Megan Rapinoe to Trump: 'Your message is excluding people'', *CNN Politics*, https://edition.cnn.com/2019/07/09/politics/megan-rapinoe-anderson-cooper-trump-cnntv/index.html, 10 July 2019.

[53] The World, 'Ada Hegerberg, first female Ballon d'Or winner: 'A huge step forward'', *The World: Sports*, https://www.pri.org/stories/2019-01-11/ada-hegerberg-first-female-ballon-dor-winner-huge-step-forward, 11 January 2019.

[54] BBC News, 'BBC reveals 100 great British heroes', *BBC News: Entertainment*, http://news.bbc.co.uk/1/hi/entertainment/tv_and_radio/2208532.stm, 2 August 2002.

[55] BBC Gloucestershire, 'Boy Scout founder Lord Baden-Powell 'executed PoW'' *BBC News: England*, http://news.bbc.co.uk/1/hi/england/gloucestershire/8403956.stm, 9 December 2009.

[56] BBC News, 'BBC reveals 100 great British heroes'.

[57] L Givetash, 'White House compares Trump-Churchill leadership styles, and historians scoff', *NBC News*, https://www.nbcnews.com/news/world/white-house-compares-trump-churchill-leadership-styles-historians-scoff-n1224556, 6 June 2020.

[58] J Charmley, '*Churchill: The End of Glory: A Political Biography*', (London, Faber, 2009)

[59] R Toye, '*Churchill's Empire: The World That Made Him and the World He Made*', (London, Pan, 2010).

[60] J Cheng-Morris, 'Tory MP compares Boris Johnson to Alexander the Great – 'He's saved our democracy'' *Yahoo! News*, https://uk.news.yahoo.com/boris-johnson-compared-alexander-great-132504961.html, 30 December 2020.

[61] Florence Griswold Museum, 'The Great Americans: Portraits By Jac Lahav', *Florence Griswold Museum*, https://florencegriswoldmuseum.org/jac-lahav/, 9 February 2019.

[62] S Scott, 'New data reveals UK knows "shockingly little" about Black British history', *Bloomsbury News*, https://www.bloomsbury.com/uk/connect/latest-news/new-data-reveals-uk-knows-shockingly-little-about-black-british-history/, 27 October 2023.

[63] D Sandbrook and T Holland, 'Young Churchill: Born to Lead', *The Rest is History*, Goal Hanger Podcasts, 239, 2022.

[64] D J Hall, 'Bulldog Churchill: The Evolution Of A Famous Image', *International Churchill Society*, https://winstonchurchill.org/publications/finest-hour/finest-hour-106/bulldog-churchill-the-evolution-of-a-famous-image/, 29 August 2013.

[65] W Dockter, 'Pigs, poodles, and African lions - meet Churchill the animal-lover', *The Telegraph*, https://www.telegraph.co.uk/news/winston-churchill/11370727/Pigs-poodles-and-African-lions-meet-Churchill-the-animal-lover.html, 27 January 2015.

⁶⁶ M Lazaris, 'Crufts 2020: The positives and the problems', *RSPCA*, https://www.rspca.org.uk/-/a-guest-blog-written-by-our-passionate-vet-and-animal-lover-dr-michael-lazaris, 7 January 2021.

⁶⁷ D G O'Neill, J Elliott, D B Church, P D McGreevy, P C Thomson, and D C Brodbelt, 'Chronic kidney disease in dogs in UK veterinary practices: prevalence, risk factors, and survival', *Journal of Veterinary Internal Medicine*, 27, 4, (2013), p.814–21.

⁶⁸ L L Farrell, J J Schoenebeck, P Wiener, D N Clements, and K M Summers. 'The challenges of pedigree dog health: approaches to combating inherited disease', *Canine Genetics and Epidemiology*, 2, 1, (2015), p.1–14.

⁶⁹ C Toureille, 'Top dog!' *Daily Mail*, https://www.dailymail.co.uk/femail/article-6792295/Crufts-Day-4-glossy-pooches-owners-nervously-await-Best-Show.html, 10 March 2019.

⁷⁰ Crufts, 'Interview with Crufts Best in Show winner, 2019', https://www.crufts.org.uk/blogs/interview-with-crufts-best-in-show-winner-2019/, 1 December 2020.

⁷¹ *Country Life*, 'Dukes and their dogs', https://www.countrylife.co.uk/articles/dukes-dogs-britains-aristocracy-just-mad-canine-friends-rest-us-171496, 23 December 2017.

⁷² E West, 'Staffordshire Bull Terriers: Why the Underclass is Bad for the Environment', http://blogs.telegraph.co.uk/news/edwest/100006300/staffordshire-bull-terriers-why-the-underclass-is-bad-for-the-environment/, 2009, cited in D McCarthy, 'Dangerous dogs, dangerous owners and the waste management of an "irredeemable species"', *Sociology*, 50, 3, (2016), p.560–75.

⁷³ K Nelson, 'The dog breed most likely to bite you has been revealed', the *Independent*, https://www.independent.co.uk/news/uk/home-news/dog-breed-most-likely-attack-bite-you-revealed-a7166296.html, 3 August 2016.

⁷⁴ H J Nast, 'Loving . . . whatever: Alienation, neoliberalism and pet-love in the twenty-first century', *ACME: An International E-Journal for Critical Geographies*, 5, 2, (2006), p.300–27.

⁷⁵ P Hubbard and A Brooks, 'Animals and urban gentrification: Displacement and injustice in the trans-species city', *Progress in Human Geography*, 45, 6, (2021), p.1490 1511.

⁷⁶ ViaGen Pets, 'The Worldwide Leader In Cloning The Animals We Love', https://viagenpets.com/, 2021.

⁷⁷ Microsoft News (2020). 'Hairdresser welcomes cloned French bulldog to make his quarantine bearable'https://www.msn.com/en-gb/news/world/hairdresser-welcomes-cloned-french-bulldog-to-make-his-quarantine-bearable/vi-BB12EEF9, 15 April 2020.

⁷⁸ S Swart, 'Dogs and dogma: A discussion of the socio-political construction of Southern African dog "breeds" as a window onto social history', *South African Historical Journal*, 48, 1, (2003), p.190–206.

[79] J Doble, 'Can Dogs be Racist? The Colonial Legacies of Racialized Dogs in Kenya and Zambia', *History Workshop Journal*, 89, 1, (2020) p.68–89.

[80] L Van Sittert and S Swart, *Canis Africanis* (Brill, Leiden: 2008).

[81] R Bray, I Gooskens, S Moses, L Kahn, and J Seekings, *Growing Up in the New South Africa: Childhood and Adolescence in Post-Apartheid Cape Town*, (University of Cape Town: 2011).

[82] J M Coetzee, *Disgrace*, (Secker & Warburg, London: 1999)

[83] I Dande and S Swart, 'History, politics and dogs in Zimbabwean literature, c. 1975–2015', Tydskrif vir Letterkunde, 55, 3, (2018), p.152–73.

[84] S Chinodya, *Can We Talk and Other Stories* (Weaver Press, Bulawayo: 2017).

[85] T Maluleke. 'I am an African and I grieve for my dog Bruno', *Mail and Guardian*, https://mg.co.za/article/2015-03-06-i-am-an-african-and-i-grieve-for-my-dog-bruno/ 6 March 2015.

[86] G Baderoon, 'Animal likenesses: dogs and the boundary', *Journal of African Cultural Studies*, 29, 3, (2017), p. 345–61.

[87] G Raddi, 'Universities and the NHS must join forces to boost student mental health', the *Guardian*, https://www.theguardian.com/education/2019/feb/15/universities-and-the-nhs-must-join-forces-to-boost-student-mental-health, 15 February 2019.

[88] A Gani, 'Tuition fees "have led to surge in students seeking counselling"', the *Guardian*, https://www.theguardian.com/education/2016/mar/13/tuition-fees-have-led-to-surge-in-students-seeking-counselling, 13 March 2016.

[89] S Miriyala, 'Pass/Fail Grading Systems in Medical School', *American Association for Anatomy*, https://anatomy.org/AAA/News-Journals/Newsletter-Articles/Pass-Fail-Grading-Systems-in-Medical-School.aspx?_zs=iinWO1&_zl=T5PT5, 2021

[90] Swedish Council for Higher Education, 'The Swedish higher education system', ww.uhr.se, 2007.

[91] HESA, 'What are HE students' progression rates and qualifications?' https://www.hesa.ac.uk/data-and-analysis/students/outcomes, 31 January 2023.

[92] S Weale, 'Proportion of students in England awarded first-class degrees soars', the *Guardian*, 19 November 2020.

[93] OfS, 'Analysis of degree classifications over time – changes in graduate attainment from 2010–11 to 2018–19', *Office for Students*, https://www.officeforstudents.org.uk/publications/analysis-of-degree-classifications-over-time-changes-in-graduate-attainment-from-2010-11-to-2018-19/, 19 November 2020.

[94] S Gamsu and M Donnelly, 'Social Network Analysis Methods and the Geography of Education: Regional Divides and Elite Circuits in the School to University Transition in the UK', *Tijdschrift voor economische en sociale geografie*, 112, 4, (2020), p.370–386.

95 D Bishop, 'NSS and teaching excellence: the wrong measure, wrongly analysed', *Times Higher Education*, https://www.timeshighereducation.com/blog/nss-and-teaching-excellence-wrong-measure-wrongly-analysed, 4 January 2016, and A Buckley 'How much are your NSS results really telling you?' *WONKHE*, https://wonkhe.com/blogs/how-much-are-your-nss-results-really-telling-you/, 20 March 2019.

96 J H S Cheng, and H W Marsh, 'National Student Survey: Are differences between universities and courses reliable and meaningful?', *Oxford Review of Education*, 36, 6, (2010), p.693–712.

97 OfS, 'The National Student Survey: Consistency, controversy and change', *Office for Students*, https://www.officeforstudents.org.uk/publications/the-national-student-survey-consistency-controversy-and-change/, 19 February 2020.

98 C McCaig, 'The marketisation of English higher education: A policy analysis of a risk-based system', (Emerald: Leeds, 2018).

99 School of Global Affairs, '100 Black Women Professors NOW programme', *King's College London*, https://sspp.newsweaver.com/sga-news/1pe4eglnr3t1n49gezdcfq?email=true&lang=en&a=6&p=5943908 5&t=30007613, 25 May 2021.

100 W Evans, 'Bullying is a feature of UK research universities, not a bug', *Times Higher Education*, https://www.timeshighereducation.com/opinion/bullying-feature-uk-research-universities-not-bug, 30 August 2023.

101 D Sayer, 'Five reasons why the REF is not fit for purpose', the *Guardian*, https://www.theguardian.com/higher-education-network/2014/dec/15/research-excellence-framework-five-reasons-not-fit-for-purpose, 15 December 2014, and K Lesnik-Oberstein, 'Marketisation "is wrecking teaching and research"', *Times Higher Education*, https://www.timeshighereducation.com/blog/marketisation-wrecking-teaching-and-research, 12 June 2015.

102 R Harris, (2019). 'The Certain Uncertainty of University Rankings', *RPubs*, https://rpubs.com/profrichharris/convincing_stories1, 1 November 2019.

103 NL Times, 'Utrecht University chose not to be included on the Times Higher Education rankings', https://nltimes.nl/2023/09/29/utrecht-university-chose-included-times-higher-education-rankings, 29 September 2023.

104 R Ghazali, 'Sheffield student slams process to shut down Department of Archaeology as "unethical"', *The Star*, https://www.thestar.co.uk/education/sheffield-student-slams-process-to-shut-down-department-of-archaeology-as-unethical-3277758, 18 June 2021.

105 D Goodhart, *The Road to Somewhere: The Populist Revolt and the Future of Politics* (Hurst, London: 2017).

106 J Grove, 'Stefan Grimm inquest: new policies may not have prevented suicide', *Times Higher Education*, https://www.timeshighereducation.

com/news/stefan-grimm-inquest-new-policies-may-not-have-prevented-suicide/2019563.article, 9 April 2015.

[107] The Tab, "'They treat us like shit": Professor Grimm's email sent weeks after his death', https://thetab.com/uk/imperial/2014/12/02/they-treat-us-like-shit-professor-grimms-email-sent-weeks-after-his-death-7076, 2 December 2014.

[108] Imperial College London, 'Statement on Professor Grimm', https://www.imperial.ac.uk/news/162449/statement-professor-stefan-grimm/, 4 December 2014.

[109] BBC, 'Ofsted chief admits culture of fear around school inspections', *Sunday with Laura Kuenssberg*, https://www.bbc.co.uk/news/live/uk-politics-65358122, 23 April 2023.

[110] R Adams, 'Ofsted's "simplistic judgments" no longer fit for purpose, schools experts warn', the *Guardian*, https://www.theguardian.com/education/2023/nov/04/ofsteds-simplistic-judgments-no-longer-fit-for-purpose-schools-experts-warn, 4 November 2023.

[111] Ibid.

[112] M Frazer, 'The unintended consequences of pursuing an 'outstanding", *Cambridge University Press and Assessment*, https://www.cem.org/blog/the-unintended-consequences-of-pursuing-an-outstanding, 6 October 2017.

[113] B Jeffreys, 'Work-related suicide probe call after death of head teacher Ruth Perry', *BBC News*, https://www.bbc.co.uk/news/education-65651606, 22 May 2023.

[114] Instituto Nacional De Estatistica, 'Tourism Statistics', 2016, https://www.ine.pt/xportal/xmain?xpid=INE&xpgid=ine_publicacoes&PUBLICACOESpub_boui=299820469&PUBLICACOESmodo=2, 2017.

[115] Reuters, 'Foreign tourism to Portugal sets new record in May, helped by US visitors', https://www.reuters.com/world/europe/foreign-tourism-portugal-sets-new-record-may-helped-by-us-visitors-2023-06-30/, 30 June 2023.

[116] S Kule, 'Lisbon Emigration: Why millennials are moving to the Portuguese capital in their droves', the *Independent*, https://www.independent.co.uk/travel/europe/lisbon-emigration-tourism-millennials-freelancers-digital-nomad-portugal-airbnb-a7967376.html, 5 October 2017.

[117] L Morrison, 'Why this is Europe's best work-and-play capital', *BBC Business Traveller*, https://www.bbc.com/worklife/article/20160419-europes-best-work-and-play-city, 20 April 2016.

[118] F Dunlop, '7 reasons Lisbon could be coolest capital in Europe', *CNN Travel*, https://edition.cnn.com/travel/article/lisbon-coolest-city/index.html, 25 August 2017.

[119] A Goss, 'Barcelona bar none', *Financial Times*, 20 August 2023.

[120] J Temperton, 'Web Summit ditches Dublin for Lisbon', Wired, https://www.wired.co.uk/article/web-summit-dublin-lisbon-2016, 23 August 2015.

121 P Cosgrave, 'The Next Chapter', Web Summit, https://websummit. com/blog/the-next-chapter/, 23 September 2015.

122 A Davies and A Brooks, 'Interpellation and Urban transformation: Lisbon's sardine subjects', *Social & Cultural Geography*, 22. 7, (2021), p.956–978.

123 Turismo de Lisboa, 'Plano Estratégico para o Turismo na Região de Lisboa 2015–2019', https://www.am-lisboa.pt/documentos/1518980510Y8fG-P7vq7Qv09AI7.pdf, 1 October 2014, p.19–25.

124 L Nofre, Í Sánchez-Fuarros, J C Martins and P Pereira, 'Exploring Nightlife and Urban Change in Bairro Alto, Lisbon', *City & Community*, 16, 3, (2017), p.330–344, p.330.

125 Sovereign, 'Residency In Portugal: Portugal Passive Income (D7)', Visahttps://www.sovereigngroup.com/portugal/private-clients/ residency-in-portugal/portugal-passive-income-d7-visa/, 2024.

126 K Peddicord, 'Killing The Golden (Visa) Goose', *Forbes*, https://www. forbes.com/sites/kathleenpeddicord/2023/08/29/killing-the-golden-visa-goose/, 29 August 2023.

127 Portugal News, 'The Golden Visa Program is NOT over', https://www. theportugalnews.com/news/2023-10-19/the-golden-visa-program-is-not-over/82442, 19 October 2023.

128 A I P Esteves, M L C Fonseca,. and J S M Malheiros, 'Labour market integration of immigrants in Portugal in times of austerity: resilience, in situ responses and re-emigration', *Journal of Ethnic and Migration Studies*, 44, 14, 2018, p.2375–2391.

129 Euronews, 'The Dark side of Tourism: Lisbon's "terramotourism"', https://www.euronews.com/2017/09/19/lisbon-s-tourism-magnet-is-kicking-out-local-residents, 9 December 2019.

130 Fundação José Neves, (2023). '*Área Metropolitana de Lisboa: Salários*', Brighter Future, https://brighterfuture.joseneves.org/raio-x-regioes?_ga=2.147040882.450956960.1670884727-1920835700.1670884727, 2024.

131 M Pereira and P Nunes, 'Thousands protest in Portugal over housing crisis', *Reuters*, https://www.reuters.com/world/europe/thousands-protest-portugal-over-housing-crisis-2023-04-01/, 2 April 2023.

132 S Tulumello and A Colombo, 'Inclusive communities, exclusionary city, planning? Mapping condominos fechados semi-quantitatively in Lisbon, Cascais (and Barreiro)', In 'Changing societies: legacies and challenges', *Ambiguous inclusions: inside out, outside in, Vol 1.* (Imprensa de Ciências Sociais, Lisbon: 2018), p.481–507.

133 Davies and Brooks. 'Interpellation and Urban transformation'.

134 L F G, Mendes, (2012). 'Nobilitação urbana marginal enquanto prática emancipatória: Alternativa ao discurso hegemónico da cidade criativa?' *Revista Crítica De Ciências Sociais*, 99, 1, (2012), p.51–72.

135 A Carmo and A Estevens, 'Urban citizenship(s) in Lisbon: examining the case of Mouraria', *Citizenship Studies*. 21, 4, (2017), p.409–424.

[136] A Cócola Gant, 'Holiday Rentals: The New Gentrification Battlefront', *Sociological Research Online*, 21, 3, (2016) p.1–9.

[137] Quoted in E Mondlane, *The Struggle for Mozambique* (Penguin, London: 1969), p.79.

[138] A Brooks, *Clothing Poverty: The Hidden World of Fast Fashion and Second-Hand Clothes* (Zed, London, 2019).

[139] Ibid.

[140] M Leitenberg, 'Deaths in Wars and Conflicts in the 20th Century', Occasional Paper #29, Cornell University Peace Studies Program, 2006.

[141] J Hanlon, 'Mozambique: Police death squad jailed, but those at top protected', *Club of Mozambique*, https://clubofmozambique.com/news/mozambique-police-death-squad-jailed-but-those-at-top-protected-by-joseph-hanlon-163863/, 24 June 2020; Amnesty International 'Mozambique', https://www.amnesty.org/en/countries/africa/mozambique/, 2024.

[142] H Pérez Niño and P Le Billon, 'Foreign aid, resource rents, and state fragility in Mozambique and Angola', *The Annals of the American Academy of Political and Social Science*, 656, 1, (2014), p.79–96.

[143] World Bank, 'Mozambique GDP growth', https://data.worldbank.org/indicator/NY.GDP.MKTP.KD.ZG, 7 January 2021.

[144] BBC News, 'Mozambique: From Marxism to market', https://www.bbc.co.uk/news/world-africa-21655680, 25 March 2013.

[145] UNDP, 'Human Development Report 2010', https://hdr.undp.org/system/files/documents/human-development-report-2010-summary-english.human-development-report-2010-summary-english, 2010.

[146] World Bank, 'Mozambique: Net official development assistance and official aid received (current US$)', https://data.worldbank.org/indicator/DT.ODA.ALLD.CD?end=2018&start=1992, 7 January 2021.

[147] J Hanlon and M Mosse, 'Mozambique's Elite – Finding its Way in a Globalized World and Returning to Old Development Models', UNU-Wider, Working Paper No. 2010/105, September 2010.

[148] L Nhachote, 'Mozambique's "Mr Guebusiness"', *Mail and Guardian*, http://mg.co.za/article/2012-01-06-mozambiques-mr-guebusiness, 6 January 2012.

[149] WTO, 'Trade Policy review: Mozambique', https://www.wto.org/english/tratop_e/tpr_e/tp154_e.htm, 26 January 2001.

[150] A Brooks, 'Networks of Power and Corruption: The Trade of Japanese Used Cars to Mozambique', *Geographical Journal*, 178, 1, (2012), p.80–92.

[151] A Brooks, 'Was Africa rising? Narratives of development success and failure among the Mozambican middle class', *Territory, Politics, Governance*, 6, 4, (2018), p.447–467.

[152] A M Pitcher, *Transforming Mozambique: The Politics of Privatization, 1975–2000*, (Cambridge University Press: 2003).

[153] A Brooks, 'Riches from Rags or Persistent Poverty? The Working Lives of Secondhand Clothing Vendors in Maputo, Mozambique', *Textile*, 10, 2, (2012), p.222–237.

154 UNDP, Human Development Report 2021/2022, https://hdr.undp.org/system/files/documents/global-report-document/hdr2021-22pdf_1.pdf 2022.

155 N Cook, 'Mozambique: Politics, Economy, and U.S. Relations', Congressional Research Service, https://www.everycrsreport.com/files/20190820_R45817_066c7037af7aa7f83c9e625767b9c8697c1ec2e8.pdf, 20 August 2019.

156 United Nations, 'Strongly Condemning "Wanton Brutality" of Reported Massacres in Northern Mozambique, Secretary-General Urges Authorities to Investigate, Hold Perpetrators Accountable', https://www.un.org/press/en/2020/sgsm20409.doc.htm, 10 November 2020.

157 B Nhamirre, 'Cross-border cooperation could curb kidnappings in Mozambique', *ISS Today*, https://issafrica.org/iss-today/cross-border-cooperation-could-curb-kidnappings-in-mozambique, 1 March 2023.

158 UNHCR, 'Civilians bear the brunt of violence in Mozambique's Cabo Delgado', https://www.unhcr.org/uk/news/briefing/2020/11/5fae44df4/civilians-bear-brunt-violence-mozambiques-cabo-delgado.html, 13 November 2020.

159 The Archbishop of Canterbury, 'Archbishop of Canterbury meets Prime Minister of Mozambique and victims of conflict' https://www.archbishopofcanterbury.org/news/news-and-statements/archbishop-canterbury-meets-prime-minister-mozambique-and-victims-conflict, 21 November 2022.

160 Amnesty International, 'Mozambique: Video showing soldiers burning corpses is latest evidence of atrocities in forgotten war in Cabo Delgado' https://www.amnesty.org/en/latest/news/2023/01/mozambique-video-showing-soldiers-burning-corpses/, 11 January 2023.

161 J Hanlon and T Smart, *Do Bicycles Equal Development in Mozambique?* (James Currey, Oxford: 2008).

162 G Gudgin, 'UN Human Development Index', the *Irish Times*, https://www.irishtimes.com/opinion/letters/un-human-developmentindex-1.4444925, 26 December 2020.

163 UNDP, Human Development Reports, https://hdr.undp.org/data-center/country-insights#/ranks, 17 January 2024.

164 J Hickel, 'The sustainable development index: Measuring the ecological efficiency of human development in the anthropocene', *Ecological Economics*, 167, 106331, (2020).

165 Le News, '1 in 20 suffer material deprivation in Switzerland' https://lenews.ch/2023/05/05/1-in-20-suffer-material-deprivation-in-switzerland/, 5 May 2023.

166 J D Sachs, *The End of Poverty: Economic Possibilities for Our Time* (Penguin, London: 2006); D Nayyar, *Catch Up: Developing Countries in the World Economy* (Oxford University Press: 2013); UN, 'Leaving no one behind', https://sustainabledevelopment.un.org/content/documents/2754713_July_

PM_2._Leaving_no_one_behind_Summary_from_UN_Committee_ for_Development_Policy.pdf, July 2018.

[167] T Marshall, *Prisoners of Geography*, (Elliott and Thompson, London: 2015), p.259.

[168] J M Blaut, *The colonizer's model of the world*, (Guilford Press, New York: 1993).

[169] T Parsons, *The system of modern societies*, (Prentice Hall, Upper Saddle River, New Jersey: 1971).

[170] Mondlane, *The Struggle for Mozambique*.

[171] F Fukuyama, *Falling behind: Explaining the development gap between Latin America and the United States*, (Oxford University Press: 2008).

[172] D Chakrabarty, *Provincializing Europe: Postcolonial thought and historical difference*, (Princeton University Press: 2008).

[173] N Smith, *Uneven development: Nature, capital, and the production of space*, (The University of Georgia Press: 2008).

[174] W Rodney, *How Europe underdeveloped Africa*, (Bogle-L'Ouverture Publications, London: 1972).

[175] H-J Chang, *Bad Samaritans: The Guilty Secrets of Rich Nations and the Threat to Global Prosperity*, (Random House Business, London: 2008).

[176] A Brooks and C Herrick, 'Bringing relational comparison into development studies: Global health volunteers' experiences of Sierra Leone', *Progress in Development Studies*, 19, 2, (2019), p.97–111.

[177] UNDP, *Human development report 2014*. (United Nations Development Programme: 2014).

[178] J Crompton, T P Kingham, TB Kamara, et al., 'Comparison of Surgical Care Deficiencies between US Civil War Hospitals and Present-Day Hospitals in Sierra Leone', *World Journal of Surgery*, 34, (2010), p.1743–1747.

[179] The World Bank, World Development Indicators: Health systems, http://wdi.worldbank.org/table/2.12, 2024.

[180] M Jerven, 'An unlevel playing field: national income estimates and reciprocal comparison in global economic history', *Journal of Global History*, 7, 1, (2012), p.107–128.

[181] Reuters, 'Clinton warns against "new colonialism" in Africa,' https://www.reuters.com/article/us-clinton-africa-idUSTRE75A0RI20110611, 11 June 2011.

[182] J Anderlini, 'China is at risk of becoming a colonialist power', *Financial Times*, https://www.ft.com/content/186743b8-bb25-11e8-94b2-17176fbf93f5, 19 September 2018.

[183] L Newson, 'Pathogens, places and peoples: geographical variations in the impact of disease in early Spanish America and the Philippines', *Technology, Disease and Colonial Conquests, Sixteenth to Eighteenth Centuries*, 2, (2001), p.167–210.

[184] J Seabrook, *The Song of the Shirt: The High Price of Cheap Garments, from Blackburn to Bangladesh*, (Hurst Publishers, London: 2015).

[185] Brooks, *The End of Development*.

[186] N Mirumachi, *Transboundary Water Politics in the Developing World*, (Routledge, Abingdon: 2015).

[187] X Jinping, 'The Rejuvenation of the Chinese Nation Is a Dream Shared by All Chinese', *Qiushi: CPC Central Committee Bimonthly*, http://en.qstheory.cn/2020-10/04/c_541843.htm, 4 October 2020.

[188] D Carrington, 'The world's most toxic town: the terrible legacy of Zambia's lead mines', the *Guardian*, https://www.theguardian.com/environment/2017/may/28/the-worlds-most-toxic-town-the-terrible-legacy-of-zambias-lead-mines#:~:text=Kabwe%20is%20the%20world's%20most,to%20be%20poisoned%20every%20day, 28 May 2017.

[189] A Brooks, 'Spinning and Weaving Discontent: Labour Relations and the Production of Meaning at Zambia-China Mulungushi Textiles', *Journal of Southern African Studies*, 36, 1, (2010), p.113–132.

[190] *The Economist*, 'Not as bad as they say', https://www.economist.com/middle-east-and-africa/2011/10/01/not-as-bad-as-they-say, 1 October 2011.

[191] UNCTAD, 'Investment flows in Africa set to drop 25% to 40% in 2020', https://unctad.org/news/investment-flows-africa-set-drop-25-40-2020, 6 June 2020.

[192] IMF, 'World Economic Outlook, October 2020: A Long and Difficult Ascent', https://www.imf.org/en/Publications/WEO, 7 October 2020.

[193] Banned and Challenged Books, '100 Most Challenged Books of the Past Decades', https://www.ala.org/advocacy/bbooks/frequentlychallenged-books/top10, 2024.

[194] T Tapp, 'Women Wear 'Handmaid's Tale' Costumes At Ruth Bader Ginsburg Vigil To Protest Trump And McConnell's Actions' *Deadline*, https://deadline.com/2020/09/women-wear-handmaids-tale-costumes-at-vigil-to-mourn-ruth-bader-ginsburg-protest-trump-and-mcconnells-actions-1234581707/, 21 September 2020.

[195] The Times of Israel, ''Handmaid's Tale' author nods at inclusion in Israel protests', https://www.timesofisrael.com/handmaids-tale-author-nods-at-inclusion-in-israel-protests/, 20 March 2023.

[196] D Kirka, 'Protesters greet Netanyahu as he meets UK leader in London', AP, https://apnews.com/article/uk-israel-netanyahu-a85c110fd24d25ec38688d791047492f, 24 March 2023.

[197] B Plett Usher and A Zurcher, 'Stakes are immense as Biden presses Israel to change course', *BBC News*, https://www.bbc.co.uk/news/world-middle-east-67788359, 23 December 2023.

[198] J Rose, 'You made me do it', *London Review of Books*, 45, 23, 30 November 2023.

[199] F Heller, 'Spain's Sumar leader calls out 'Israeli apartheid' against Palestinian people', *Euractiv*, https://www.euractiv.com/section/politics/

news/spains-sumar-leader-calls-out-israeli-apartheid-against-palestinian-people/, 12 October 2023.

[200] Protect Journalists, 'A statement by journalists', https://www.protect-journalists.com/, 9 November 2023.

[201] N Mandela, 'Address by President Nelson Mandela at International Day of Solidarity with Palestinian People, Pretoria', *South African Government*, http://www.mandela.gov.za/mandela_speeches/1997/971204_palestinian.htm, 4 December 1997.

[202] BDS, 'Israeli Apartheid Week', https://bdsmovement.net/law, January 2023.

[203] BDS, 'What is BDS', https://bdsmovement.net/, 2024.

[204] R Falk and V Tilley, 'Israeli Practices towards the Palestinian People and the Question of Apartheid', *Palestine and the Israeli Occupation, Issue No. 1*, (United Nations, Beirut: 2017), p.64.

[205] T Goldenberg, 'A former Mossad chief says Israel is enforcing an apartheid system in the West Bank', *AP*, https://apnews.com/article/israel-apartheid-palestinians-occupation-c8137c9e7f33c2cba7b0b5ac7fa8d115, 6 September 2023.

[206] ICC, 'Rome Statue of the International Criminal Court', https://www.icc-cpi.int/sites/default/files/RS-Eng.pdf, 2011.

[207] I Pappé, *Israel and South Africa: The many faces of apartheid.* (Zed, London: 2015).

[208] R Sabel, 'The Campaign to Delegitimize Israel with the False Charge of Apartheid' *Jewish Political Studies Review*, 23,3/4, (2011), p.18–31.

[209] Amnesty International, 'Israel's Apartheid Against Palestinians', https://www.amnesty.org/en/latest/campaigns/2022/02/israels-system-of-apartheid/, 1 February 2022.

[210] M Srivastava, 'Israel reacts to 'apartheid' label from Amnesty International', *Financial Times*, https://www.ft.com/content/870ab8ec-fd92-41b2-b9fa-41cd530b9cda, 1 February 2022.

[211] K Bird, 'Why Are U.S. Jews Still Calling Jimmy Carter an Antisemite?', *Haaretz*, https://www.haaretz.com/us-news/2021-09-15/ty-article-opinion/.premium/why-is-jimmy-carter-still-called-an-antisemite/0000017f-dbc8-db22-a17f-fff96f400000, 15 September 2021.

[212] P McMichael, 'Incorporating comparison within a world-historical perspective: An alternative comparative method', *American Sociological Review*, 55, 3, (1990), p.385–397.

[213] Human Rights Watch, 'A Threshold Crossed: Israeli Authorities and the Crimes of Apartheid and Persecution' https://www.hrw.org/report/2021/04/27/threshold-crossed-israeli-authorities-and-crimes-apartheid-and-persecution, 27 April 2021.

[214] C Murray, 'Class, gender and the household: The developmental cycle in Southern Africa', *Development and Change*, 18, 2, (1987), p.235–249.

215 J Díaz, 'Make Margaret Atwood Fiction Again', *Boston Review,* https://www.bostonreview.net/articles/literature-culture-margaret-atwood-junot-diaz-make-margaret-atwood-fiction-again/, 29 June 2017.

216 Murray, 'Class, gender and the household'.

217 S Jones, 'South Africa's external trade in the 1980s', *South African Journal of Economic History*, 9, 2, (1994), p.110–126.

218 A Mackinnon, *'The making of South Africa: Culture and politics'*, (Pearson, Boston: 2012), p.239.

219 J Sharp and A Spiegel, 'Women and wages: Gender and the control of income in farm and Bantu households', *Journal of Southern African Studies,* 16, 3, (1990), p.527–549.

220 L Evans, 'Gender, generation and the experiences of farm dwellers resettled in the Ciskei Bantustan, South Africa, ca 1960–1976', *Journal of Agrarian Change*, 13, 2, (2013), p.213–233.

221 M Lurie, A Harrison, D Wilkinson and S A Karim, 'Circular migration and sexual networking in rural KwaZulu/Natal: Implications for the spread of HIV and other sexually transmitted diseases', *Health Transition Review*, 7, 3, (1997) 17–27.

222 T L Sall, 'The Rainbow Myth: Dreaming of a Post-racial South African Society', *Institute for Global Diaologue: Occasional Paper 73*, 1 October 2018, p.5.

223 M Vickery, *Employing the Enemy: The Story of Palestinian labourers on Israeli settlements*, (Zed Books: London, 2017).

224 A Ross, *Stone men: The Palestinians who built Israel*, (Verso, London: 2019).

225 Vickery, *Employing the Enemy*.

226 Y Berda, *Living emergency, Israel's permit regime in the occupied territories*, (Stanford University Press: 2017).

227 M Griffiths and A Brooks 'A relational comparison: The gendered effects of cross-border work in Palestine within a Global Frame', *Annals of the American Association of Geographers*, 112, 6, (2022), p.1761–1776.

228 D Matthews, 'The Land Act Legacy Project Collection' *SAHA (South African History Achieve)*, http://www.saha.org.za/landact1913/transcript_of_interview_with_florence_senna_mongake.htm, 22 September 2013.

229 Ibid.

230 Anonymous. Excerpt from *'Race Relations News'*, South African Institute of Race Relations, 5, 41 (1978).

231 B Bozzoli, *Women of Phokeng: Consciousness, life strategy, and migrancy in South Africa, 1900–1983*. (Heinemann, Portsmouth, NH: 1991).

232 M Griffiths and J Repo, 'Biopolitics and checkpoint 300 in occupied Palestine: Bodies, affect, discipline', *Political Geography,* 65, 2018, p.17–25.

233 T Bhattacharya, *Social reproduction theory: Remapping class, recentering oppression*, (Pluto Press, London: 2017).

234 S Hall, 'Race, articulation, and societies structured in dominance'. In *Sociological theories: Race and colonialism*, ed. C. Guillaumin, (UNESCO, Paris: 1980), p. 305–345.

235 A Mackinnon, *The making of South Africa: Culture and politics*, (Pearson, Boston: 2012).

236 S Dubow, 'South Africa's Racist Founding Father Was Also a Human Rights Pioneer' *The New York Times*, https://www.nytimes.com/2019/05/18/opinion/jan-smuts-south-africa.html, 18 May 2019.

237 Congressional Research Service, 'U.S. Foreign Aid to Israel', https://crsreports.congress.gov/product/pdf/RL/RL33222/49, 1 March 2023.

238 S Polakow-Suransky, *The Unspoken Alliance: Israel's Secret Relationship with Apartheid South Africa*, (Knopf Doubleday Publishing Group, New York: 2011).

239 D Cammack, 'South Africa's war of destabilisation'. *South African Review-SARS* 5, (1990), p.191–208.

240 Mackinnon, *The making of South Africa*.

241 N Klein, *The shock doctrine*, (Penguin, London: 2007).

242 M Farah and M Abdallah, 'Security, business and human rights in the occupied Palestinian territory', *Business and Human Rights Journal*, 4,1, (2019) p.7–31. 22–23.

243 Ibid.

244 H Klifa, 'Stock prices of major defence companies surge in wake of October 7th attacks in Israel', *Action on Armed Violence*, https://aoav.org.uk/2023/stock-prices-of-major-defence-companies-surge-in-wake-of-october-7th-attacks-in-israel/, 13 November 2023.

245 D Welsh, *The Rise and Fall of Apartheid* (Jonathan Ball Publishers, Johannesburg and Cape Town: 2009).

246 Statistics South Africa, 'How Unequal is South Africa?' https://www.statssa.gov.za/?p=12930, 4 February 2020.

247 O Mildenhall, 'Paddy Hopkirk and the Mini that won the Monte Carlo Rally', *Auto Express*, https://www.autoexpress.co.uk/mini/89423/paddy-hopkirk-and-the-mini-that-won-the-monte-carlo-rally, 31 December 2014.

248 Harry's Garage, '2020 MINI Electric real-world review; flawed but fun', https://www.youtube.com/watch?v=BgEE3fB0ddY, 26 June 2021.

249 Harry's Garage, 'Will the 2030 ban & dash to electric cars spell the end for classics in UK?', https://www.youtube.com/watch?v=1CUA2imRYRM, December 2020.

250 S Hargreaves, 'Batteries vs oil: A comparison of raw material needs', *Transport & Environment*, https://www.transportenvironment.org/publications/batteries-vs-oil-comparison-raw-material-needs, 1 March 2021.

251 J Jolly, 'Fossil fuel cars make "hundreds of times" more waste than electric cars', the *Guardian*, https://www.theguardian.com/business/2021/mar/01/fossil-fuel-cars-make-hundreds-of-times-more-waste-than-electric-cars?CMP=Share_AndroidApp_Other, 1 March 2021.

252 J Ambrose, 'Aston Martin in row over "sock puppet PR firm" pushing anti-electric vehicle study', the *Guardian*, https://www.theguardian.com/

business/2020/dec/02/aston-martin-pr-firm-anti-electric-vehicle-study, 2 December 2020.

253 RAC Foundation, 'UK petrol and diesel consumption', https://www.racfoundation.org/data/volume-petrol-diesel-consumed-uk-over-time-by-year, 2021.

254 M DeBord 'If VW deceived consumers about its diesel cars, then it has a huge problem', *Yahoo News*, https://in.news.yahoo.com/vw-deceived-consumers-diesel-cars-150000093.html, 19 September 2015.

255 *Financial Times*, 'Electric vehicles may not be the climate answer after all', https://on.ft.com/3dgomTh, 15 February 2021.

256 R Hotten, 'Volkswagen: The scandal explained', BBC News, https://www.bbc.co.uk/news/business-34324772, 10 December 2015.

257 C Rogers, 'Judge Slaps VW With $2.8 Billion Criminal Fine in Emissions Fraud', *Wall Street Journal*, 21 April 2017.

258 P Kågeson, P 'Cycle-Beating and the EU Test Cycle for Cars', *European Federation for Transport and Environment*, 98(3), https://www.transportenvironment.org/sites/te/files/media/T&E%2098-3_0.pdf, 1998.

259 A Stamm, '"We Choose to Go to the Moon" and Other Apollo Speeches', *Smithsonian Air and Space Museum*, https://airandspace.si.edu/stories/editorial/we-choose-go-moon-and-other-apollo-speeches, 2019.

260 M Mazzucato, *Mission Economy: A Moonshot Guide to Changing Capitalism* (Penguin, London: 2020).

261 P Stevens, '"This is our generation's moonshot," Energy Secretary Granholm says of fighting climate change', *CNBC*, https://www.cnbc.com/2021/04/23/our-generations-moonshot-energy-secy-granholm-on-climate-change.html, 23 April 2021.

262 O Schwartz, 'Could Microsoft's climate crisis "moonshot" plan really work?', the *Guardian*, https://www.theguardian.com/environment/2020/apr/23/microsoft-climate-crisis-moonshot-plan, 23 April 2020.

263 Nature Portfolio, 'Japan's moonshot project to capture carbon', https://www.nature.com/articles/d42473-020-00521-1, 2021.

264 Mazzucato, *Mission Economy*.

265 J Ghosh, 'Lessons from the Moonshot for fixing global problems', *Nature*, https://www.nature.com/articles/d41586-021-00076-1, 2021.

266 Brooks, *The End of Development*.

267 BBC Radio 4, *39 Ways to Save the Planet*, https://www.bbc.co.uk/programmes/m000qwt3, 2021.

268 Movie Body Counts Boards, 'Where Eagles Dare (1968)', https://moviebodycounts.proboards.com/thread/1565/where-eagles-dare, 14 April 2008.

269 A Hirsch, 'If you talk about Russian propaganda, remember: Britain has myths too' *The Guardian*, https://www.theguardian.com/commentisfree/2018/mar/21/russia-propaganda-skripal-britain-churchill, 21 March 2018.

270 J Holland, *The War in the West: A New History* (Bantam Press: London, 2015).

[271] G Dyer, *Broadsword Calling Danny Boy* (Penguin: 2018, London), p.10.

[272] The Argus, 'Looking back: Recalling the days of Battlefield Brighton', https://www.theargus.co.uk/news/10462107.looking-back-recalling-the-days-of-battlefield-brighton/, 4 June 2013.

[273] V Chaudhary, A Osborn and J Arlidge, 'England's glory night marred by fans' riots', *The Observer*, https://www.theguardian.com/uk/2000/jun/18/footballviolence.football, 18 June 2000.

[274] R Hattersley, 'Catastrophe at Charleroi', *the Guardian*, https://www.theguardian.com/football/2000/jun/20/euro2000.sport1, 20 June 2000.

[275] Storey, D. 'England's '10 German bombers' song should be consigned to the dustbin of history', *i News*, https://inews.co.uk/sport/football/england-10-german-bombers-song-consigned-dustbin-of-history-1873673, 26 September 2022.

[276] A Costello, 'How a string of failures by the British government helped Covid-19 to mutate', the *Guardian*, https://www.theguardian.com/commentisfree/2020/dec/22/uk-government-blamed-covid-19-mutation-occur?CMP=Share_AndroidApp_Other, 22 December 2020.

[277] BBC News, 'Coronavirus: UK got vaccine first because it's "a better country", says Gavin Williamson', https://www.bbc.co.uk/news/uk-politics-55175162, 4 December 2020.

[278] ADL, 'Why is Putin Calling the Ukrainian Government a Bunch of Nazis?' https://www.adl.org/resources/blog/why-putin-calling-ukrainian-government-bunch-nazis, 3 April 2022.

[279] United States Holocaust Memorial Museum, 'The Holocaust in Ukraine', https://www.ushmm.org/information/exhibitions/online-exhibitions/ukraine, 2024.

[280] ADL, 'Why is Putin Calling the Ukrainian Government a Bunch of Nazis?'

[281] ISW, 'Russian Offensive Campaign Assessment, September 5, 2023' https://www.understandingwar.org/backgrounder/russian-offensive-campaign-assessment-september-5-2023, 5 September, 2023.

[282] GOV UK, 'About the AI Safety Summit 2023', https://www.gov.uk/government/topical-events/ai-safety-summit-2023/about, 2023.

[283] R Browne, 'British Prime Minister Rishi Sunak pitches UK as home of A.I. safety regulation as London bids to be next Silicon Valley', *CNBC: Tech*, https://www.cnbc.com/2023/06/12/pm-rishi-sunak-pitches-uk-as-geographical-home-of-ai-regulation.html, 12 June 2023.

[284] P Guest, 'Britain's Big AI Summit Is a Doom-Obsessed Mess', *Wired*, https://www.wired.co.uk/article/britains-ai-summit-doom-obsessed-mess, 23 October 2023.

[285] R Frisk, 'How the poppy became a symbol of racism', *Independent*, https://www.independent.co.uk/voices/poppy-racist-war-remembrance-day-b1955812.html, 11 November 2021.

[286] S McDonell, 'Why China censors banned Winnie the Pooh', *BBC News*, https://www.bbc.co.uk/news/blogs-china-blog-40627855, 17 July 2017.

[287] See for example: *Daily Mail* 'Hit video game which compared China's President Xi to Winnie the Pooh is pulled from sale again – after being banned by Beijing', *Mail Online*, https://www.dailymail.co.uk/news/article-9064355/Taiwanese-horror-game-Devotion-pulled-calling-Chinas-President-Xi-Winnie-Pooh.html, 17 December 2020.

[288] A Syed, 'Liz Truss Is Now the Shortest-Serving Prime Minister in U.K. History', *Time*, https://time.com/6223441/shortest-serving-uk-prime-minister-liz-truss/, 20 October 2022.

[289] S Ratcliffe, *Oxford Essential Quotations (4th ed)*, (Oxford University press, 2016).

[290] BBC News, 'Piers Morgan mocks Daniel Craig for carrying baby,' https://www.bbc.co.uk/news/uk-45873664, 16 October 2018.

[291] D Kurtzleben, 'Why Trump's authoritarian language about 'vermin' matters', *NPR*, https://www.npr.org/2023/11/17/1213746885/trump-vermin-hitler-immigration-authoritarian-republican-primary, 17 November 2023.

[292] Ibid.

[293] R Ben-Ghiat, 'Trump's "Vermin" Speech Echoes Fascist Rhetoric', *Lucid*, https://lucid.substack.com/p/trump-really-doesnt-want-you-to-call, 13 November 2023.

[294] N Standley, 'Ofsted seen as toxic and schools should self-evaluate, says inquiry', *BBC News*, https://www.bbc.co.uk/news/education-67449711, 20 November 2023.

[295] Sky News, 'Israel-Hamas war: Next step is to 'eradicate this Nazi Hamas', says former Israeli PM', https://news.sky.com/video/israel-hamas-war-next-step-is-to-eradicate-this-nazi-type-hamas-says-former-israeli-pm-naftali-bennet-12983273, 12 October 2023.

[296] A Shatz, 'Vengeful Pathologies', *London Review of Books*, 2 November 2023.

[297] I Deutscher, 'On the Israeli-Arab War', *London Review of Books*, 1, 44, July/August, 1967.